REDCOATS AND COURTESANS

The Birth of the British Army
(1660–1690)

George Monck, 1st Duke of Albemarle (1608–1670). The Hero of the Restoration. Studio of Sir Peter Lely c 1665–6. *(By courtesy of the National Portrait Gallery, London)*

REDCOATS AND COURTESANS

The Birth of the British Army
(1660–1690)

Noel T. St. John Williams

BRASSEY'S (UK)
London • New York

First English edition 1994

UK editorial offices: Brassey's, 33 John Street, London WC1N 2AT
UK orders: Marston Book Services, PO Box 87, Oxford OX2 ODT

USA orders: Macmillan Publishing Company, Front and Brown Streets,
Riverside, NJ 08075

Distributed in North America to booksellers and wholesalers by the
Macmillan Publishing Company, NY 10022

Library of Congress Cataloging in Publication Data
available

British Library Cataloging in Publication Data
A catalogue record for this book is
available from the British Library

Hardcover 1-85753-097-7

Typeset by M Rules
Printed in Great Britain by
Bath Press

For my grandchildren,
Anthony, Richard and Antonia

Contents

Preface

Redcoats and courtesans? My story will tell of the birth of the modern British army, in which I have spent the best part of my professional life, and of how and why it began. It will chronicle its dramatic growth within the space of two reigns, from a small force of foot and horse guards, which Charles II raised and paid out of his own pocket to protect his person and safeguard his throne, to a standing army of over three dozen famous regiments. This army saw active service on the Continent, in the colonies and on the African mainland, where at Tangier it would win the first battle honour to be inscribed on a British regimental colour.

It is a story of wars, plots and rebellions, of fire and plague, of love and romance, and of two kings. One, nationally popular because of his failings, was accused by his contemporaries of frivolity, indolence and debauchery; of neglecting the business of government for the pursuit of pleasure;[1] and of being the political plaything of favourites and mistresses. He excused himself in the belief that 'God would never damn a man for allowing himself a little irregular pleasure'.[2] The other king, his brother, would lose his kingdom, according to his critics, not on account of his vices, for which he would do penance for having spent most of his life in almost a perpetual course of sin, but because of his virtues, his firmly held convictions and his deep religious faith.[3]

Both monarchs surrounded themselves with able ministers, colourful courtiers and a bevy of beautiful and exciting ladies. Their portraits, expressing the luxuriant sensuousness of the Restoration world,[4] can still be admired in royal palaces, stately homes and the National Portrait Gallery. The names and exploits of Buckingham, Rochester, Monmouth, Churchill and Judge Jeffreys, of Barbara Castlemaine, Frances Stuart, Nell Gwynn and Louise de Keroualle, have been immortalised in the diaries and chronicles of the times – Pepys, Evelyn, Gramont, Clarendon and Bishop Burnet. These and many others play their parts in the story of 30 exciting years, characterised by political intrigue, petticoat diplomacy and a licentious court.[5]

The setting for much of the story is London, which, until it was largely destroyed by the Great Fire of 1666 and rebuilt under Sir Christopher Wren, was the medieval city known to Chaucer and Shakespeare. The home of the kings and the centre of their court was the old palace of Whitehall, once owned by Cardinal Wolsey and confiscated by the jealous Henry VIII. It was destined to be almost completely destroyed by another fire at the end of the seventeenth century: its remains, except for the Banqueting Hall,[6] lie today under the government departments of Whitehall. But visitors will recognise Stuart London in Wren's churches, Albemarle and Downing Streets, Richmond Terrace, Horse Guards Parade, Chelsea Hospital, Somerset House, Scotland Yard, Drury Lane Theatre, Pall Mall – and the ducks in St James's Park.[7]

So much for the stage and the players in my story! I have attempted to place the army in its political and social setting, and to show how the events in which the regiments were engaged were shaped and influenced not only by the sovereigns but also by the men and women who surrounded them. Under Charles II the army was never a political force and remained loyal to its king; under James II it suffered divided loyalties – Protestant against Catholic, English against Irish, courtier against professional officer – and England lost a dynasty. The control and retention of a standing army in peacetime became one of the main constitutional quarrels between Stuart kings and Parliament, until finally resolved in the Glorious Revolution of 1688–89.[8]

So dramatic were the events, so momentous the times and so varied and complex the characters involved in my story, that perhaps I may be forgiven by my readers for any preference in selection or personal bias in the telling. As one historian has rightly said,[9] no one has ever written of the Stuarts with moderation and balance; it is impossible to do so.

Acknowledgements

This book owes much to the printed sources listed in the references. The author thanks the following for their help and for permission to reproduce copyright material: Mr Angus Madders and the staff of Chester Public Library; The King's Own Border Regiment [Colonel L I Cowper, *The King's Own Story*]; Lady Antonia Fraser, *King Charles II*, Weidenfeld and Nicolson; Ronald Hutton, *Charles II* by permission of Oxford University Press; Emeritus Professor J R Jones, *Country and Court*, Arnold and *Charles II: The Royal Politician*, Allen and Unwin; Dr John Childs, *The Army of Charles II*, Routledge and Keegan Paul; *The Army, James II and the Glorious Revolution*, Manchester University Press and *The British Army of William III*, Manchester University Press; Professor John Miller, *Catholic Officers in the late Stuart Army*, article in the English Historical Review; Arthur Bryant, *The Letters, Speeches and Declarations of Charles II*, Cassell and MacMillan Publishing Company, New York; Bryan Bevan, *Charles II's French Mistress*, Robert Hale; H and C Adams, *A History of the British Army Vol I*, Major Book Publications; Latham and Matthews (ed) *The Diary of Samuel Pepys*, by permission of Bell and Hyman now Unwin, Hyman, an imprint of HarperCollins Publishers Ltd; Violet Wyndham, *The Protestant Duke*, Weidenfeld and Nicolson; H A L Fisher, *A History of Europe*, Arnold and NFER Nelson; Arthur Bryant, *King Charles II*; Collins an imprint of HarperCollins Ltd; G Huehns (ed), *Clarendon: Selections from the History of the Rebellion*, by permission of Oxford University Press; Enid Routh, *Tangier: An Outpost of Empire*, John Murray (Publishers) Ltd; David Ogg, *England in the Reign of Charles II* and *England in the Reign of James II and William III*, by permission of Oxford University Press; Arthur Bryant, *Restoration England*, Collins, an imprint of HarperCollins Publishers Ltd; Cyril Hartmann, *The King, My Brother*, William Heinemann Publishers Ltd; Patrick Morrah, *Restoration England*, Constable.

The author also wishes to thank his publishers Brassey's (UK) Ltd for their courtesy and help, especially Jenny Shaw and Angela Clark; Cherry Ekins for editorial comment and suggestions, and Janet and David Taylor and Lesley Armstrong for the word processing.

List of Illustrations

1

Our Trusty and Well-Beloved George Monck

On New Year's Day 1660, General George Monck, appointed by Oliver Cromwell to be his commander-in-chief in Scotland, left his headquarters at Coldstream and began a march on London. This march would restore the exiled Charles II to his throne, separate Scotland from England again as an independent kingdom, and lead to the creation of today's British army.

Who was this soldier – a vile traitor or the hero of the Restoration? Monck was condemned by some as a military adventurer who took advantage of every political wind that blew: a base renegade, loyal neither to his King nor his Parliament. Others would hail him as 'the father of his country', a model of military virtues, decisive in action, and the arbiter of events which only he could control. Some would see him as second only to the future Duke of Marlborough in his acquisition of honours, wealth and property; a man cursed to marry, after a long and unlawful familiarity, 'a woman of the lowest extraction, a mean and contemptible creature, with little wit and less beauty', whom he feared more than an army.[1] All would acknowledge him, however, as a man whose life was full of excitement and drama, of pageantry and political intrigue, with even a touch of romance and love.

The events which led to Monck's march on London can be traced back to 1642, when for the first time in nearly 160 years there was war in England. No armed invader threatened her shores; but inside the country Cavalier fought Roundhead in a disastrous civil war, the one in support of the rightful king, the other on behalf of the elected Parliament.[2] The Long Parliament wanted to rule the nation by controlling its councils of state, its finances, the church and the army. Charles I was determined to resist these demands, to maintain the autocracy of the English crown and his right to dissolve Parliament at his will.

Both parties needed armies, which at that time did not exist. The King could rely on a loyal gentry, whom he commissioned to raise regiments of foot and especially of cavalry. Parliament was supported by the London trained bands, the ports and the navy. Both sides competed for the local militia. The war lasted for five years and ended with the supremacy of Parliament, thanks largely to Oliver Cromwell, who created and led a disciplined and dedicated professional force of some 22,000 well-paid and well-fed soldiers in the New Model Army.[3]

A second civil war broke out in 1648, when Royalists revolted in Wales, Kent and Essex, and Charles called on the Scots to invade. Cromwell defeated the Scots at Preston, while General Fairfax put down the risings in the south. Unable to negotiate with or trust the King, Cromwell decided on his execution, which took place on 3 September 1649. The Long Parliament was 'purged' by Colonel Pride, leaving a 'Rump' of army sympathisers to set up a Commonwealth of England with the army, without a King or a House of Lords.

During 1649–50 Cromwell subdued Ireland with terrible massacres at Drogheda and Wexford, which the Irish remember to this day.

In 1651, Charles II returned to England from exile on the Continent and attempted to regain his throne with the help of the Scots. One Scots army was defeated at Dunbar, and another at Worcester; Charles himself escaped from the battlefield in disguise and fled to France with a small band of devoted followers. At the end of 1653 Cromwell was proclaimed Lord Protector and ruled as uncrowned king for the next five years, supported by the New Model Army. The three kingdoms of England, Ireland and Scotland were united into a single Commonwealth. But this Commonwealth structure and the army's solidarity fell apart on Cromwell's death in 1658. At that point, General George Monck stepped into the limelight.

Monck was born in Devon in 1608, descended at many removes from a bastard son of Edward IV. At the early age of 17, he showed his mettle by thrashing the county sheriff for the unjustified arrest of his father, as he set out to pay his respects to Charles I. To avoid the inevitable court proceedings, George volunteered for an expedition to Cadiz commanded by his kinsman Sir Richard Grenville, the naval hero and captain of the *Revenge*. Two years later, he risked his life passing through the French army besieging the Huguenot garrison of La Rochelle carrying a letter from the King to the Duke of Buckingham.[4] He was rewarded with an ensign's commission, and 'being a younger brother, he entered into the life and conditions of a soldier'.[5]

Monck later commanded his own regiment in Ireland, where he won a number of engagements and gained the reputation of being the most beloved by his soldiers of any officer in the army. His concern for the welfare of his soldiers and for sharing their privations, which became features of his military career, was to earn him the affectionate title of 'Old George'.

Captured at the Battle of Nantwich (1644), fighting for Charles I in the Civil War, Colonel Monck was imprisoned for treason by order of the House of

Commons. During his two-year captivity in the Tower of London he fell in love with his seamstress/laundress, the 25-year-old Nan Clarges,[6] who was kind to him in a double capacity – assisting him in his dire need (the King sent him £100) and bearing his child. In 1652 Monck married her, despite her scolding tongue and lack of breeding, but to their credit no breath of scandal was ever to hurt either of them at the bawdy court of Charles II.[7]

Cromwell thought highly of Monck's military talents, released him from the Tower and appointed him military governor of Ulster. On 13 August 1650 Cromwell gave him a regiment of his own, composed of five companies of each of two regiments, originally formed in 1645 as part of the New Model Army. Thus was formed the oldest of our existing national regiments, the one complete relic of the famous New Model Army, and the one surviving corps which fought under Oliver Cromwell. It would become even more famous later under the name of the Coldstream Guards.[8] Monck served Cromwell well at Dunbar and in 1651 was appointed commander-in-chief of the Parliamentary troops in Scotland. Two years later, as general-at-sea, he gained naval victories against the Dutch.

Believing the Stuart cause was lost, although probably remaining a Royalist at heart (as were his brother and all his relations), Monck while in Scotland developed a personal loyalty to Cromwell, his superior officer and paymaster. Just before his death in September 1658, Cromwell wrote to Monck, with a touch of wry humour:

> There be some that tell me there is a certain cunning fellow in Scotland called George Monck, who is said to lie in wait there to introduce Charles Stuart: I pray you, use your diligence and send him to me.[9]

After Cromwell died, England fell into turmoil. The people feared another civil war and were tired of military rule and high taxes. 'Long before the breath was out of Oliver's body, a pleasure-loving nation was yearning for a release from the grim restraint of compulsory godliness.'[10] Many hoped for a return to the old order of rule by King and Parliament. The Royalists hoped Cromwell's death would lead to the restoration of the monarchy, with Monck 'the instrument best able to effect the King's restoration'.[11]

But Richard Cromwell had been nominated by his father as his successor and ruled for a few months as Protector. He proved a mere figurehead, unfit to rule, and was ousted in April 1659 by a group of Cromwell's major-generals led by Lambert and Fleetwood, Cromwell's son-in-law. They formed a council of state to rule the country in conjunction with the resurrected Parliamentary Rump; but they failed to establish a civil government and quarrelled amongst themselves. The population was hostile to the army, whose leaders were divided and whose discipline and morale were steadily deteriorating as its arrears of pay continued to accumulate. The state was bankrupt, unable to pay debts of over £2,000,000.

Between 1656 and 1658 Charles had established a government in exile – a small court with a council at Bruges – and in England and Scotland ineffective Royalist networks plotted insurrection. While Cromwell ruled and kept his army under control, all Charles's efforts to dislodge him were weak and unsuccessful; but after Cromwell's death, as England descended into confusion and near anarchy, Charles planned with French help to land at Rye on 1 August 1659. If the country rose in support, he would then take possession of Maidstone and Rochester. Charles wrote appealingly, promising rewards to many of the influential men during Richard Cromwell's Protectorate, including Monck – he wanted Monck to use his army in Scotland to support the planned rebellion. To Sir John Grenville, nephew of the unfortunate Sir Richard, Charles wrote:

> It is in his power to do me so great service that I cannot easily reward, but I will do all I can, and I do authorise you to treat with him . . . and whatever he shall promise to any of his officers, or the army, under his command, I will make good and perform upon the word of a king.[12]

But Monck refused to receive Charles's letter and set about keeping the Scots quiet, while the Rye project petered out through lack of commitment by France and Royalist disarray in England. The council of state learned of Charles's plans and, as a precaution, raised 14 regiments, each of 1,000 men, and called out the militia. Lambert was appointed commander-in-chief, marched to Westminster and on 13 October 1659 expelled the republican Rump remnant of the Long Parliament. Once again England was under the rule of a military dictatorship – a committee of safety comprising 23 military officers.

Monck, in Scotland, opposed Lambert's actions and the rule of a military junta without public support or constitutional authority. He firmly believed that the military arm should be subordinate to the civil. He wanted a stable government and was convinced this could only be achieved through the return of the King and a loyal Parliament. He wrote to the Speaker of the House of Commons:

> I am not one of those that seek great things, having had my education in a Commonwealth, where soldiers received and obeyed commands but gave none . . . Obedience is my great principle and I have always, and ever shall, reverence the Parliament's resolution in civil things as infallible and sacred.[13]

Monck knew how unpopular Cromwell's military despotism had been and how bitterly the people had hated rule by his major-generals. He saw that Lambert and Fleetwood were seeking similar autocratic power. He realised that, if he kept his head and the loyalty of his troops (and he ensured they received their pay regularly, in contrast to Lambert's men), he alone could save the country from the oppression of his brother officers – he could provide the opportunity for the people to decide how they wished to be governed.

The remoteness and isolation of Monck's regiments in Scotland proved to be an advantage, despite the fact that all his actions were spied upon. Lambert arranged for officers to go to Scotland to spread propaganda and undermine Monck's authority. Monck had these agents arrested or carefully watched, while he played for time by sending a delegation to London to negotiate for the return of the Rump.

Before leaving Scotland on his historic march to London, Monck took resolute action by occupying Edinburgh and the border fortresses. He arrested and cashiered any officers, supporters of Lambert, whose loyalty he could not guarantee. He reminded his two regiments that they were the paid servants of Parliament and that their duty was to defend the civil authority[14]. He wrote to the military leaders begging them to submit to Parliament or face the consequences. The City of London feared it would have to find the money to pay Lambert's soldiers, provide free accommodation for them and submit to their plundering. In a final letter to the Speaker, Lenthall, on 22 October 1659, Monck wrote:

> I am resolved as a true Englishman to stand and assert the liberty of Parliament . . . and to avoid the shedding of blood.[15]

On 23 November Lambert arrived at Newcastle to command the forces assembling there for an advance into Scotland. By mid-December the two armies were only 30 miles apart – but the situation of the two generals was very different. Throughout the crisis Monck had succeeded in keeping his army united and disciplined. The soldiers were carefully briefed on their duties and potentially mutinous units were disbanded. Officers, disloyal to him or whose allegiance was suspect, were either removed, sent to remote commands, or left behind in Scotland. This thorough preparation paid off.

Lambert's army, on the other hand, without pay and quarrelling amongst themselves, quickly became demoralised and unwilling to fight. Officers loyal to the Rump seized control of the Portsmouth garrison: the fleet declared for Parliament and blockaded the Thames. This collapse in the south undermined all Lambert's plans. The council of officers met for the last time on 23 December 1659 and three days later the Speaker reassembled the Rump; but, in notifying Monck, he did not invite the general to come to London.[16]

Despite the end of the crisis, Monck decided to cross the Tweed on

1 January 1660 with a formidable force of about 7,000 men, including his own regiments of foot and horse. He marched with a great train of his officers and gentlemen of the county (Yorkshire) attending him, the bells ringing in every town through which he passed.[17] On the way, he was joined by the Parliamentarian General Fairfax and a number of English regiments, leaving Lambert a general without soldiers. At York, Monck was deluged with petitions for a free Parliament, but he still had not committed himself in public to restoring the monarchy. To have done so would probably have caused a mutiny in the army, which was republican and anti-Stuart.

Slowly the long columns of marching men mounted the Hampstead hills and London opened up before them. Monck realised there was no alternative to restoring the King and hinted that this was his ultimate aim to his chaplain and biographer, Gumble. Samuel Pepys, just beginning to write his famous diary in his humble lodgings in Axe Yard, near to what is now Horse Guards Parade, noted that Monck kept on his mask to the end, to the perplexity of both friends and enemies.

> All the world is at a loss to think what Monck will do: the city saying that he will be for them, and the Parliament saying he will be for them.[18]

On 3 February he marched into Whitehall, to suppress anarchy, enforce due obedience to the laws, and secure that respect for the civil government with which the country's welfare and happiness were so closely interwoven.[19] His great march south had taken just over a month. In the Palace of Whitehall he set up his headquarters and declared himself for the City, the Rump and free elections. Pepys saw the soldiers 'march by in very good plight and stout officers', but noted they wanted their promised back-pay and would create mischief if they didn't get it.[20]

The Rump was fundamentally hostile to Monck, both as an independent military politician and as a popular hero. Hoping to force him into conflict with his supporters in the City, the Rump ordered Monck to demolish the City gates and subdue the Londoners to obedience. On 11 February Monck ordered his army to take up quarters in the City but then sent a sharp protest to the Rump, demanding free elections and reminding them that a dissolution must come by 6 May. The Rump's attitude infuriated the City and antagonised Monck's officers. It proved the beginning of the end of the Rump and Monck became, in effect, the uncrowned king of England; but he wisely resisted the temptation to take absolute power. Pepys recorded that common joy was everywhere, church bells rang, the soldiers were given drink and money, bonfires were lit and the Rump was roasted.[21]

The Rump imprisoned Lambert in the Tower, and on 25 February appointed Monck commander-in-chief of the three separate forces of the kingdom –

England, Scotland and Ireland. They also appointed him joint commander of the fleet with Pepys's cousin and patron, Admiral Edward Mountagu, later created Earl of Sandwich by Charles II. On 6 March Monck was feasted at the Mercer's Hall, but still remained silent about his true intentions, still outwardly a true republican. Any hint that he intended to restore Charles would have provoked discontent and threatened his authority with his troops. Pepys noted that 'the Parliament seems to be strong for the King, while the soldiers do all talk against'. Clarendon, assessing the situation, wrote to Charles on 28 March:

> The army is not yet in a temper to hear your name publicly: but doubt not in a short time they will be so modelled that the General may answer for their perfect obedience.[22]

Monck and Charles were now secretly corresponding. To Sir John Grenville (later the Earl of Bath), the royal emissary, Monck said that he was not only ready to obey Charles's commands but to sacrifice his life and fortune in his service. Charles wrote to Monck:

> I cannot think you wish me ill, for you have no reason to do so: and the Good I expect from you will bring so great a Benefit to your Country and to your self that I cannot think you will decline my interest. I will leave the way and manner of declaring it entirely to your own judgement and will comply with the advice you shall give me. Your affectionate friend, Charles R.[23]

The actual process of restoration took just over two months. On 16 March 1660 the Rump of the Long Parliament at last dissolved itself. On 1 April, Pepys reported that the soldiers at Dunkirk were drinking the King's health in the streets. Three days later, Charles issued his famous Declaration of Breda 'to heal the wounds of the past 20 years', offering a general pardon to the regicides and promising freedom of conscience, confirmation of land titles and the settling of arrears of army pay. He promised the army that they would be received into his service upon as good pay and conditions as they then enjoyed,[24] (a condition which he was unable to fulfil when Parliament insisted on the disbandment of Cromwell's army).

In the middle of elections for a new Convention Parliament, Lambert escaped from the Tower during the night of 9 April. He let himself down with a rope tied to his window, while his chambermaid put on his night cap and got into his bed to fool the warder. The general (whose daughter Mary only six months previously had been considered as a suitable bride for the King – she eventually married the second Duke of Buckingham) was still a rallying point for discontent, so Monck had him pursued. He was captured at Edgehill and returned to the Tower, where he remained for the rest of his life.

Monck's officers wanted him to declare publicly for the King before Parliament met, so the glory would be his and the army's. But Monck declined, reminding them of their promise, and of his declared determination, to keep military power obedient to civil authority. 'Wait a little longer for the right moment,' he told them.

The new Convention Parliament met on 25 April, with Generals Monck and Fairfax (who had broken with Cromwell over the execution of Charles I) elected as members of Parliament. Some MPs indulged in the bitterest invectives against the murderers of their late sovereign.[25] On 1 May, Monck's brother, Nicholas, brought a letter from Charles, together with his Declaration of Breda, appealing for unity. The letter was addressed 'to our trusty and well-beloved George Monck to be communicated by him to the Parliament and Council of State and to the officers of the armies under his command'. Similar but separate letters were addressed to Lords, Commons, the fleet and the City. The same day both Houses formally read the letter and Charles's declaration, and drafted a reply, voting unanimously that the Constitution of England lay in King, Lords and Commons. Monck read the letter and declaration to his officers, who received it with great joy.

As the nation waited, Pepys recalls that in London men were upon their knees in the streets, drinking the King's health. But in Deal, where guns were fired in salute, 'the soldiers of the Castle threatened but durst not oppose'; while the King was happy to leave it to Monck, 'who can now do the business or at least can hinder it'.[26]

On 8 May, Charles was proclaimed King with a great deal of pomp in the palace yard at Whitehall and at Temple Bar and an invitation was sent to King Charles II to resume the throne of his ancestors. The country went wild with joy and Parliament voted £50,000 to the King and £10,000 to the Duke of York (Charles's brother, James). These sums were supplemented by gifts from men of all political persuasions, who hastened to the King at Breda to procure indemnity for the past or to anticipate favours to come. The army sent a loyal address.

Thus Monck had brought about what he may have all along intended, a bloodless revolution. Not a shot was fired and no foreign soldier set foot on English soil. It was his supreme achievement. Even the noted chronicler of the period, the Earl of Clarendon (Charles's faithful follower Hyde, whom he rewarded for his long service and wise council with an earldom, land, and the Chancellor's Great Seal after the Restoration), no lover of Monck, acknowledged that the General managed the business with wonderful prudence and dexterity.[27] Charles, writing to Monck from Breda, spoke of his impatience to return, saying:

I must acknowledge your extraordinary affection to me and your discreet conduct of this great work, in which you have had to do with persons of such different humours and contrary affections, which you have wonderfully composed.

Charles embarked on the finest ship in the navy, renamed the *Royal Charles* in his honour, and Monck rode to Dover to meet his sovereign. As the fleet bringing the King back to England reached the Dover Roads, Charles sent Monck, 'the sole pillar of the King's confidence', a message saying he would not land until the General himself received him. Characteristically, he added, 'I pray bring Mrs Monck with you'.

The King, with the Dukes of York and Gloucester and others in his suite (including Samuel Pepys, who had been appointed secretary to the fleet commander), landed at Dover in the afternoon of 26 May. They were greeted by crowds of nobility and people. Monck was the first to be received by the King, kneeling on the crowded beach in loyal duty. Charles embraced and kissed him. After a reception by the mayor and the governor of Dover Castle, Monck travelled beside the King and his brothers in the royal coach to Canterbury. Here Charles was welcomed by the cathedral bells and several troops of horse of the aristocracy, clad in very rich apparel, commanded by the Duke of Buckingham and the Earls of Oxford, Lichfield and Derby. Lining the route were regiments of the Kentish militia. Monck was presented with the Order of the Garter (the basis of the badge of the Coldstream Guards). Admiral Edward Mountagu, who had brought the navy over to the King's side, received the same honour and was made Earl of Sandwich. Charles visited the cathedral, spent a night at Rochester and inspected his ships at Chatham.

At Blackheath on 28 May, the King, now mounted on horseback, was welcomed by the army, above 50,000 strong of horse and foot, drawn up by Monck in the King's honour. The General presented the chief officers to kiss the King's hand, 'which grace they received with all humility and cheerfulness',[28] while the troops shouted approval. The cavalcade moved along the Old Kent Road, over London Bridge and into the City through crowded streets. Then it was the turn of the Lord Mayor of London, the sheriffs and aldermen, and the whole City militia, to welcome him.

In the Banqueting Hall of the Palace of Westminster, the Speaker of the House of Commons gave a loyal address. In reply, Charles promised to preserve the laws and liberties of his people, with the Protestant religion next to his life and crown – the very issues which would dominate his reign. William Cavendish, the first Duke of Newcastle, advised the King to patrol the counties with troops and to remember always that it was with the army and not the lawyers or clergy that the King's power rested. Parliaments were justifiable only if the King was able to control them – another warning of the troubles to come!

It can never be said that the New Model army actively supported the restoration of Charles – rather, it stood aside and did not oppose it. Had it not been for the power and influence of General Monck, who removed all the leading republican officers and men before Charles set foot in England, this largely Cromwellian army would almost certainly have demanded that Charles suffered the same fate as his father. It was Monck who carried the soldiers with him.[29] Thus, concluded Clarendon, in this wonderful way did God put an end in one month to a rebellion which had raged for nearly 20 years.[30]

Monck received the thanks of his sovereign in tangible form. Charles gave him a palace, large grants of land, and a pension of £7,000 a year. He made him a privy councillor, master of the horse, gentleman of the bedchamber, lord lieutenant of Ireland, and joint admiral of the fleet with Mountagu. (The Duke of York was made lord high admiral.) On 3 August 1660 he gave him his commission as captain-general and commander-in-chief of all the King's forces. At Canterbury Monck had been awarded the highest and rarest order of chivalry the monarch can bestow – the Garter – for his princely blood and signal services.[31] Now Charles created him Duke of Albemarle, the title deriving from land held in Normandy by his Plantagenet ancestors. His patent of nobility read 'Victor sine sanguine' – an apt title for a general who had restored his King without bloodshed.[32]

2

Enter King and Royal Mistress

Charles entered London on his thirtieth birthday, after 17 years of exile. Standing in the Strand, John Evelyn, a fervent Royalist, watched the King ride into his capital at the head of his Life (or Horse) Guards and five regiments of foot soldiers:

> above 20,000 brandishing their swords and shouting with unexpressable joy: the pavements strewn with flowers, the bells ringing, the streets festooned and the fountains running with wine: the Mayor [General Brown], the Aldermen, the Companies in their liveries with banners and chains of gold: Lords and nobles clad in gold and velvet, Ladies at the windows and on the balconies, trumpets, music and crowds of people so great that the procession took seven hours in passing the city from two o'clock in the afternoon till nine o'clock at night, and all this had been achieved by the very army that had rebelled against him. It was the Lord's doing![1]

So enthusiastic was the welcome that Charles, reflecting on the day's events, whimsically remarked that it must have been his own fault he had been so long abroad, for he had not met anyone that day who had not professed to have always desired his return. But, alas! Instead of showing his gratitude to heaven by prayers and thanksgiving for his miraculous restoration, Charles passed the night in the palace of Whitehall in the arms of his mistress, Barbara Palmer, who had arrived in his retinue from Holland. As Andrew Marvell, tutor to Cromwell's nephew and later a great favourite of Charles II, wrote:

> In a slashed doublet then he came ashore,
> and dubbed poor Palmer's wife his royal whore.[2]

Barbara Palmer was a member of the Villiers clan, which has made its mark on the affairs of England from the Norman Conquest to the present day.[3] She was born in 1640 in the parish of St Margaret's, Westminster,[4] the daughter of a Royalist officer, Colonel-General Viscount Grandison. At the age of 29 he was mortally wounded at the head of his regiment, fighting for Charles I at the siege of Bristol in 1643.[5] His daughter 'was prepared for the King's bed the very first day he lay at Whitehall, seduced from her loyalty to her husband and enticed into the arms of the happily restored Prince',[6] recorded the contemporary Abel Boyer. Gilbert Burnet, later Bishop of Salisbury, confirmed that Charles 'had her' the first night he arrived in London.[7] Nine months later their first child, Anne Fitzroy, was born[8] and Barbara became recognised at court as the King's official mistress.

The role of royal mistress, or *maîtresse en titre* at the French court, had existed as long as the institution of monarchy itself. The function of most queens was to provide the heir to the throne, while the monarch sought his sexual pleasures elsewhere. Throughout history kings have been subjected to abnormal upbringings and loveless marriages for reasons of state, starved of a normal family life and forced to live, with little privacy, in a court surrounded by courtiers and attendants, by pomp and etiquette, by formality and ceremony.

Louis XIV built and furnished his splendid palace at Versailles for such a court; a temple fit for the Sun King and a model for Europe. In its beautiful promenades and secluded arbours, amidst its classical statues and cascading fountains, and in neighbouring Fontainebleau, Louis could seduce Louise de la Vallière, the Queen's maid of honour. He also charmed Henrietta (Minette), Charles's sister, the 17-year-old pleasure-seeking bride of Louis's brother, the notoriously homosexual Duc d'Orléans. In such settings, Louis established his court, lived with his mistresses, and raised the last and most powerful, Madame de Maintenon, almost to the status of a queen.

There was never a shortage of candidates anxious to share a royal bed, whisper on the royal pillow, and use their charms to further their own (or someone else's) ambitions. Intrigue and mistress went hand in hand and, since the King held absolute power and was the fount of all high office, civil, military and ecclesiastical, the stakes were high for petticoat diplomacy. Royal mistresses were therefore not merely 'pretty faces and heavenly bodies', but an integral part of English and European political, military and social history.[9]

Charles loved women: he loved being in their company, fondling, kissing and making love to them. 'I am well acquainted with a little fantastical gentleman called Cupid,' he wrote to his sister Minette. For their part, women offered themselves to his embraces for obvious mercenary reasons, but also because he was physically attractive to them. According to Barbara Palmer, who had every reason to know, he was a good lover, being well endowed to give women pleasure.[10] Prince Visconti wrote that many women, both married and single, had told him that to be loved by their King involved no wrong to husband, father, or even God himself.

Charles, one of the most attractive of all our English kings, inherited his dark, romantic good looks from his mother's Italian ancestors. His Stuart charm came from his father, Charles I, and his strong sexuality from his maternal grandfather, Henri IV of France. It is not surprising, therefore, that he enjoyed so many women and entertained so many mistresses, although he was said to have had an eye for beauty but little time for romance. Lord Halifax, who knew him well, recollected:

> His inclinations to love were the effects of good health and a good constitution, with so little of the seraphic as ever man had. I am apt to think that his passions stayed, as much as ever man's did, in the lower region.[11]

Gilbert Burnet, in his well-known portrait of the King drawn from life in 1683, blamed Charles for his love of pleasure and his vast experience with women, together with the great influence they had in all his affairs, both at home and abroad. Not only the women themselves had great power but his court was full of pimps and bawds, and all matters in which one desired to succeed had to be put in their hands.[12]

Historians have readily admitted Charles's sexual proclivities and the number of his mistresses, his love of pleasure, often before business, and the frivolities and low moral standards of his court. But they have been more interested in the extent to which Charles (and James after him) was influenced by his women in political and diplomatic circles and in policy and decision making. Halifax wrote:

> A mistress, either dexterous herself, or well instructed by those that are so, may be very useful to her friends (or equally very damaging to her enemies), not only in the immediate hours of her ministry, but by her influence and insinuations at all times. Mistresses were recommended to him, and it was resolved generally by others, whom he should have in his arms, as well as whom he should have in his Councils.

Pepys in his diary frequently echoed the complaints of Charles's ministers and courtiers: that the King was 'only governed by lust and women and rogues about him'.[13] Louis XIV and his court certainly believed it.

But modern writers support another view. Years of exile had taught Charles the value of compromise and dissimulation, and that little value was to be gained from a strict adherence to principles. Bishop Burnet said Charles trusted no one (a lesson he had learned as a refugee) and had the greatest art of concealing himself of any man alive. He thought no man was sincere, no woman honest, and no one served him out of love. Clarendon, who knew him better than most, thought he lived with his ministers as he did with his mistresses: he used them, but he was not in love with them. He tied himself no more to them than they did to him. According to the historian J.P. Kenyon Charles's mistresses were simply sexual toys, for the bed not the Cabinet and their influence on politics was negligible.[14] But from the court there flowed an endless stream of offices, favours and titles; and in the awarding of these, the King's favourites played their part.

Barbara Palmer (1640–1709), though not the first of Charles's mistresses, was certainly the most influential in the early years of his reign. Her wealth of dark auburn hair, deep blue eyes and voluptuous figure had early in her life made her the object of various young gentlemen's affections.[15] At the age of 15 she became the mistress of Philip Stanhope, second Earl of Chesterfield, who with Buckingham and other Royalists was seeking to restore the monarchy. Three years later (14 April 1659), she was married off to the Royalist Roger Palmer, educated at Eton and King's College, Cambridge, a law student of the Inner Temple and heir to a considerable fortune. This loveless marriage did not affect Barbara's romantic intrigue with Chesterfield (later to become Colonel of the Buffs from 1682–4).

Unaware of her duplicity, Palmer took her to Holland early in 1660 to offer his support and £1,000 to Charles, joining the growing number of Royalists similarly seeking place and preferment, willing to trade financial help for future favours. He had to return to London for business reasons, leaving his wife behind at the court Charles had established at Breda, and there she encountered the 29-year-old future King. She was ten years younger, and when a woman of Barbara's seductive charms and blatant sensuality met the equally amorous and amoral future King the result was inevitable. Before long Charles was writing to her husband, thanking him for his financial support and adding mischievously, 'You have more title than one to my kindness'.[16] Six weeks after Charles's return to England, Pepys stood listening a long while to the 'great doings of music' at the house next door, and noted somewhat belatedly 'the King and Dukes of York and Gloucester at the house of General Whalley with Madame Palmer, a pretty woman that they have a fancy to make her husband a cuckold'.[17]

At first the lovers used to meet in the Palmers' house in King Street, Westminster, conveniently backing onto the Privy Garden at Whitehall palace. But soon Charles installed Barbara in her own apartments inside the palace, beside Lord Sandwich's lodgings and close to his own. Before very long she was reigning over the court at Whitehall, where her greed, bad temper and promiscuity were to become notorious. From the admittedly biased Bishop Burnet she earned the reputation of being most enormously vicious and ravenous, foolish and imperious, very uneasy to the King and always carrying on intrigues with other men.[18]

During the early years of Charles's reign, Barbara exhibited all the traits of a born courtesan and strengthened her hold over the King, whom Pepys believed 'at the command of any woman like a slave and cannot command himself in the presence of a woman he likes'. Despite her passionate and aggressive qualities, which in private had their attractions but which in public could be degrading, she bound the King to her for longer than any other woman. She would exercise considerable political influence as the ally of Arlington, who began his career as a minion of the royal mistress,[19] and as the enemy of Clarendon. She accepted bribes and favours from all and sundry to provide for her own and her children's future.

To mollify her husband and reward his mistress, Charles created Roger Palmer Earl of Castlemaine,[20] but with succession to the title confined to the heirs of Barbara's body – for reasons everybody knew, according to Pepys. The official declaration, tongue in cheek, said it was 'in consideration of her noble descent, her father's death in the service of the crown and by reason of her personal virtues'. Gibbs described it more forthrightly as the wages of prostitution.[21] Without her exotic presence, Whitehall might have been a better place, but it would certainly have been a duller one.[22]

3

The Birth of the Army and a Royal Marriage

One of the first actions of the newly-restored King was to rid himself of the army: although it obeyed Monck, now Duke of Albemarle, it had been raised to serve Parliament against the monarchy. Army pay was in arrears, and the soldiers were restless and highly unpopular with the public. So, on 13 September 1660, Charles gave his assent to two Acts of Parliament to disband the Cromwellian army of 65,000 men.

The first Disbandment Act provided that all officers and men who were in pay on 25 April 1660, and had not deserted since that date, would receive their full arrears and a bonus of an extra week's pay from the King's own purse. A second Act, 'for the speedy disbanding of the Army and garrisons of this Kingdom', provided for the disbandment of one regiment at a time, the order being decided by lot. The names of the regiments and garrisons were placed in a glass and drawn out by members of the Privy Council. The last regiments to be disembodied would be those of the Dukes of York, Gloucester and Albemarle. Albemarle was given charge of the operation, and it was expected that disbandment would be completed by the early months of 1661.

The Cromwellian army generally accepted its fate willingly. Albemarle had already dismissed dissenting officers and men, and the King's Declaration of Breda promising to pay their arrears won them over. An Order of the House of Commons on 17 December 1660 made provision for the maimed and disabled. To ease the return to civilian life of some 40,000 officers and men, legislation exempted those willing to practise a trade in their own locality or to open a shop from the rigorous apprenticeship requirements. The King and wealthier citizens employed many disbanded soldiers to build their houses and gardens, and some were used to build the canal in St James's Park. Pepys commented:

> Of all the old army now, you cannot see a man begging about the streets. You shall have this captain turned a shoemaker; the lieutenant, a baker; this a

brewer; that a haberdasher; this common soldier, a porter; and every man in his apron and frock, etc, as if they never had done anything else.[1]

By Christmas the New Model Army, 'the bravest, the best disciplined and the soberest army that had been known in these latter ages' had ceased to exist, except for the Coldstream regiment and Albemarle's own regiment of horse.[2] As Fortescue wrote – Charles II was fortunate in having a soldier like Albemarle who understood soldiers and a man who understood men to carry out such a dangerous task.

On St Valentine's Day, 14 February 1661, Albemarle assembled the survivors of Cromwell's Model army on Tower Hill to finish its disbandment. Four commissioners appointed by the King congratulated the 1,000 infantry and 170 cavalry drawn up on parade for being instrumental under General Monck in restoring the King to his throne. The soldiers were promised all their arrears of pay, and then enlisted into the King's service. The troops cheered, were formally disbanded, laid down their arms, and picking them up again were immediately embodied into the new army 'as an extraordinary Guard to his Royal Person, whom God long preserve in health and happiness'.[3]

Albemarle's regiment became the Lord General's Regiment of Foot Guards (later the Coldstream Guards),[4] and his regiment of horse became the Lord General's Troop of Life Guards. Albemarle himself was appointed captain general and commander-in-chief. Military historians claim that today's standing army was actually born at 10 o'clock in the morning of St Valentine's Day 1661 on Tower Hill (although its birth certificate had been issued a couple of weeks earlier).[5]

One matter left unfinished after the Restoration was the fate of the regicides. Charles had signed a general pardon 'for all treasons, felonies and similar offences' committed since the execution of his father in 1649, except for 49 named persons 'for their execrable treason in sentencing to death or signing the instrument for the horrid murder or being instrumental in taking away the precious life of the late sovereign Lord Charles'. The first of the executions took place on Saturday 13 October 1660, witnessed by Pepys and a vast crowd.

> I went to Charing Cross to see Major General Harrison hanged, drawn and quartered – he looking as cheerfully as any man could do in that condition. He was presently cut down and his head and heart shown to the people, at which there was great shouts of joy.

General Harrison had sat as one of the judges at the trial of Charles I. Colonel Francis Hacker, who had actually supervised the execution on the scaffold, did not defend himself at his trial except to say, 'I was a soldier and under command'. He and others followed Harrison in quick succession. Charles himself witnessed some of the executions. When 10 had suffered, the King wrote to Clarendon, 'I am weary of hanging – let it sleep'. The rest were reprieved and taken back to prison.

Then Parliament turned its attention to the dead. Evelyn recorded the final scenes before thousands of spectators on 30 January 1661:

> The carkasses of Cromwell, Bradshaw [one of the judges] and Ireton [Cromwell's son-in-law] were dragged out of their superb tombs (in Westminster among the kings) to Tyburn and hanged on the gallows from 9 in the morning till 6 at night, beheaded, and then buried beneath it in a deep pit.

The Restoration heralded a period of general rejoicing, to which the King's easy charm and approachability contributed. In the early months his popularity increased, and his coronation, arranged by Parliament under Clarendon's supervision, aroused the greatest enthusiasm. It took place on St George's Day, 23 April 1661. Early the previous day, Charles went by barge to the Tower of London, traditional starting point for coronation ceremonies, and from there rode back to Whitehall in state. On the glorious day itself, Charles was cheered by crowds as he rode, robed and bare-headed, from Whitehall to Westminster Hall, and thence on foot to the Abbey. The procession was led by the Duke of York's Horse Guards.

Evelyn witnessed the colourful spectacle, which has formed the basis for subsequent coronations to this day. He describes a magnificent train on horseback, as rich as embroidery, velvet, cloth of gold and jewels could make them and their prancing horses, proceeding through streets strewn with flowers, houses hung with rich tapestry, windows and balconies full of ladies; the London militia lining the ways to Westminster, with loud music, the bells ringing and speeches and joyful acclamations en route. When the King entered the Abbey, the clergy brought out the regalia and, with the peers in their robes and coronets, paid homage to Charles, seated on a throne before the altar. The King was then presented to the people before he took the oath, swearing to maintain the Protestant religion, the Magna Carta and the laws of the land. After the banquet which followed, the King returned to Whitehall by river in a triumphal barge.

The next important event was the King's marriage. To cement his unstable throne, Charles needed a wife to provide an heir – and he needed money. Marriage could provide a rich dowry, as well as useful dynastic alliances. During his exile he had made several attempts to find a wife, but all the ladies he had approached had fought shy of marrying a penniless and homeless wanderer with poor prospects for the future.[6] But marriage with the reigning sovereign of England was quite a different matter – now he could take his pick of almost any princess in Europe.

The English people preferred him to choose a Protestant bride. Ministers led by Clarendon carefully scrutinised the incomes and religions of a number of eligible ladies; the King studied also their persons. Both France and Spain were anxious to provide a bride, preferably Catholic, to strengthen their friendship: their ambassadors presented Charles with a whole litany of marriages, offering to endow almost any Saxon, Danish and even Dutch princess 'into whose bed Charles might legally wish to romp'.[7] Charles, remembering both Spanish promises and German ladies, whom he considered 'dull and foggy', brushed aside their offers and looked more closely at the princess of a little nation struggling for independence against Spain.

Portugal was in need of mercenaries and willing to pay heavily for an English alliance. In the previous century she had led the world in maritime enterprise: she had tapped the wealth of Guinea in gold, ivory and slaves; coasted round Africa; and opened up a new route to riches and empire in the Spice Islands of the East Indies. Now she was rich in trade and overseas possessions, and had a princess available in the shape of Catherine of Braganza, daughter of King Juan IV. Louis XIV of France was supportive, hoping for a new ally in his perpetual struggle against Spain, and offered Charles 300,000 pistoles (£50,000) to conclude the marriage. Portugal, in return for permission to enlist British troops for her defence, offered Charles the richest dowry any bride had ever brought to England: over half a million pounds in ready cash; Tangier, key to the Mediterranean; and Bombay, with trading rights in the East Indies.

England's oldest ally, by sacrificing two possessions she could no longer hold, saved the rest of her crumbling empire but gave English merchants the key to India and eventually to the vast colonial expansion of the nineteenth century. Louis XIV, beside using his influence and gold to negotiate the marriage treaty, also reassured the anxious Charles (whose interest in the marriage was not solely financial) by painting Catherine as a lady of great beauty and admirable endowments, whom at one time he had even considered marrying himself.

The marriage treaty was signed on 23 June 1661, with the dowry guaranteed as promised. As a result, 4,000 troops were despatched to Portugal in May 1662 (the month of the actual marriage), and shortly afterwards took part in the defeat of a Spanish offensive in Portugal.

Charles broke the news to his newly-elected Parliament on 8 May 1661: 'I have often been put in mind by my friends that it was high time to marry . . . and I think you do not desire me to be an old bachelor'. The Commons, mostly composed of Cavalier squires and well acquainted with their sovereign's partiality for women, broke into laughter. 'I can now tell you', continued the King, 'not only that I am resolved to marry but to marry the daughter of Portugal'. They were not entirely enthusiastic about his choice; but a Popish

Queen was better than no Queen at all, and all England hoped for an heir to secure the throne. Perhaps, too, the King would now settle down to a less extravagant life-style!

In the year which passed before the marriage was consummated, the King's passion for Barbara Palmer (now Lady Castlemaine) visibly increased. She was accepted publicly as the King's official mistress, and Pepys was already complaining of the lewdness and beggary of the court. To show her hold over the King, Barbara announced that for the imminent birth of her next child she would 'lie in' at Hampton Court. This magnificent royal palace had been handed over to the crown by Cardinal Wolsey in 1525 with all its wealth and splendour to appease his jealous master, Henry VIII. It was the palace where Charles planned to spend his honeymoon.[8]

When Catherine arrived at Portsmouth in May 1662, shy and sick after her voyage, she was escorted into harbour by the Duke of York, as lord high admiral, and a retinue of courtiers. Charles was not there to greet her. He was dining and supping daily with Barbara, who was eight-and-a-half months pregnant with their first son, Charles.[9] Pepys noted that 'the King and she did send for a pair of scales and they did weigh one another: and she being with child was said to be the heaviest'.[10]

When Charles arrived five days later, he found his bride ill in bed with a fever. Nevertheless, they were married the following week, on 21 May, first secretly in her bedroom in accordance with her Catholic rites and then publicly by the Anglican Bishop of London. In announcing the news to his sister, Minette, he wrote, 'I hope I shall entertain my wife at least better the first night than your husband did you'. He did, and the wedding night was a success. The delighted Charles wrote to his mother-in-law, 'I am the happiest man in the world and the most enamoured'. To Clarendon he confided that he had consummated the marriage and Clarendon noted that the King had very good satisfaction in the Queen, who had beauty and wit enough to make herself very agreeable to him.[11]

Catherine (1638–1705) was in fact a small, frail woman, eight years younger than Charles, with an olive-tinted complexion, a pleasant rather than a pretty face, and frumpishly dressed. To Clarendon, Charles continued, 'I must be the worst man living, if I be not a good husband'.[12] He promised to contain himself within the strict bounds of virtue and conscience and banish Barbara from his bed. Chesterfield, who had been appointed chamberlain to the Queen and was in constant attendance upon her, knew Charles and Barbara intimately and was not convinced by Charles's marital vows and honeymoon intentions!

The honeymoon was spent as planned at Hampton Court, the stateliest, healthiest and most luxurious of the royal palaces outside London. Charles had redecorated and refurbished it, adding a bridal bed of crimson and silver velvet, and had bought back many of the tapestries, pictures and pieces of furniture sold during the Commonwealth. The King and Queen travelled there in a superb chariot drawn by six horses, followed by a long procession of carriages containing officers and ladies of the royal household, servants, and baggage.

The nobility, gentry and ladies of the court were presented to Catherine, many of the latter hoping the Queen would put Lady Castlemaine's nose out of joint,[13] when she eventually returned to court after the birth of her child. One evening the Duchess of York came in the royal barge from London, with a flotilla of courtiers, maids of honour, servants and musicians. She entered through Anne Boleyn's Gateway to pay her homage, and then the whole royal family sat down to drink the Queen's favourite beverage, tea, a custom she introduced into England. To quote the contemporary poet, Edmund Waller, 'The best of queens and best of herbs we owe to Portugal!'[14]

4

The Growth of the New Army

Charles and his court had watched the orderly disbandment of the Cromwellian army with favour. These soldiers, given their background, were dangerous companions, and many of the plots and rumours of plots during the early months of Charles's reign were attributed to them. But the King realised that to secure his throne and restore public confidence in the new order, a small permanent force, loyal to himself and independent of Parliament, was necessary.

On 23 November 1660, Charles commissioned the loyal and trusted Colonel John Russell to raise a regiment of foot guards to protect the King's person. Russell was the son of the fourth Earl of Bedford, who had fought during the Civil War as colonel of Prince Rupert's Guards, and was imprisoned in the Tower after an abortive rising in 1658. The regiment consisted of 12 companies, each of 100 men, the first of which was to be known as the Sovereign's Company. The King's Royal Regiment of Foot Guards (from 1815 known as the Grenadier Guards), being a royal regiment, was given precedence on the English establishment over the older Coldstreamers. Today it ranks as the senior infantry regiment of the British army.[1]

The following month the King's Foot Guards were posted 'at all corners of London and the Palace to secure the government against plots which had been discovered'. Just as the regiment was being formed, an insurrection arose. Insignificant in itself and quickly suppressed, it justified the King's attempt to retain a small force of 'guards and garrisons'.

The plot involved about 50 supporters of General Lambert, calling themselves Fifth Monarchy men, a non-conformist sect believing in 'the Second Coming and the binding of the kings of the earth in chains and their nobles with links of iron'. On 6 January 1661, in St Paul's Cathedral, they killed a man who supported King Charles rather than King Jesus, and then attacked the Lord Mayor and his musketeers. Soon the King's Foot Guards, the City militia and eventually Albemarle's Coldstream regiment arrived to capture their leader, Captain Venner, a wine cooper from Massachusetts, and the survivors. But so alarmed was the government, both to protect the sovereign and to maintain law and order, that Parliament agreed on the captain general's advice to supplement Lord Russell's regiment of Foot Guards with three more regiments.

So, on 26 January 1661, Charles signed a Royal Warrant authorising the establishment of the first standing army in the country. It is often called the birth certificate of the British army, and provided for the First and Second Foot Guards, the Life Guards and the Royal Horse Guards, numbering 374 officers and 3,200 men, at an annual cost of £122,500.[2] (In addition to these four regiments, there were 28 garrison companies of foot soldiers stationed in the country's forts and castles, and 250 Beefeaters[3] to be used for court ceremonials. These were added to the establishment in June 1661, and also charged to the King's account.)

During his exile, Charles had a personal bodyguard of 80 Royalist gentlemen who had held commissions in the army of Charles I. The Duke of York and Monck had similar troops of bodyguards. On 26 January 1661, after the Venner insurrection, the King formed them into the Life Guards of three troops of cavalry: The King's Own, The Duke of York's and the Duke of Albemarle's.

The first two troops, according to the military historian Sir John Fortescue,[4] were composed of men of both birth and education. For more than a century they were rightly called 'gentlemen of the Life Guards': every trooper in the ranks was the personal servant and bodyguard of his monarch, and answerable to no one except his own officers. They were nearly all men of private fortune, and often paid substantial premiums for the right to serve in this *corps d'élite*. Mounted on splendid black horses, they were magnificently dressed and equipped, almost entirely at their own expense. When they rode out as the King's escort they were accompanied by the drums, trumpets and hautboys (oboes) of their own band.

In February 1661 the twentieth Earl of Oxford, Aubrey de Vere, one of the six peers who had invited Charles to return as King, was ordered to raise the regiment of Royal Horse Guards. They were also known as the Blues (after their uniforms of Oxford blue), and Oxford himself became their colonel and remained so until 1688.

In addition, Charles recalled some Scottish mercenaries in the French service, the Royal Ecossais Regiment (first raised by Sir John Hepburn in 1633, and traditionally regarded as the ancient bodyguard of Scottish kings) to become the Royal Regiment of Foot. Their colonel was George Douglas, Earl of Dumbarton, and the regiment was commonly known as Dumbarton's. It would be the senior regiment of the line, under the title of the Royal Scots.[5]

Later, on 1 October 1661, the Earl of Peterborough was asked to raise a new regiment of foot to garrison Tangier (known as the Second Foot or The Queen's Regiment) and a troop of horse (The Tangier Horse or First Royal Dragoons). Fortescue comments that the oldest regiments of the British army trace their continuous history in the service of the crown to 1660–1661 and to the odd combination of the Fifth Monarchy plot and a Roman Catholic dowry (Tangier).[6]

In Dunkirk, which Cromwell had captured from Spain in 1657, some 6,000 foot soldiers and 600 garrison troops had been unaffected by the disbandment of the New Model Army, except that Cromwell's republican officers were replaced by Royalist sympathisers. But the King had insufficient money to retain the garrison, which cost £130,000 a year to maintain, and the troops were in any case viewed with deep suspicion in England as a possible invasion force; so in October 1662 Charles sold Dunkirk to France for 5 million livres (£400,000).

Amongst the garrison were men from The Royal Regiment of Guards, raised in 1656 and commanded by Lord Thomas Wentworth. It consisted entirely of officers, most of whom had followed Charles into exile and served him in the English regiment of infantry raised by General Wilmot, the first Earl of Rochester. Such was their devotion to Charles that they had accepted commissions in this regiment at ranks lower than those they had previously held in the Royalist forces during the Civil War. When Charles sailed to Dover to recover his crown, Wentworth accompanied him as a privy councillor and left his regiment behind in Dunkirk.

But now these loyal troops (some 500 pikemen clothed in buff, and 700 musketeers in red coats) were brought to England to be amalgamated with Lord Russell's First Foot Guards. They were taken on the English establishment in 1665, making the regiment some 24 companies strong,[7] and giving a distinguished origin to the future Grenadier Guards.

Some Dunkirk cavalry were incorporated into the Duke of York's troop of Life Guards; other troops were sent to Tangier, to Portugal, or to serve as mercenaries in the French army as the Duke of York's regiment. The remainder were disbanded, thus removing any political danger from this last reservoir of Cromwell's New Model Army abroad.

The Convention Parliament, its work of restoration and pardon accomplished, was dissolved. Its replacement, the Cavalier Parliament, was opened by the King on 8 May 1661, a few weeks after his coronation, and would last almost to the end of his reign, being finally dissolved in 1679. Its members were chiefly Royalists, Cavalier gentry and landowners, with a sprinkling of merchants, lawyers and military officers out for revenge and compensation. They immediately set about passing the so-called Clarendon Code between 1661 and 1665. The code was a series of penal laws against their Puritan opponents – the non-conformist middle and lower classes – which would divide

England into bitter rivalry between Anglican church and dissenters, including Presbyterians and Quakers.

Those who refused to accept the Anglican communion and prayer book, and to swear the oath of allegiance and supremacy, were excluded from municipal office. Puritans were expelled from their non-conformist livings, and imprisoned and transported to the colonies for attending their religious meetings. Their clergymen and schoolmasters were forbidden to live within five miles of any town or city.

Many left hearth and home to face the storms of the Atlantic, settling on the shores of Massachusetts, rather than see the communion table in their village church moved to the east end, where it savoured of the abomination of the Catholic mass.[8] Thus the New England colonies were founded, firmly planting on American soil the English language and the three distinguishing features of English life – the Congregational church, the town council and the village school.[9]

Justices of the peace would vigorously enforce these terrible laws until the Glorious Revolution of 1689, executing the Clarendon Code without royal mercy or court favour. This was unlike the even more terrible laws against Catholics, still largely a legacy of the harsh legislation of Elizabeth I, which could be mitigated by royal declarations of indulgence (as in 1687 and 1688). Laws such as the Clarendon Code were responsible for many of the plots and informers like Titus Oates, for the distrust and hatred of Popery, and for the hundreds of imprisonments, transportations and worse which bedevilled the reigns of the Stuarts.

From early times, it had been the duty of able-bodied men to muster for the defence of the kingdom when invasion threatened. This ancient tradition and feudal obligation evolved into the militia, spread over England, Scotland and Ireland. It was a citizen force, under the authority of lords-lieutenant and the local gentry of the shires, responsible to Parliament and not the crown, and acting largely as a riot force in peacetime. Its strength after the Restoration was about 90,000 men, of whom only 6,000 were cavalry.

On 30 July 1661 the Cavalier Parliament passed the Militia Act, confirmed by others in 1662 and 1663, which declared:

> the sole supreme government, command and disposition of the militia and of all the forces by sea and land, and of all forts, is, and by the laws of England ever was, the undoubted right of his majesty . . . and that both or either of the Houses of Parliament cannot, nor ought to, pretend to the same.[10]

These Acts declared, without equivocation, that the King had control of all the military forces, but made no mention of a standing army. This was an issue which would be the subject of fierce controversy in the coming decades, until finally resolved in the Mutiny Act of 1689. The Militia Act made clear, too, that Parliament had no right to raise soldiers or levy war against the crown; in order to protect the crown, all officers and soldiers were to take the oaths of allegiance and supremacy.

The Disbandment Act allowed the King to raise as many soldiers as he wished, provided he paid for them – in fact, confirming the ancient prerogative of the crown. Parliament would later claim that, by passing the Militia Act, it had opened the way to military government and supported an absolute monarchy. The cry of 'No standing armies' would be loudly heard in the 1670s, and Parliament under the Whigs would seek to establish the principle supported by Monck, that military power should be subordinate to the civil.[11]

In June 1662 Barbara Castlemaine (Barbara Palmer before Roger Palmer's ennoblement) gave birth to her first son, Charles Fitzroy. A week later Barbara deserted her indignant husband and moved to the house of her uncle, Colonel Edward Villiers, at Richmond. She took most of their possessions with her: every dish and piece of clothing out of the house, and all the servants except the hall porter, according to Pepys. She considered the handsome settlements she had obtained for Roger – a peerage, the marshalship to the King's Bench Prison, an estate in Ireland and a seat in the Irish House of Lords – a fair exchange for her freedom. Roger went to France, with the avowed intention of entering a monastery, but thought better of it.[12]

Despite his promise to Catherine to be a good husband, Charles could not keep away from his radiant mistress and was determined to regularise her position at court now that she was of noble rank. To confirm her status he included her name as lady of the Queen's bedchamber in a list of appointments to the Queen's household. This was the second highest in ranking of the few royal posts which could be given to a woman. (The highest, that of first lady, mistress of the robes and keeper of the privy purse to the Queen, Charles had already given to the Countess of Suffolk, sister of Barbara's father.)

To Charles's surprise the normally docile Queen, forewarned of Barbara Castlemaine's reputation by her mother, the Queen Regent of Portugal, was outraged when she saw Barbara's name included in her household list. Angrily she struck it out, refusing in this way to honour officially the King's mistress; with rage and tears, she refused Charles's request to reinstate it. Charles was determined to fulfil his promise to Barbara and gave Clarendon, one of the few friends the Queen had, the unenviable task of persuading Catherine to accept the nomination.

The Chancellor thoroughly disapproved of the King's relationship with Barbara and her hold over him. He loathed her person and her very name, which he refused to use in his autobiographical history, calling her instead 'the lady of youth and beauty, with whom the King had lived in great and notorious familiarity, since his arrival in England'. To Charles he courageously pointed out that in England, contrary to France, if a woman prostituted herself even to the King, she was regarded as being no better than a common whore, as Anne Boleyn had discovered. And even in France the King's mistresses were 'women of quality, who had never been tainted by any other familiarity'.[13]

But Charles was adamant, defending Barbara's name with more loyalty than accuracy as he warned Clarendon:

> not to meddle any more with what concerns my Lady Castlemaine. I am resolved to go through with this matter whatever the consequences and whosoever I find to be my Lady Castlemaine's enemy in this matter, I do promise to be his enemy as long as I live. I have undone this lady,and ruined her reputation and I am obliged in conscience and honour to repair her to the utmost of my power.[14]

If necessary, he said, he would return the Queen and her ladies to Portugal. Faced by such threats Clarendon protested no more, and persuaded the Queen that the only way to keep her husband's affection was to yield. At length the Queen surrendered, even showering on her rival every mark of attention. Soon, noted Clarendon, the lady came to the court, was lodged there and was every day in the Queen's presence and the King in continual conference with her.[15]

Charles was devoted to Barbara and courtiers competed for her patronage; poets, warriors and nobles paid her compliments; strumpets and great ladies imitated her coiffure, her dress and the imperious way she held her head. In the tour at Hyde Park her coach was escorted by the greatest in the land. Every afternoon was a party and every night a ball, with Barbara sitting beside the King in brilliant attire, radiant with happiness and so lovely that Charles, in unrestrained rapture, stopped every few minutes to kiss her. He took her to church with him and, regardless of precedence, seated her in the pew beside his own. In April 1663 he moved Barbara again to new apartments in the Holbein Gate, the upper storeys of which commanded a lovely view over St James's Park. She was at the peak of her power.[16]

In return, Charles was kind, courteous and grateful to the Queen, though his gratitude fell short of fidelity. For a time at least, he tried to do his duty to her, although he found little in her to attract him physically. For some years it would be his practice to spend the evening with his mistresses and then return to the marital bed seeking an heir. Judging by his success in producing progeny[17] (Charles prided himself on being the father of a not inconsiderable number of his loyal subjects), it was not for lack of effort on his part that his wife failed the succession. The failure, in fact, distressed both of them. Barbara, on the other hand, was soon pregnant again –she would produce five children recognised by the King.[18]

In the early years of her marriage, hoping for children, the Queen sought help in the various watering places of England, of which Bath and Tunbridge were then the most famous. In July 1663 the court went to Tunbridge, about the same distance from London as Fontainebleau is from Paris. During the season it became the general rendezvous of all the pleasure-seeking and handsome of both sexes. The company, though numerous, was always select; since those who repaired there for entertainment exceeded the number who went for health. Everything there breathed mirth and pleasures; constraint was banished, familiarity was established upon the first acquaintance, and joy and pleasure were the sole sovereigns of the place.[19]

The company were accommodated in little, clean and convenient cottages within a mile-and-a-half radius of 'the Wells', where they met in the morning to drink the waters. On one side of the shaded walk was a row of shops, plentifully stocked with all manner of toys, lace, gloves and stockings; on the other was the market, where young, fair, fresh-coloured country girls, with clean linen, small straw hats and neat shoes and stockings, sold game, vegetables, flowers and fruit. Here one could live as one pleased; here, likewise, was gambling and no want of amorous intrigue.

In September the court went to Bath, from which Charles wrote to Clarendon that his wife was very well pleased with the bath, and he hoped the effects would be as she desired.[20] But Catherine was to be disappointed, having frequent miscarriages. Later in the reign she despaired of bearing children, especially as the King neglected her more and more for his mistresses.

The Queen was not equipped by nature or upbringing to play any part in public affairs, and in time she faded into the background, amusing herself in the evening with the fashionable card game of basset, with music, and seeking consolation in her religion. She remained genuinely in love with her husband, accepting his numerous liaisons with quiet dignity. In later years, she resided mostly at Somerset House, leaving her husband with even more freedom to indulge his nature.

5

The Palace of Whitehall

Charles's principal residence in London, and the centre of his court, was the sprawling old palace of Whitehall, the historic site of today's government departments. A visiting Frenchman described the palace in 1665 as a more commodious habitation than the Louvre, for it contained above 2,000 rooms and lay between a fine park and a noble river.[1] For nearly 40 years, from the Restoration until it was destroyed by fire in 1698, it enjoyed a splendour unmatched in its annals. Many key events of the Stuart reigns took place within the confines of the palace. Charles I stepped out of one of the windows of the Banqueting Hall to meet his executioner; there Charles II brought his bride, and died in the royal bedchamber. James II and his Queen, Mary of Modena, with their unfortunate infant son, were smuggled out of one of the palace's dark passages to make their escape to France; while William and Mary were proclaimed King and Queen of England in Whitehall. Popular imagination has been enthralled down the ages with both the glamour and romance of Whitehall's miraculously restored King, and its colourful courtiers and famous court beauties – Barbara Castlemaine, Frances Stuart, Nell Gwynn and Louise de Keroualle all had apartments in the palace.

In reality, the palace was a warren of rooms and apartments, galleries, courtyards and gardens. It contained the homes, offices and workplaces not only of the royal families but also of the principal ministers of state, courtiers, chaplains, maids of honour, mistresses, servants high and low – in short, of all the gilded army of fashionable and upper-class society which surrounded the English throne. Of immense size, the palace in the days of Charles II extended along the river and in front along the present Parliament Street and Whitehall Street as far as Scotland Yard; and on the other side of those streets to the turning into Spring Gardens beyond the Admiralty, looking into St James's Park.[2] Today, all that remains above ground is the Banqueting Hall.

Once the palace of Cardinal Wolsey had stood here; but Henry VIII, jealous of his subject's ever-increasing magnificence, confiscated the property, changing its name from York Place to Whitehall, and established it in 1530 as his royal residence. Here he celebrated his marriages to Anne Boleyn (1533) and Jane Seymour (1536), and extended the palace by acquiring the area of today's Horse Guards, demolishing hundreds of squalid houses in the process.

During the Commonwealth troops had been billeted in the palace and a gun battery placed at the Holbein Gate. But in May 1659 Whitehall, which had lain looted and empty since the death of Cromwell, was put up for sale to pay off the soldiers' arrears of pay. It attracted no buyers. Charles occupied it immediately on his return and it quickly became the private, social and political centre for the King and his courtiers to play out their daily lives.

On the south side, the palace began with the bowling green and the privy garden. Next came the Banqueting Hall, built by Inigo Jones for Charles I, with its beautiful Rubens ceiling. The hall was used for the audiences of ambassadors, touching for the King's Evil,[3] and the distribution of Maundy money to the poor at Easter. Beside it stood the palace gate and tower, which gave access to the Great Hall or presence chamber. Built by Cardinal Wolsey and neglected during the Commonwealth, this chamber under Charles II became once again the scene of festivity, dancing and plays.[4]

The centre of this courtly village was the long Stone Gallery, overlooking the sun dial and privy gardens, the hub of the King's government. On its walls hung the King's paintings, a kind of National Gallery open to all-comers. Yet the crowds which thronged the gallery did not come to see the pictures: the velvet curtains across the doors would part and the King himself would pass through the host of place-seekers, preferment hunters and sightseers, followed by a group of ministers from bedchamber or council chamber.

From the Stone Gallery, guarded doors opened into the royal apartments, built round three sides of a small court or garden. In the Council Chamber the great committees of state sat in debate, while in the withdrawing room the waiting lords warmed their hands before a wood fire. Beyond was the holy of holies, the King's bedchamber, reserved for its carefully selected staff, princes and important councillors. The most secret affairs of state were transacted here at all hours of the day and night. In 1682 a new bedchamber was built for the King, its ante-room hung with tapestries illustrating the adventures of Don Quixote. Yet even here, where Charles slept with his pampered spaniels, the King enjoyed little privacy, though entry was strictly limited by court etiquette.

Up a tiny flight of stairs lay the King's closet, opened by the King's private key. In this room Charles kept his treasures – pictures by Titian, Raphael and

Holbein, jewels, crystal vases, rare cabinets, and his collection of enamelled clocks and watches. Nearby, completed in 1668, were his laboratory, his library of 1,000 volumes, his maps and sea charts, and some mathematical instruments.[5]

In 1532 Henry VIII built the King's Gate, and about the same time Holbein designed and erected the Holbein Gate with its beautiful embattled towers. This connected the tennis court, cock-pit and bowling green with the palace. Pepys, appointed clerk of the King's ships and a member of the navy board first constituted by Henry VIII, had a room in the Holbein Gate. As apartments for the royal mistress, it afforded quick and easy access to the King's chambers.

Below it, through the tall stone archway separating the two sides of the palace – the river or east side, and the park side on the west – ran a muddy lane called King Street,[6] which linked Charing Cross[7] with Westminster, the Houses of Parliament and the Abbey. The Street was so narrow that there were frequent quarrels between coachmen and carters trying to pass one another. Pepys noted such a quarrel on 27 November 1660, which resulted in one of Lord Chesterfield's footmen being killed in a brawl. Later in Charles II's reign, Sir George Downing,[8] one of his ministers, developed property in the area (today's Downing Street commemorates his name).

It was not in the King's private apartments, nor even in the ante-room, where foreign ministers daily waited his return from his walk in St James's Park, but in the Banqueting Hall and the Chapel Royal that England saw its King. He dined in state a little after mid-day, raised on a dais, while the lords of the household served him on bended knee and all England looked on from the galleries to share the pageantry. The bountiful supply of food at the King's tables was a source of wonder and amazement to foreigners: not only were noblemen and gentlemen subjects lavishly entertained, but even strangers were admitted to the privileges of the King's officers.

> Besides divers dishes provided every day for the King's honour, 240 gallons of beer a day were allowed at the Buttery Bar for the poor, besides all the broken meat, bread etc. gathered into baskets and given to the poor at the Court gates by the King's grooms.[9]

And every Sunday morning a stream of citizens flowed westwards by boat or coach to see the King at prayers. Pepys was a frequent visitor to the Chapel Royal, curtained to separate the monarch from the ladies of the bedchamber, who sat on either side. They listened to the new organ, which Charles introduced, and heard the long sermons the King endured. 'My Lord, My Lord', cried one preacher to the sleeping Lauderdale, 'you snore so loud you will wake the King!.'[10]

In 1670 Charles provided apartments for his mistress, Louise de Keroualle, near to the Stone Gallery; rooms occupied later by their son, the Duke of Richmond, and remembered today in Richmond Terrace. On 4 October 1683, Evelyn visited Louise's quarters, which were among the most splendidly furnished in Whitehall. He described the rich and splendid furniture of her apartment, twice or thrice pulled down and rebuilt to satisfy her prodigal and expensive pleasures. He saw the beautiful French tapestries, embroidered with copies of the palaces of Versailles and St Germain, hunting scenes and exotic landscapes; Japanese cabinets, screens, pendulum clocks, great vases of wrought plate, tables, stands, chimney furniture, sconces and braziers all of massive silver and without number, besides some of Charles's best paintings. The apartments were ten times the richness and glory of the Queen's, whose bedchamber contained nothing but some pretty pious pictures and books of devotion.[11] Evelyn walked through the gallery into Louise's dressing room, within her bedchamber, where she was in her morning loose garments, her maids combing her hair, newly out of her bed, Charles and the gallants standing about her.[12] On 10 April 1691 Evelyn would record the fire which finally destroyed the palace and burned down these apartments, together with 'other lodgings of such lewd creatures who debauched both King Charles II and others and were his destruction'.[13]

Distributed around the royal apartments were the lodgings of the maids of honour, the Queen's seamstress and Barbara, Countess of Suffolk, mistress of the Queen's robes. Here, too, were the privy stairs, guarded by a faithful servant, which allowed the King to enter his apartment from the river.[14]

North of the Great Court lay an area called Scotland Yard, devoted to servicing the Palace – the bakehouse, spicery, buttery, laundries, the King's coal yard and the department of works. It derived its name from a palace which once occupied the site, built for the reception of Scottish kings when they visited London to pay homage for their fiefdoms. John Milton had a small apartment there in 1650.

Sir John Denham, who had fought bravely for his King during the Civil War, died in his residence in Scotland Yard in 1668, when surveyor of the King's works. He received this appointment as a reward for the confiscation of his property, and his imprisonment and exile, during the Commonwealth. Denham's pretty, 18-year-old wife became the mistress of the Duke of York, who openly visited her at her husband's house and courted her at the palace. Her early death in 1667 gave rise to the unfounded suspicion that the jealous Duchess had poisoned her with a cup of chocolate. Neighbours believed the 50-year-old Denham was the culprit, and the fury of the populace was only appeased by a sumptuous funeral he provided for her at St Margaret's, Westminster.[15] After Denham's death he was succeeded by Sir Christopher Wren, who held the post for the next 50 years.

Among those who resided in the Palace during Charles II's reign were the Duke and Duchess of Albemarle. They lived in apartments overlooking the park; apartments which had been occupied by Cromwell before he became Protector. Cromwell's son-in-law, General Fleetwood, lived in Wallingford House, on the site of the present Admiralty House. On Charles's Restoration, the Duke of Buckingham, whose vast estates were restored by the King (still remembered in Villiers Street), took over Wallingford House and established there a Board of Admiralty. In other parts of the palace lived the Dukes of Monmouth, Lauderdale and Ormonde, Prince Rupert, Earl Rochester, Lord Peterborough, and a number of ladies of whom we know little, like Mrs Kirk, Lady Sears and Mrs Chiffinch. Across the park the Duke of York held his own court in St James's Palace.

The present buildings of the Horse Guards stand on the site of an old guard-house, put up originally in 1641 for the gentlemen pensioners who formed the guard (there being no standing army before the reign of Charles II). In 1663-4 a much larger barracks was built, occupying almost the whole of the tiltyard site, to accommodate the Horse Guards and part of the Foot Guards. A court-yard in front led into the street of Whitehall, with sentry boxes on either side of the entrance.[16]

The tiltyard in Henry VIII's time was a place for noblemen and others 'to exercise themselves in jousting, turning and fighting at barriers'.[17] Henry watched the tournaments on what is now Horse Guards Parade, from the splendid gallery he built overlooking it. It was used as a place for tournaments and pageants under Elizabeth I, who also commanded the bear, the bull and the ape to be baited in the tiltyard. In Hendrick Dankaert's 1680 painting of the tiltyard and Horse Guards, Charles II is strolling through St James's Park with his courtiers and spaniels. Behind is a detachment of Coldstream Guards, who are carrying at their head their colonel's colour. In the background the Banqueting Hall can be seen, with the lodgings of the Duke of Albemarle to the right (See plate 8).

In September 1660 disbanded soldiers were employed to build a canal through St James's Park and Charles began to stock the lake with ducks and birds, whose descendants still fascinate modern Londoners and visitors. Beyond the lake he planted trees and flowers, and filled the park with deer, antelopes and Arabian sheep to delight his own and future generations. The King would take his exercise in the park, which helped to preserve his superb health and good humour; talking to all-comers, feeding his birds, or playing on the Pall Mall court he built for that popular game. Fond of outdoor pursuits, Charles had a bowling green near the river and constructed a new tennis court in 1662 to help to reduce his weight.[18]

With the King in residence, Whitehall was the focus of political intrigue and of fashionable society. In the early months all England flocked there –

ruined Cavaliers begging grants and favours, mayors with loyal addresses and gifts, politicians seeking places, and ordinary people to see their King and kiss his hands, or touch his person to cure them of their ills. Half the jobbing and half the flirting of the metropolis went on under his roof, wrote Lord Macaulay.

6

The Court

Royalty stood at the centre of the whole system of patronage and power: access and proximity to the King's person were the goals of courtiers, politicians and military alike. Ministers, mistresses, favourites, adventurers, priests, physicians, foreign visitors and diplomats – all who could gain access to the court and personal contact with their sovereign – sought to obtain or use such influence to advantage; guiding or prejudicing his mind or feelings for or against policies, individuals and supplicants for favours.[1] Even lesser attendants and menial body servants could obstruct, spread ill-reports or do harm. And mistresses had a special role to play within the intimate confines of the bedchamber, with their favourable opportunities for pillow talk and petticoat diplomacy.

One lowly-placed but trusted servant who performed many services for the King, as both special agent and procurer-general, was William Chiffinch. In 1666 he succeeded his brother as page in the King's bedchamber, and soon became so well trusted that only he had a duplicate key to the King's private closet. Under his skilful management, eavesdropping became a profession and the backstairs a political institution, for much of Charles's policy was made in corners behind locked doors.[2] Chiffinch guarded Charles's private stairs, which were also a means by which nocturnal visitors could be smuggled into the royal bed. The contemporary Roger North wrote:

> Under Chiffinch the backstairs might properly be called the spy-office, where the King spoke with particular persons about intrigues of all kinds. He fished out many secrets and discovered men's characters, which the King could never have obtained by any other means.[3]

Lord Halifax, a senior minister of Charles II with first-hand experience, claimed that the King had backstairs to convey information to him, as well as for other uses. 'I do not believe he trusted any man – or any woman'.[4]

Chiffinch loyally supported the King, his mistresses and his favourite courtiers, feathering his own nest in the process. With his wife, he distributed French gold, secret service monies and other inducements on behalf of his master, to high and low alike. He would serve and outlive both Charles II and James II, dying in 1691 a comparatively wealthy man. He left his estate to his daughter Barbara, whose many suitors included Lord Plymouth, Lord Shrewsbury and Sir William Clifton. Barbara finally married in 1681, Colonel Edward Villiers (uncle of Barbara Castlemaine) and became Lady Villiers, Countess of Jersey.[5]

After his restoration Charles was able to reward many of those who had shared his exile or supported his cause, giving them honours and high household, civil or military posts. Besides Monck (Albemarle), Hyde (Clarendon) and Mountagu (Sandwich), Anthony Ashley Cooper, who had been a Royalist colonel of horse during the Civil War and then a field marshal on the Parliamentary side, was restored to royal favour and became Earl of Shaftesbury and Chancellor of the Exchequer. Sir Edward Nicholas was made Charles's first secretary of state, later replaced by Sir Henry Bennet ennobled as Lord Arlington, and James Butler became Duke of Ormonde and lord lieutenant of Ireland, gaining the return of his Irish estates and large grants of land as reward for the fortune he had spent on the King.

One of the first to be rewarded was John Wilmot, second Earl of Rochester. His father had been general of the King's cavalry during the Civil War and had also helped Charles escape after the battle of Worcester, disguised as the manservant of Colonel Lane's sister Jane. During Charles's exile Rochester had been one of his chief advisers and carried out a number of secret and diplomatic missions for him. The perils they had shared earned the King's gratitude – a legacy Wilmot left to his son. Charles gave the younger Wilmot a pension, the post of a gentleman of the bedchamber, and made him a naval commander. In this role he showed courage in a number of engagements against the Dutch.

Rochester joined the intimate circle of the King's most dissolute associates and accompanied Charles on many of his amorous adventures. His practical jokes and ribald wit spared neither the King nor his ministers and mistresses. He was dismissed from the court at least once a year, but Rochester so fascinated the King that Charles would soon restore him to favour again. For slipping into the King's pocket, for instance, such lines as:

> was ever Prince's Soul so meanly poor,
> To be a slave to every little whore?
> (A Satyr)

– he was sent to cool his heels in the Tower for a spell!

Military commands were given to 'our right trusty and right well-beloved cousin,' Aubrey de Vere, Earl of Oxford (colonel of the Blues), Robert Sidney and the Earl of Chesterfield (colonels of the Buffs), and Henry Mordaunt, Earl of Peterborough (colonel of the Queen's Regiment), to name but a few. In the three years after his restoration some 160 former Royalist army officers and around 30 families of those deceased were rewarded by the King.

To these were added soldiers of fortune, who had placed their swords at the service of foreign monarchs during Charles's wars. Needy and self-seeking adventurers were disgorged from the taverns and brothels of France and the Low Countries, where they had whiled away the Commonwealth years gambling, roistering and wenching. Now they were returning – the worthier to help unselfishly in the reconstruction of the monarchy, the less worthy to join in the eager competition for royal favour.[6]

For 150 years after the Restoration, monarchs would continue to commission men of proven loyalty from the ranks of the peerage and gentry to command regiments of horse and foot. These regiments protected the royal person and constituted an army with which to pursue foreign policy. In return the colonels would expect to make a reasonable profit from the money they invested in their regiments, and to gain prestige and power from these stepping stones to their ambitions.

One such recipient of Charles's gratitude was the ardent Royalist Colonel Sir William Legge, who had fought for the King during the Civil War and been imprisoned in the Tower when captured in battle. He declined the earldom offered him but told the King he hoped his sons might live to deserve His Majesty's favour. Charles restored him to his posts of groom of the bedchamber and master of the armouries, and appointed him lieutenant-general of the Ordnance. The Ordnance had responsibility for the manufacture and supply of guns and munitions to both the army and the navy. Its offices were in the Tower of London, where many of Legge's staff had official lodgings, but the munitions were manufactured in gun-powder factories and gun foundries elsewhere. The Board of Ordnance controlled the appointments of all gunners and engineers, ashore and afloat, and in 1667 was made responsible for defence fortifications.[7] His eldest son, George, became Admiral Lord Dartmouth.

Another recipient was a young nobleman, John Sheffield, the third Earl of Mulgrave, who rose rapidly from captain of a troop of horse in 1667 to command an 84-gun ship in the Second Dutch War. He was colonel of the Buffs from 1673 to 1682, and became a gentleman of the King's bedchamber in 1673.[8] He was temporarily banished from the court in 1682 for having the temerity to court Princess Anne, daughter of the Duke of York, but Charles forgave him and he regained command of the Buffs from 1683 to 1684. A poet of some repute he took as his third wife an illegitimate daughter of James II by Catherine Sedley.

But neither the government nor the King could hope to reward all those who came to court or sent petitions, seeking reward or compensation for their service, sufferings or losses. This was especially true of Royalist gentry who had sold their estates to pay Cromwell's fines and so were left with grievances. One way of rewarding such old friends and supporters and repaying his huge debts was for Charles to give them large grants of land in North America, making them colonial proprietors. Six of the original Thirteen States (New York, New Jersey, the Carolinas and Pennsylvania) were founded in this way.

In 1663, for instance, Charles gave a huge area of land south of Virginia to eight important favourites. The region was called Carolina, in honour of the King. The leader of the group of proprietors was Anthony Ashley Cooper, Earl of Shaftesbury, who found he could not live even on the high salary of Chancellor of the Exchequer in Charles's extravagant court. The others were Clarendon, Albemarle, the Earl of Craven, Sir George Carteret, Lord John Berkeley and his brother Sir William Berkeley, a former governor of Virginia, and Sir John Colleton, a Royalist soldier who had fled from England to Barbados when Charles I was beheaded in 1649. The eight peers were stockholders in the Royal African and Hudson Bay companies, and were given a charter to develop North and South Carolina.

The proprietors planned to profit from their vast estates by producing such exotic products as oil, olives, sugar, silk, wine and tobacco. Captain Joseph West was appointed governor and led the expedition in 1665 to establish the province of South Carolina, between the Ashley and Cooper rivers, and the settlement of Charles Town (Charleston). Former indentured servants and other poor whites, forced out of Virginia by the low price of tobacco and negro slavery, migrated to settle and farm in the north of the province along the shores of Albemarle Sound. This area became North Carolina in 1712, and in 1729 a royal colony.

In order to discharge a debt of £16,000 inherited from his father (Admiral William Penn had once lent the money to Charles II), in 1681 the King, always short of cash, gave William Penn junior instead a huge land grant and charter. This, together with the grant of Delaware by the Duke of York in 1682 to give access to the sea, became the state of Pennsylvania, named after the Admiral. It was the last mainland colony to be founded in the seventeenth century. William Penn Junior, a convert to the Quakers, promised religious toleration and cheap land, and dissenters from England, Ireland, Sweden, France and Germany, and Jews from all over Europe, settled in the new colony. Penn made treaties with the Indians and paid them for land occupied, and trade prospered. The colony grew with such rapidity that its capital, Philadelphia, soon became the third city in the British Empire and its leading members a wealthy merchant aristocracy.

Similarly, Rhode Island, the smallest of the 13 colonies, was granted by the

King to Dr. John Clarke in 1663. Connecticut in 1662 was given to John Winthrop Junior, the eldest son of the governor of Massachusetts. In 1664 the Duke of York gave New Jersey, a sparsely settled wilderness, to his two friends and allies of the King, Lord John Berkeley and Sir George Calvert (who as governor of Jersey in the Channel Islands gave this name to the American colony). It afforded the Quakers a place where they could practise their religion in peace. In 1632 Charles I had given a charter to George Calvert (Lord Baltimore), a Catholic convert, to develop a coastal region as a home for Roman Catholics and Puritans alike. It was to become Maryland, named after Charles's mother, Henrietta Maria, the widow of Charles I.

Once again, at his marriage, Charles was inundated with appeals from importunate men and women anxious to secure positions, and thus influence, in the new royal household. Many were the wives, widows and daughters of needy Cavalier gentry and Royalist supporters, seeking reward or restitution as maids of honour or ladies of the bedchamber.

Barbara Palmer's father, for instance, was killed and his family impoverished in the King's service. In 1650 his sister, Barbara, married James Howard, third Earl of Suffolk, who acted as the earl-marshal of England at Charles's coronation. In 1662 the Countess of Suffolk was appointed first lady of the bedchamber, mistress of the robes, and keeper of the Queen's privy purse. Besides the prestige, Barbara was entitled to apartments in the palace, emoluments, and allowances of bread, beer, wine, candles and firewood throughout the year.

The posts of maid of honour were eagerly sought after. Jane Middleton, 'one of the most beautiful women in England', kept her husband and two children 'largely upon the generosity of her lovers', who included Gramont, the poet Edmund Waller, the Earl of Rochester and William Russell, standard-bearer of the First Regiment of Foot Guards.[9] She and Winifred Wells 'a big, splendidly handsome creature, with the carriage of a Goddess' were made maids of honour of the Queen. Both would share the King's bed with Barbara Castlemaine. Arabella Churchill was appointed maid of honour in the Duchess of York's household, and became the mistress of the Duke to the benefit of her brother John, the future Duke of Marlborough. Jane Middleton's younger sister, Eleanor Needham, was for several years the mistress of the Duke of Monmouth and bore him four children with the surname of Crofts.

Apart from their official duties of waiting on, and escorting, their royal mistresses, the ladies of the bedchamber and maids of honour played an important part in the politics, gossip and intrigue of court life. This was especially true of the maids of honour, who hoped their careers at court would lead to a good marriage. Young, attractive, nubile, but mostly inexperienced, they were considered fair game for the roués and lechers of the court. 'The courtiers look upon maids of honour only as amusements, placed expressly at

Court for their own entertainment', wrote the Comte de Gramont,[10] who recorded with relish the scandalous amours of the court.

Some, like Anne Temple (who would provide her husband, the middle-aged widower Sir Charles Lyttleton, with 13 children), Frances, 'la belle Jennings', and her sister Sarah, preferred marriage to court seduction. But all the maids of honour used their personal contacts with the King, his brother and the chief courtiers as opportunities to influence royal appointments, obtain favours for themselves or friends and, in rarer cases, to take part in political intrigues and events.

Perhaps the most successful of all was Clarendon's daughter, Anne Hyde, who had been appointed lady in waiting to Princess Mary (sister to Charles and James, and wife of the Dutch Prince of Orange). In Holland, James, Duke of York conceived a wild passion for her and seduced her. Finding that he had made her pregnant, James secretly married her on 3 September 1660 – making Anne the Duchess of York. The Queen Mother, Henrietta Maria, was bitterly opposed to this *mésalliance,* and the enraged Clarendon, when he learned of the marriage, declared he would rather see his daughter dead or the Duke's whore than his wife. He begged the King to send her to the Tower.

James, too, sought to repudiate the marriage, fully aware of the many new beauties thronging the court. He was encouraged by some of his friends, several of whom (like Richard Talbot, a gentleman of the Duke's bedchamber, later ennobled as the Earl of Tyrconnel) shamefully claimed to have had sexual intercourse with Anne. But Charles insisted that the marriage was legal and must stand; on the birth of his son in October 1660, James became reconciled to his fate. Clarendon was silenced by an immediate peerage and a grant of £20,000. As for Anne, she proved more regal than the Queen: Pepys wrote that the Duke 'in all things but his cod-piece is led by the nose by his wife'.[11]

The personality and tastes of the monarch determined the organisation, etiquette and tone of the court. Charles took as his model the splendid and sophisticated court of Louis XIV, which he had known and admired during his exile in France. No other court in Europe could boast such elegance and culture, and it was not long before Charles's court began to enjoy French literature, art and music, cuisine and wines, manners and fashions, and to employ French tailors, milliners and hairdressers. Even the Portuguese Queen Catherine had a French milliner 'who provided her petticoats, smocks, laces, stomachers, fans and other French bagatelles'.[12]

'The English court became in dress and manners a gross and caricatured copy of the court of Louis IV', wrote Mrs Jameson disapprovingly;[13] many contemporary Englishmen, including Evelyn, agreed. The ordinary people loathed the French and all things French, including their religion. A foreigner recorded how he witnessed a London mob, mistaking an Italian for a Frenchman, throw him into the river without a second thought.

It was in manners and fashion that French influence would be most apparent in the court at Whitehall. Cromwell and his followers, including his soldiers, had been blunt in speech and plain in dress. During the Commonwealth adultery was a crime punishable by death, swearing was fined, and drunkenness persecuted with zeal. All forms of extravagance in dress were frowned upon as sinful; the wearing of jewellery or ornament was lustful and forbidden by law.

With the Restoration came Charles and his train of dandies and coquettes, displaying in dazzling colours the fashions of the French court. English society adopted them within their means, tired of the dull clothes of the interregnum. The swashbuckling and dissolute Cavaliers swaggered and strutted in coat and doublet, in embroidered waistcoats, in velvet and satin, fine lace and red-heeled shoes. They flaunted their silken hose and ribboned garters, their feathered hats and powdered wigs and their gentlemen's right to carry a sword. They spent huge sums on their clothes – for clothes denoted social status. The Duke of Buckingham's outfit for the King's coronation, for instance, cost £30,000.

In the spring of 1660 they sauntered, scented and resplendent, through Hyde Park or the newly-opened Spring Gardens. They attended the horse races at Epsom and Newmarket, rollicked in taverns and in drunken brawls in bawdy-houses, attended bear-baitings, cock-fights, public executions and whippings. In Charles's new court of gallantry they used their tongues and swords with equal dexterity, the one to create an amorous epigram, the other to impale a rival at dawn on the point of a rapier. They danced beautifully, sang love-ditties and made love in vile, irresistible French.[14]

France dominated European military tactics, drill and battlefield manoeuvres during the seventeenth century, with army commanders like Louvois and Turenne. In the same way, French fashions influenced the dress of Charles's army, especially that of the officers. The basis was the red coat (hence the nickname), for both horse and foot, with breeches and worsted stockings often of another colour. At the beginning of the reign, coats were short and hats high-crowned. Under French influence, long coats, baggy breeches, periwigs, and an abundance of gold or silver lace and coloured ribbons were introduced. Officers wore low-crowned black hats, white shirts and cravats, fine worsted stockings, and high-heeled buckled shoes. The dress for other ranks was not much different in style, but less ornate and of cheaper material, since soldiers had to pay for their clothing out of 'off-reckonings'. The cavalry wore crimson coats with regimental facings and cloaks of red cloth. Most gorgeously dressed of all were the Life Guards in their short scarlet coats, richly laced with gold or silver, plumed beaver hats, embroidered white sashes, and rich accoutrements adorned with the royal crown and cypher.[15]

The dress of the court ladies was ornate and frankly erotic. Made of rich silk or satin, sometimes brocaded with gold and silver, the dress consisted of a wasp-waisted bodice, cut low in the bosom, open down the front and fastened with jewelled brooches or knots of riband, seemingly ready to slip off the shoulders, as in the portraits of the Duchess of Richmond and Lady Sutherland.[16] The flowing skirt gave provocative glimpses of the underpetti-coat or even more, as noted by Courtin, the French ambassador:

> There is nothing neater than the feet and ankles of the English ladies in their well-fitting shoes and silk stockings. They wear their skirts short and do not mind showing a great deal of their legs, which are perfect pictures.[17]

Green stockings were most in vogue (Lady Chesterfield's were much admired by the Duke of York), with black velvet garters, of which glimpses were often afforded, fastened below the knee by diamond buckles; where there was no silk stocking, one saw white skin, smooth as satin. Wigs were not unknown among the ladies; but their own hairstyles were generally exotic, curled over the forehead and arranged with a dazzling display of jewels or coloured rib-bons, the hair flowing luxuriously over the shoulders.[18]

To capture for posterity these gay Cavaliers and beautiful women, portrait painters abounded in Charles's court – Sir Peter Lely, Huysman, Wissing and Sir Godfrey Kneller, for example. The most famous was Lely, a native of Soest in Westphalia, where his father was garrisoned as a cavalry captain. He came to England in 1641 and painted Charles I and Cromwell, but his greatest claim to fame was to capture on canvas the licentious, fashionable society of Charles II's court.

The Duchess of York was no beauty herself, but to gratify the tastes of her husband she surrounded herself with youth and beauty. She invited Lely to paint the most handsome women of England, commencing with her own maids of honour: Frances Jennings (Duchess of Tyrconnel), Anne Temple (Lady Lyttleton), Elizabeth Hamilton (Comtesse de Gramont), and the Countesses of Falmouth and Sunderland. The list included Frances Stuart, Jane Middleton and Lady Denham, to name but a few. 'Every woman desired to have her charms immortalised by his brushes', wrote Mrs Jameson, who included many of them in her famous collection of court beauties. Many of Lely's original canvases can be seen in the National Portrait Gallery, as well as at Althorp, Euston Palace, Hampton Court Palace and Windsor Castle.

Once securely on his throne, Charles spent a great deal of his time and ener-gies during the first decade of his reign enjoying his position at the head of a young and pleasure-loving court, which carried off its immorality with cyni-cism and style. He left much of the day-to-day control of routine business to Clarendon, while he enjoyed the company of the youth of both sexes. They began to take a delight in outraging the conventions to which they had previously been subject, and to enjoy the pleasures many had been denied in the years of Commonwealth. Pepys noted[19] that gaming, swearing, women, drinking and the most abominable vices flourished at court, while the King indulged in his lusts and ease. 'It is the effect of idleness and having nothing else to employ their great spirits upon.' To the shocked Venetian ambassador, only Constantinople could match Whitehall for its corruption. Contemporary observers deplored its promiscuous immorality and irresponsible extravagance, putting much of the blame on the Merry Monarch himself, who flaunted his mistresses with joyous abandon and a cynical disregard for his critics.

The restored court did not differ greatly from that of any young or recently crowned monarch, such as Henry VIII and Louis XIV, but England had been without a court at Whitehall for nearly 20 years and people took a prurient interest in how Charles and his courtiers lived and misbehaved. Charles's lack of protocol and his affable familiarity made the scandalous doings of himself and his courtiers public knowledge.[20]

If immorality was fashionable at Charles's court, marriage itself was a much more serious business and had little to do with lust and romantic passion. Marriage for the aristocracy was a duty, for the procreation of numerous children was the ideal for most families. And since there was little prospect of divorce, the union was accepted for life. One was expected to choose a partner within one's own class, and marriage was almost always associated with money and property. Charles, writing to his beloved sister Minette in 1664, said:

> I find the passion love is much out of fashion in this country and that a handsome face without money has but few gallants upon the score of marriage.

Charles II's ambassador, Sir William Temple, married his childhood sweetheart in 1665 despite strong family opposition, a seven year wait and without breaking any of the commandments. He wrote:

> Our marriages are made, just like other common bargains and sales, by the mere consideration of interest or gain, without any love or esteem, or birth or beauty itself.[21]

Defoe's *Moll Flanders* (1683) argued that if a young woman had beauty, birth, breeding, wit, sense, manners, modesty, and all those to an extreme, yet if she had not money, she was a nobody. A contemporary proverb expressed it more colloquially: 'who marrieth for love without money, hath good nights and sorry days'.

Rich parents began to plan their children's marriages early, sometimes as soon as they were born. Nothing could strengthen a great family better than a well-planned alliance with a wealthy and influential neighbour, preferably possessing land. Charles, Barbara Castlemaine, the Churchills and other influential families sought rich and powerful partners for their children to strengthen their family positions. No father or guardian would allow his son or ward to marry a girl (or widow), however charming or attractive, who did not possess a dowry proportionate to his estate.

If a woman defied the conventions of her class, she faced disinheritance and the loss of her portion. Frances, daughter of Sir Edmund Coke, attorney general and Speaker of the House of Commons, refused to marry the hideous John Villiers and link her family with the wealthy and influential Buckinghams. Her father tied her to the bedposts and whipped her until she consented to the match. Law and custom favoured male dominance, wifely obedience, and paternalism in marriage. 'Your person is mine: I bought it lawfully in Church', wrote Fielding.[22]

Once again, Charles summed up the moral attitude of his court:

> As for husbands, Whitehall is not the place to find them: for unless money and caprice make up the match, there is little hope of being married: virtue and beauty in this respect are equally useless.[23]

Marriages for the poor were often clandestine or 'Fleet', requiring no publication of church banns or parental consent, and attractive because they were cheap and could be celebrated in the taverns around the Fleet prison. But however solemnised, marriages usually had to be delayed until the prospective husband could provide for a wife.

Weddings were popular and boisterous occasions for rich and poor alike. Ribaldry and horse-play abounded, culminating in the bride being ceremoniously undressed and the couple seen to bed by all the guests. Leaving the newly-weds to themselves, the guests would return to music, dancing, drinking and revelry until well into the early hours.

But the oldest sport of all flourished as well in the English village as in the Restoration court, both showing the same tolerant attitude towards sexual morality. What was good enough for the King was good enough for his people. Female chastity before marriage was a luxury the poor could not afford: a wedding in church might have to wait, but many a joyful union was consummated in wood or field. The parish might have to support its bastards, and its officers might punish the erring maid in the stocks or at the cart's tail, but 'no local Bumble could deprive rural England of its favourite pastime, nor Puritan oppressor root out the old traditions and pleasures of the countryside'.[24]

7

Tangier – An Expensive Wedding Present

As soon as Charles and Catherine's marriage treaty had been signed, Admiral Edward Mountagu, Earl of Sandwich, was sent to take possession of Tangier until the arrival of an English garrison. (He was also to escort Catherine to England for her wedding to the King.) Tangier controlled entry into the Mediterranean and was the principal commercial centre on the north-west coast of Africa, with a large European population. Charles rightly called it a jewel of immense value in the royal diadem.

Sandwich found the Portuguese garrison under constant attack from fanatical Moorish tribes, under their powerful leader Gayland. The Portuguese asked for his assistance, and he put 300 men ashore. It proved a masterstroke, as Pepys reported: 'Now the Spaniards' designs of hindering our getting the place are frustrated'.[1]

To garrison the new colony and secure it against Moorish attacks a sizeable force was needed, which Charles did not possess. (As we have already seen [p23–24], Charles's original army establishment of First and Second Foot Guards, Life Guards and Horse Guards took a large slice of his annual allowance from Parliament.[2]) His tiny regular army was barely capable of guarding his person, providing for ceremonial occasions and carrying out simple police duties. To mount an overseas expedition, additional troops had to be recruited.

So, on 6 September 1661, the King appointed Henry Mordaunt, second Earl of Peterborough, as governor and captain-general of all the forces in Tangier, with orders to raise one regiment of foot and a troop of 100 horse. The Tangier Regiment, as it became known, numbered 1,000 men recruited from the officers and soldiers of the disbanded New Model Army. It would in due course become 'Our most dear Consort the Queen's Regiment of Foot', with the House of Braganza's Paschal lamb emblem as its regimental crest. The 100 men who paraded on 21 October 1661 on St George's Fields, Southwark,[3] were destined to be the nucleus of the Tangier Horse, later known as the First Royal Dragoons (the Royals). Three additional regiments from the Dunkirk garrison were also placed under Peterborough's command.

But it was not until 15 January 1662 that he was able to sail for Tangier, with an expeditionary force of 2,000 foot and 500 horse. They took with them the wives of two or three hundred of the soldiers – the first time that wives had officially accompanied an English army to an overseas garrison.[4] To administer, finance and supply the garrison, Charles established a 'Committee for the affairs of Tangier', which included the Duke of York as lord high admiral, Prince Rupert, the Duke of Albemarle, General William (Earl of) Craven, and Samuel Pepys as treasurer, 'a very great honour to me'.[5] It would also prove for Pepys the source of a considerable income in profits and hand-outs from merchants and contractors, which were part of the recognised perquisites of officials at the time.

From the sea, the white-walled city, with its red tiled roofs gleaming in the African sun, looked deceptively attractive. For no sooner had Peterborough landed than he found the town derelict, with accommodation for only one-third of his troops, and under constant attacks from some 17,000 Berber rebels. Peterborough had to quarter some of his troops on the Portuguese inhabitants, already indignant at having to hand over their city. They were even more angry at the behaviour of the English soldiers, whom they accused of sacking their houses and taking public liberties with their wives and daughters.[6] Peterborough invited the Portuguese to enrol as soldiers, but they refused and left Tangier, carrying off everything of value, including doors and windows. A decaying fort named York Castle (today's Casbah) was hastily fitted up for the governor and his headquarters staff, and almost immediately became the focus of attack by a Moorish force under Gayland.

Peterborough was soon replaced by the distinguished Scottish soldier, Lord Andrew Rutherford, previously governor of Dunkirk. He was created Earl of Teviot 'to hearten him for his new post'.[7] He brought with him 400 reinforcements from the late garrison of Dunkirk and reorganised his troops into separate English and Irish regiments. Teviot (governor from 1663–1664) found the garrison demoralised by the constant attacks and the fortifications in urgent need of repair. Under his energetic leadership a line of stone redoubts was constructed beyond the town walls, which were strengthened with a number of forts. Teviot also started to build a much-needed breakwater or mole, to provide an all-weather harbour for ships. Charles offered Sir Christopher Wren a commission 'to survey and direct the works of the mole and fortifications of the citadel and town',[8] but Wren turned it down because of ill health.

Truces were agreed with Gayland, but he proved to be a treacherous enemy. In one sortie, the heavily outnumbered English troops were ambushed and lost 19 officers and 400 men killed, with Teviot among them, dying at the head of his men. To add to the garrison's problems, illness broke out, stores and provisions were low and costly, and the troops had received no pay for several months.[9]

The replacement governor, John Belasyse (1665–1667) had been a Royalist general in the Civil War, raising six regiments of horse and foot at his own expense and commanding the King's forces in the north of England. A prominent Catholic, he accepted the post only for the profit it brought, according to Pepys. Unable to take the oath of conformity, he was forced to resign his governership. During the Popish Plot scare, he was falsely accused by Titus Oates of being the commander-in-chief of a suspect Popish army and was forced to spend several years in the Tower without being brought to trial.

His successor, General the Earl of Middleton (1668–1674), had been wounded fighting for Charles at the battle of Worcester. He was captured and imprisoned in the Tower of London, but escaped in his wife's clothes and joined Charles in Paris. At the Restoration he was rewarded with an earldom and made commander-in-chief in Scotland. When he arrived in Tangier in October 1668, he found it had ceased to be a purely military outpost. Jewish and European settlers had arrived from Morocco, Spain, France and Holland, and a small but turbulent civil population now added to the difficulties of the governor's command.

Shocked by the constant drain on funds and manpower, the Tangier Committee was determined to establish the colony's prosperity through a civil government, instead of through a succession of military commanders. On 4 June 1668 Tangier was declared a free city by charter, with a mayor and corporation to govern instead of the army. One of Middleton's most important duties was to settle the inevitable disputes and disturbances which arose between the civil authorities and the army.

But his attempts to improve local standards of living by growing food, instead of importing it, failed. The mole remained uncompleted and broken by storms; and the soldiers could not pay the merchants because their pay as usual was in arrears. Middleton's urgent requests for more artificers to rebuild the mole, and more troops to face the ferocious Emperor of Morocco's Moorish armies, remained unanswered. (To protect the Mediterranean carrying trade, though, an English fleet was sent against Algiers in 1671 and 1677, and against Tripoli in 1674-1676.) Small wonder that Middleton took to drink and died in 1675, falling from his horse in a drunken stupor. Yet his soldiers loved him as a commander, and his officers had perfect trust in his generalship. He was patriotic and brave, and much the best officer the Scots had.[10]

Middleton was followed by the second Earl of Inchiquin, colonel of the Queen's Regiment (5 March 1674), who would end his career as governor of

Jamaica. During his six years as governor of Tangier (1675–1680), he was so long absent from his post that most of his duties fell on his deputy, Sir Palmes Fairborne, the only really attractive personality in a succession of idle and often corrupt administrators.

Fairborne was a highly professional soldier, who had arrived in Tangier as a captain in Lord Peterborough's Foot Regiment in 1662 and became its commanding officer in 1667. He lived in Tangier for 18 years, and never sought advancement beyond that of commanding the garrison. His whole life was embittered by the system, which left promotion to the whim or favour of a secretary of state. The constant arrears of pay, moreover, often pushed him to the verge of poverty, while anxiety on behalf of his wife and seven children led him to use every means in his power to gain some addition to his income. These included trying to buy the favour of Baron Arlington, the current secretary of state, with presents he could ill afford.[11]

Fairborne set about constructing new forts on the perimeter and strengthening the town walls; thanks to his energy and thoroughness, the city was saved from repeated Moorish attacks. But conditions had become so bad and morale so low that he had to take severe disciplinary measures within the garrison against such offences as sleeping on sentry duty, theft from comrades, and drunkenness on parade. On one occasion he was faced with a mass refusal to obey orders, until he ordered two soldiers to be marched out of the ranks and publicly shot. 'Rape, adultery, fornication and dissolute lasciviousness must be punished at discretion, according to the quality of the offence', ran his orders.

The garrison's court martial book for the period 1663–1669 has survived,[12] showing the military crimes and punishments prevalent before the Mutiny Act of 1689 gave the army a legal code of practice. It had long been recognised that, if obedience and discipline were to be maintained in troops exposed to the hardships, dangers, temptations and licence of active warfare, the ordinary laws and punishments which served to regulate civil life were inappropriate. Civil procedures were also too lengthy to be effective in the army.

During the seventeenth century several Acts set forth penalties for the special military crimes of mutiny, desertion and stealing arms, with death by hanging awarded by the civil courts and magistrates. As late as July 1678, for instance, a soldier of the Coldstream Guards was tried at the civil sessions at the Old Bailey for the felony of desertion, convicted, and sentenced to be hanged at the head of his regiment. In September 1687 a soldier of the Thirteenth Foot and another of the Grenadier Guards were hanged for desertion at Tyburn and Tower Hill respectively.[13] But for an army on active service, outside the jurisdiction of civil authorities, martial laws and military courts were established under royal prerogative to provide prompt and deterrent sentences. Corporal punishment was preferable to lengthy imprisonment;

insubordination, which could lead to the more serious crime of mutiny, was treated with great severity.

In Tangier the courts martial from 1663–1669 awarded six sentences of death for acts of neglect on sentry duty, insubordination, and violence to superiors. In five cases execution was by shooting, and in one by hanging. There were seven sentences of death for desertion and theft from comrades, all carried out by the less honourable method of hanging, which was also awarded for rape, acting as a spy, and unauthorised plunder.

For a military execution by shooting, the troops of the regiment or garrison were drawn up in a semi-circle. The prisoner, with his arms pinioned and attended by a guard and chaplain, was paraded along the whole line of troops to the blank side of the circle, where often the grave had already been dug. The prisoner then stood or knelt against a stake, to which he was bound, his eyes blindfolded and either he or the provost marshal gave the signal to fire. The troops filed past the body before returning to their quarters, or sometimes the corpse was carried three times round the parade.

When the number of offenders was inconveniently large, an example was sometimes made by selecting every tenth man by lot to suffer; or, as in Tangier on 8 September 1663, 'Two privates to throw dice on a drum-head, to be shot: he who throws the least to suffer.[14]

On 12 October 1663 Thomas Finlay, of Lieutenant Colonel Churchill's company, was sentenced 'to be whipt by the Executioner forward and backward through the Parade drawne in two ranks, his lashes to be soundly laid on, for being asleep upon the centinels post'. The punishment of whipping or scourging by the provost was performed by tying the culprit, naked to the waist, to a post and thrashing him with stout switches or birch rods. Sometimes, more seriously, he was flogged standing under the gallows with a rope about his neck, or tied upon his tiptoes by the neck to the gallows. A variation was awarded in Tangier on 17 May 1665:

> At the time of the parade to have his back stripped and to run the gauntlet of his regiment paraded with open ranks, each man furnished with a stout switch to strike the prisoner's naked back, breast, arms or where his cudgel should light as he marched down the lanes.

To drown the prisoner's cries, drums were beaten during the punishment. Other punishments awarded were branding for murder, boring the tongue with a red-hot iron for blasphemy, and imprisonment on bread and water. William Merriday was condemned in Tangier to ride the wooden horse with four muskets tied to his heels and a pair of shoes about his neck, for the crime of selling his shoes. Another soldier, found drunk at his post, was sentenced 'to be tied necke and heels, with his head forced between his knees by two muskets, and kept there for an hour, till the blood gushed out of his nose, mouth and ears'.

On 30 December 1676, Charles ordered a survey of the city and garrison,[15] which was costing about £140,000 a year to maintain.[16] This was a considerable drain on the King's private purse, since Parliament refused to make any provision for Tangier's defence. The survey showed the total inhabitants numbered 2,225, of whom 50 were army officers, 1,231 other ranks, with 302 army wives and children. Foreigners numbered 130; there were 156 mole workers; 200 wives and children of citizens; 70 widows and single women; and the remainder were priests, servants and a number of slaves in His Majesty's bagnio (a sort of prisoner-of-war camp where the 'slaves' were employed on building the mole or ransomed, according to the practice of the Barbary pirates). Amongst the buildings listed was a hospital and an army school, in which the King thought fit to employ Richard Reynolds, Master of Arts and Fellow of Sidney Sussex College (Cambridge) in his service as a schoolmaster.[17]

Social distinctions were strongly marked: the governor and principal officers of the garrison and their families formed the upper circle, followed by municipal dignitaries, merchants, ministers, doctor and schoolmaster. The attractive climate and short two-week sea journey from Falmouth made Tangier a pleasant place for courtiers and their ladies to visit. There were balls and banquets, cards and music, pretty walks and gardens, and a popular resort called White Hall, 'where the ladies, officers and the better sort of people do refresh and divert themselves'.

On a fine spring afternoon on the mole, officers in their loose grey (a concession to the climate) or red coats, breeches and hose to match, could be seen strolling in the company of English ladies dressed in flowing gowns of French or Italian silk, one or two with feathered hats and perfumed gloves from Madrid. Riding by would be troopers of the Tangier Horse in their black helmets and cuirasses (with no such tropical dress concessions), worn over red coats and black thigh-length boots.[18]

From time to time business or curiosity brought out some great personage from England, with money in his pocket and a few court gallants and ladies in his train. Tangier society would then throw itself into the enjoyment of dances and entertainments with such whole-hearted frivolity that the Moors remarked, 'if you give the officers a ball and the common soldiers a bottle of wine, you may do what you will with an Englishman'.[19]

1680 proved a black year for the garrison. The Earl of Ossory was appointed governor-general, but died before he could take up his appointment. The fortifications fell into disrepair; illness laid low the latest batch of recruits, 'very sad creatures, some old men and two of them women in men's clothes';[20] and enemy sappers gradually dug their way beneath the outlying forts. A short

Charles II seated in his Garter Robes. Sir Peter Lely. *(Reproduced by kind permission of the Duke of Grafton and Courtauld Institute of Art)*

Barbara Palmer (née Villiers), Duchess of Cleveland (1640–1709) as the Madonna and Child. Sir Peter Lely c 1665–75. *(By courtesy of the National Portrait Gallery, London)*

Queen Catherine of Braganza (1638–1705). Dirck Stoop c 1660. Dressed in the 'monstrous fardingales' of her native Portugal. She later adopted French court fashions. *(By courtesy of the National Portrait Gallery, London)*

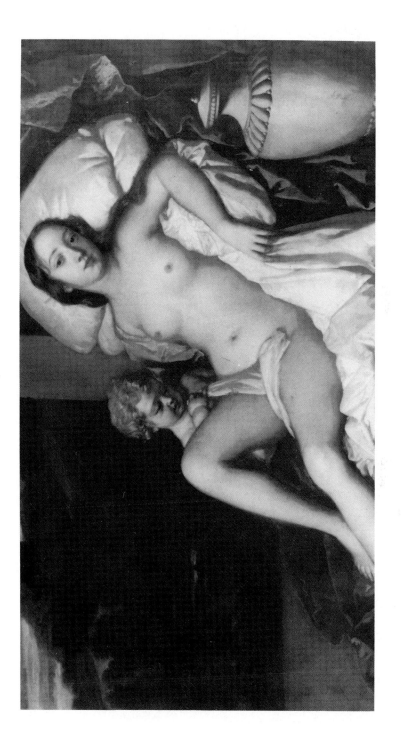

Barbara Palmer, Countess of Castlemaine, with Henry Fitzroy, 1st Duke of Grafton. Sir Peter Lely c 1665. Private collection. *(By courtesy of the National Portrait Gallery, London)*

The Execution of the Regicides, 13–19 October 1660. Contemporary Engraving. *(By permission of The Trustees of the British Museum)*

Top The Duke of York's Troop of Horse Guards, Coronation of Charles II, 22 April 1661. Wenceslaus Hollar. (*By permission of The Trustees of the British Museum*)

Below State Trumpeters at the Coronation of James II, 23 April 1685. (*By permission of The Trustees of the British Museum*)

Whitehall Palace and Horseguards Parade. Hendrick Dankaerts. *(By kind permission of His Grace, The Duke of Roxburghe)*

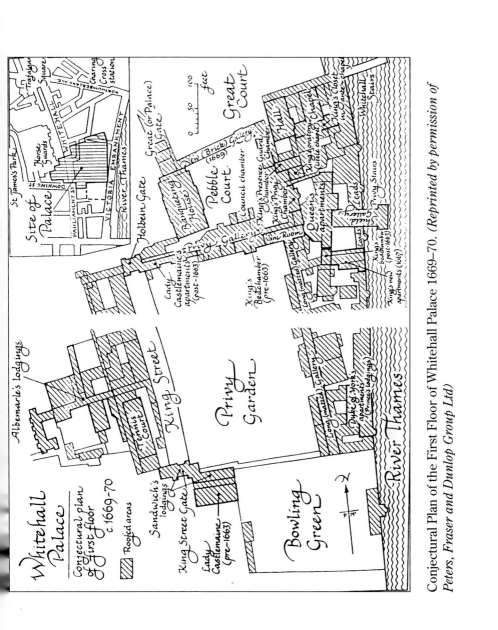

Conjectural Plan of the First Floor of Whitehall Palace 1669–70. (Reprinted by permission of Peters, Fraser and Dunlop Group Ltd)

Tangier c 1665. Wenceslaus Hollar. *(By permission of The Trustees of the British Museum)*

Key   1 *The Upper Castle*   2 *York Castle*   3 *Portuguese Church*   4 *James Fort*   5 *Catharine Port*   6 *Catharine Fort*
      7 *Charles Fort*   8 *Whitehall*   9 *York Fort*   10 *The Mole*   11 *Eastern Tower*   12 *Fountain Fort*

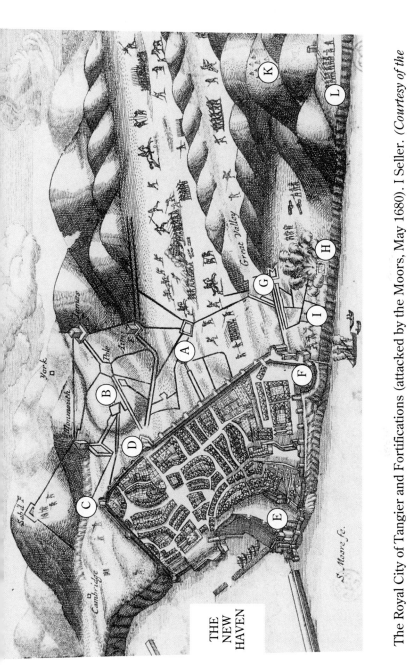

THE NEW HAVEN

The Royal City of Tangier and Fortifications (attacked by the Moors, May 1680). I Seller. (*Courtesy of the Director, National Army Museum, London*)

Key A Whitehall   B Bridges   C Irish Battery   D Port Catharine   E York Castle
F Upper Castle   G Charles Fort   H Henrietta   I Whitby   K Moores
L Teviot slain 16 May 1664

Top Nell Gwynn (1650–87). Simon Verelst c 1670. Private Collection.
(By courtesy of the National Portrait Gallery, London)

Below James II and Anne Hyde c 1665. Sir Peter Lely. *(By courtesy of the National Portrait Gallery, London)*

FIELD OFFICER 1680   OFFICER TANGIER 1680   PIKEMAN 1680

MUSKETEER 1680   GRENADIER 1684   DRUMMER 1685

English Regimental Uniforms in the reign of Charles II. Mrs L I Cowper. *(By kind permission of the Museum of the King's Own Royal Regiment [Lancaster])*

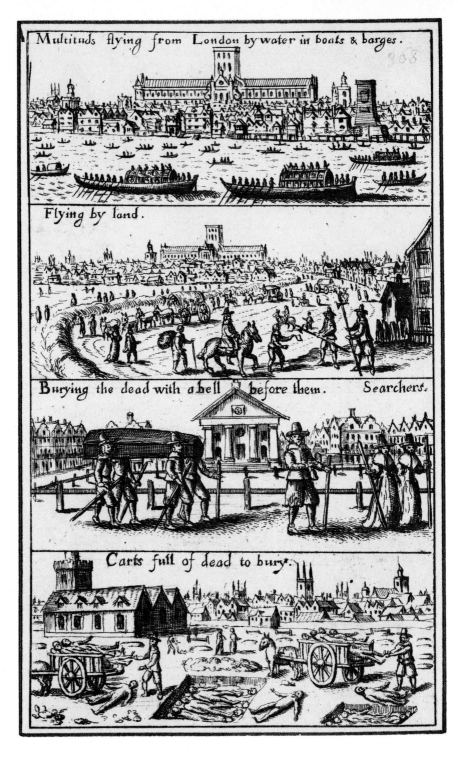

Scenes of the Plague of London. Woodcut Broadsheet c 1665. *(By permission of The Master and Fellows, Magdalene College, Cambridge)*

truce was arranged, but the English had to agree to return to the original Portuguese boundaries of the town, surrendering all their added fortifications.

The gravity of the situation at last forced Parliament to pay for and fit out a strong relief force to bring the garrison's strength up to 3,200 foot and 600 horse. Twelve companies of the Earl of Dumbarton's regiment (First Foot, the Royal Scots) were sent out from Ireland. A further foot regiment was raised on 13 July 1680, the Second Tangier, 'with many brave Volunteer Gentlemen, encouraged to undertake this noble enterprize in the Service of their King and country, by that hopeful youth the Earl of Plymouth,' and sent to Tangier. In addition a 600-strong composite battalion, called the King's Battalion, was formed from the Grenadier and Coldstream Guards, the Maritime and Musgrave's Regiments, placed under the command of Colonel Edward Sackville of the First or King's Regiment of Foot Guards, and sent to the garrison.[21]

The reinforcements arrived in Tangier just in time to support a sortie led by Fairborne to recover lost ground and reoccupy the outlying forts. The attack completely surprised the enemy, but a well-aimed bullet mortally wounded Fairborne in the moment of victory. Sitting on a chair on the ramparts of the Upper Castle, he survived long enough to see the garrison march back into town to celebrate the victory, won at the cost of barely 100 casualties. For their part in the fighting, 'Tangier 1680' is emblazoned on the colours of the First Foot – their first battle honour. Charles conferred on them the title of The Royal Regiment of Foot (The Royal Scots). Colonel Sackville took over the temporary command of the garrison, until failing health necessitated his return to England.

The next commander-in-chief and lieutenant governor (1682) was the most colourful of all the governors, Colonel Percy Kirke. He was a professional soldier, who had served under Turenne, and with Churchill and the Duke of Monmouth at Maestricht. In July 1666, with the help of the Duke of York, he had obtained an ensign's commission in the lord admiral's Maritime Regiment (the yellow-coated regiment from which the Marines originated); and was later a subaltern in his brother-in-law's regiment of horse, the Earl of Oxford's Blues.

He came to Tangier in command of the Second Tangier Regiment (later the King's Own Royal Lancaster Regiment), to replace the regiment's first colonel, Charles Fitz-Charles, Earl of Plymouth, also known as Don Carlos, a son of King Charles by Catherine Pegge (the daughter of a Derbyshire squire, whom Charles had met on one of his early travels). Tired after a day's fighting in Tangier, the young Colonel Plymouth had decided to spend the night of 1 October 1680 in a roofless fort. It began to rain and he caught a chill, from which he died a month later. His body was embalmed and returned to England to be buried in Westminster Abbey.

Plymouth's regiment meanwhile sailed from Plymouth under Kirke's command, with Major Charles Trelawney as his deputy, losing one officer and 50 men of disease during the month's journey. They did not learn of their colonel's death until they arrived in Tangier on 28 December. According to custom, the regimental colours were immediately placed in mourning, and so remained until the news of Percy Kirke's appointment to the colonelcy was received in Tangier.[22] Lord Macaulay in his *History of England* called Kirke a bully, coward, bungler, liar, libertine, butcher, embezzler and traitor. But, although this was undoubtedly true in some respects, the facts do not substantiate all these accusations. Imagine the state of mind of a modern officer on being given command of a garrison of 2,000 men, none of whom had been paid for a year, in a station in constant danger of attack by a superior force, and with no facilities for recreation, poor food, inferior equipment, inefficient medical and non-existent welfare services.[23]

During the truce which followed the siege of Tangier in 1680, Kirke made friends with the Emperor of Morocco, Ismail, who would rule his country for 55 years. 'He would excel all mankind in barbarity and murder, inventing every day a new pastime of cruelty', wrote an Embassy official.[24] He would kill a slave to test the edge of a new weapon, spear a dozen negroes or strangle a woman or two from his harem as a *divertissement*, and even the lives of his sons were not safe from his cruelty. Despite his hatred of all foreigners, Ismail took a liking to Kirke and swore 'there never would be Bullet shot against Tangier, so long as Kirke was in it'.[25] They exchanged gifts, the Emperor sending Kirke 12 cows and a Christian woman in return for some Irish greyhounds. Ismail confirmed his vow that, if none but Kirke and his wife (Lady Mary Howard, daughter of the fourth Earl of Suffolk) should be left alone in Tangier, he would not betray Kirke. But in the negotiations for the release of prisoners from his bagnio at Meknes, which was reputed to hold 30,000 slaves, including 2,500 Christians and 70 prisoners-of-war, Ismail demanded too high a price for their ransom, so that only a few could ever be redeemed from the terrible fate of a galley slave.[26]

Despite the Emperor's vows of eternal friendship, Kirke did not trust him and kept the garrison in constant readiness to resist attack. Out of a total of some 1,200–1,400 men, 400 would be on guard every night, and no soldier was ever allowed more than three nights running in bed 'lest he should fall into idle ways'. The Castle, built on a rock some 200 feet above sea level, was strongly fortified and in good repair, but only three of the numerous forts built upon the surrounding sand-hills remained. The rest were either in ruins or in the hands of the Moors. York Castle housed the ammunition and stores, carried there by garrison troops from the Water Gate, where the provisions were unloaded from ships.[27]

Pepys, who disliked Kirke intensely, recorded in colourful, if exaggerated, detail all the gossip and scandal associated with him. He thought he was the most foul-mouthed man he had ever met, as he and his officers publicly boasted of their amorous affairs and how they defamed every woman who yielded to their invitations:

> The Governor, Kirke, is said to have got his wife's sister with child and, while he is with his whores at his bathing house, his wife, whom he keeps in by awe, sends for her gallants and plays the jade by herself at home.[28]

According to Bishop Ken, chaplain of Lord Dartmouth's fleet, Kirke caused a scandal by seeking to obtain the post of garrison chaplain at Tangier for a Mr Roberts, the brother of his current mistress. Kirke's morals were appalling, but probably no worse than those of many of his contemporaries. He kept mistresses in an age when that was normal, with royal precedents and the examples of the court and his fellow officers. As a contemporary broadsheet expressed it:

> Those foolish things called wives are grown unfashionable and the keeping of a miss the principal character of a fashionable, well-bred gentleman.[29]

The strength of the garrison dwindled rapidly. Over half the officers were on prolonged leave, some of them 'having other employments at home and more taken with the satisfaction of being with their friends, never intending to return'.[30] Five officers of Kirke's regiment, for example, were given permission to return home in two visiting frigates, because 'they were in great extremity for want of pay, being 16 months in arrears'.

The men were decimated by sickness and short of rations. In October 1682, nearly 24,000 pounds of Irish meat had to be thrown into the sea, 'so extremely corrupted', that it was both unserviceable and 'of a noisome smell'. Such rations were responsible for frequent outbreaks of scurvy, which with the tainted water and hard drinking caused uncounted deaths among the garrison.[31] For Kirke's men there was little amusement or recreation to relieve the boredom, except sitting on the seashore catching fish to supplement their diet, playing cards or dice, or drinking and whoring in the taverns, many of which were kept by soldiers' widows.

The women, too, came under strict military discipline. On 25 June 1664, for example, a woman was convicted at Tangier for inciting to mutiny. She was sentenced to be gagged and receive 50 lashes on her bare back, 10 each at five different locations, and to be expelled from the garrison by the first available ship, being whipped also from the prison to the water-side. A court tried Elizabeth Harrold, accused of 'threatening her husband to be his death and beating him by breaking his head and other harms'. Her sentence was 'to be stripped at the Cross and to receive 24 stripes on her naked back by the executioner'.[32] There was a house of correction, a pillory, stocks and a ducking stool 'for scolds and evil-tongued women'. Most fearsome of all was the whirligig, 'a wooden cage on a pivot, whose amazing velocity made brawling and loose women very sick and emptied their bodies through every aperture'. Such a bawd was awarded this punishment 'for the too frequent bestowal of her favours'; the punishment performed 'to the delight of the jaded troops'.[33]

Records, including Charles's survey of 30 December 1676, show a number of soldiers' wives living in the garrison: some had come from England, other couples had married locally 'even though they have wives and husbands living in other places'. The Roman Catholic Portuguese monks complained that Kirke had forbidden them to marry soldiers to local women without his permission, 'which he refused, thus encouraging immorality'. But in this he was only following a growing army practice. Soldiers, upon pain of being cashiered, were not permitted to marry without official permission, from at least 1670 and this remained army marital policy for the next 200 years. It was not a question of religion, but simply that the army preferred single men.[34]

For some time Parliament had been concerned about the cost of maintaining the garrison and the difficulties of constructing the mole. As early as 1680, the King had threatened to give up Tangier unless supplies were voted for it. The mole, intended to provide a safe harbour for shipping, had proved a costly illusion. Merchant ships continued to be harassed by Barbary pirates, and captured crews were regularly sent as slaves to the Emperor's bagnios. Tangier, moreover, was regarded as a nursery for a Popish army,[35] since Irish troops had been employed to guard it and several of the governors had been Catholics. The Popish Plot in England had intensified the dread of Catholicism, and the King's frequent appeals for more troops to increase the size of the garrison renewed suspicions that a standing army was being retained in Tangier to ensure a Catholic succession and absolute monarchy.

On 20 December 1680, the House of Commons petitioned the King to give his assent to a Bill of Exclusion to disinherit the Duke of York; adding that, unless and until the bill was passed, Parliament could not give any supplies to Charles. The King refused to sacrifice his brother's right of succession to save Tangier. Finally, in 1683, Charles gave Admiral Dartmouth (who in the intervals between commanding at sea was Captain General of Portsmouth and Master General of Ordnance)[36] secret orders to abandon Tangier. Dartmouth was to level the fortifications, destroy the mole and harbour, and evacuate the troops. Pepys was summoned to accompany the expedition as Dartmouth's adviser on matters concerning the civilian population.

In August 1683 Dartmouth, given the rank of admiral of the fleet and captain-general in Tangier, sailed from Plymouth ostensibly to succour the garrison but in truth 'on a voyage for the destroying and deserting of Tangier'.[37] After 21 years of occupation, Pepys found the place a sink of iniquity and corruption, with few women of quality or beauty, except the mayoress and her two sisters. In the whole place there was nothing but vice of all sorts, swearing, drinking, cursing and whoring, the women as bad as the men.[38]

While the mole was being demolished, Pepys and the lawyers cleared the town of European inhabitants and dealt with compensation claims for the loss of their property. All the forts and walls were mined for last-minute destruction. Soldiers and sailors carried stores on board the ships and sufficient water for the journey. Lord Dartmouth addressed the garrison officers and told them the King intended to keep the two Tangier regiments on a permanent establishment. He praised them for their service, and blamed the abuses in Tangier on 'the Worth of the men, the smallness and arrears of their pay and the leanness of the place'.[39]

One of Dartmouth's chief concerns was the evacuation of sick soldiers 'and the many families and their effects to be brought off'. The hospital ship *Unity* sailed for England on 18 October 1683 with 114 invalid soldiers and 104 women and children under the care of John Eccles, 'usher and writing master of the school and gunner', who had served the garrison school for seven-and-a-half years. The military families were quartered at Falmouth on an allowance of three pence a day to each soldier's wife, until the arrival of the battalion. The disabled soldiers were sent to the newly opened Royal Hospital at Chelsea.

The main force of 2,830 officers and men and 361 wives and children finally completed the demolition of the mole and fortifications, and evacuated the garrison during the early months of 1684. The Second Tangier Regiment left on 13–14 February for Plymouth with some 600 men and 30 wives and children. The Earl of Dumbarton's regiment went into quarters at Rochester, and Trelawney's regiment to Portsmouth. Colonel Kirke returned home with Lady Mary and their two children, to be stationed with the Queen's First Tangier Regiment at Pendennis Castle. Their eldest son would also become colonel of the 'Lambs', and succeed his father as keeper of the palace at Whitehall. Lord Dartmouth, a relative of the Villiers, Dukes of Buckingham, carried out his work in Tangier very effectively, and was the last to leave. The King rewarded him with a gift of £10,000, and authority to hold a fair twice a year and a market twice a week at Blackheath.[40]

Before leaving, Dartmouth was able to purchase the release of many English prisoners from Ismail's bagnio, including several officers and about 40 men, some of whom had spent 10 years in the hands of the Moors. As the last soldiers embarked and the flag was hauled down, the besieging Moors took possession of the ruined town. In due course, Britain would replace Tangier with the more useful and defensible Gibraltar (1704) and the magnificent harbour of Port Mahon in Minorca (1763), which ensured British control of the Mediterranean. But Tangier had cost nearly two millions of royal treasure and many lives had been sacrificed in its defence. It had proved an expensive wedding present for the King.

8

Royal Pleasures and Military Affairs

New Year's Eve 1662 was celebrated with a grand ball at the palace. Pepys watched the scene with great pleasure, noting the ballroom crammed with fine ladies, the greatest of the court. The King, a fine dancer, called for the first tune, *Cuckolds All A-Row*, an old dance of England, and led out the Duchess of York; the Duke of York danced with the Duchess of Buckingham; James Crofts, the Duke of Monmouth, with Lady Castlemaine.[1] A few weeks earlier Pepys had seen the Queen for the first time,

> with Mr Crofts, the King's bastard, a most pretty spark of about 15 years old who, I perceive, do hang much upon my Lady Castlemaine, and is always with her; and I hear the Queen is mighty kind to him.[2]

James Crofts, alias Fitzroy, alias Scott, was born at Rotterdam in April 1649. This child of sin, who was destined to be the plaything of the goddess of fortune,[3] was the son of Charles and Lucy Walter, whom Charles had made his mistress during his exile in Holland. Charles summoned his mother, now the Queen Dowager, from Paris to London soon after his marriage. She brought with her Charles's beloved son, on whom he conferred a dukedom early in the New Year.

Pepys reported that the duke was in such splendour at court and so dandled by the King that some believed, if the King should have no child by the Queen (of which there was as yet no appearance), he would be acknowledged for a lawful son.[4] From the beginning, the King showed his affection for the young Duke of Monmouth, heaping honours and offices upon him. With his good looks and charming manners, he early became a powerful influence at court and in the political arena. Dryden later wrote:

Of all his numerous progeny was none
So beautiful, so brave as Absalon [Monmouth]:
With secret joy, indulgent father viewed
His youthful image in his son renewed;
To all his wishes nothing he denied.[5]

In years to come, ministers of state – Arlington, Clifford, Lauderdale, Buckingham and especially Shaftesbury – paid homage to him and used his influence to further their own aims and policies. He became popular with the common people, who elevated him to the status of a national hero. As the King's favourite son he became the Protestant hope for succession to the throne.[6] He rose rapidly to the top of his chosen military profession, and became personally responsible for the safety of his sovereign and comman-der-in-chief of his army.

Meanwhile, Pepys was complaining that there was nothing but lechery at court from top to bottom. The King, by his daily dalliance in public with his mistress and by showing so much favour to his favourites, was risking his popularity with his people. Charles spent his evenings in Barbara's apartments,

supping at least four or five times every week with my Lady Castlemaine and most often stays till the morning with her and goes home through the garden all alone privately and that so the very sentries take notice and speak of it.[7]

The King was infatuated with Barbara, while she was accused of unbelievable depravities, although still aged only 22. 'It is strange how the King is bewitched by this pretty Castlemayne,' complained Pepys, saying she had all the tricks of Aretin (a sixteenth century pornographer), and used them to give him plea-sure.[8] The court resented her because she thought herself superior to the rest of mankind, wrote Gramont.

Encouraged by her, the King sought younger ministers, like Bennet and Berkeley, as the trusted companions of both his amorous adventures and his state business. Sir Henry Bennet (later Earl of Arlington) seldom spoke in Parliament or council, but worked tirelessly in private. 'His knowledge of the King's temper and of a courtier's arts and his readiness to serve and encourage Charles in his dissolute habits secured his position.'[9] It was typical of his methods that, as soon as he took over Sir Edward Nicholas's apartments in Whitehall (reserved for the secretary of state), he had a door built to give him secret access to a staircase leading directly to the King's private rooms. Clarendon called him a master of backstairs intrigue.

Barbara Castlemaine's intimate evening gatherings in her apartments pro-vided the ideal opportunities for the clique of ministers to influence the King and oppose Clarendon. It was Barbara who in 1662 persuaded Charles to replace the dutiful and loyal Sir Edward Nicholas as secretary of state by Bennet,[10] whose influence with the King grew as Clarendon's declined. Sir Charles Berkeley, whom the King loved every day with more passion, according to Clarendon, was promoted keeper of the King's privy purse, and with his intimate friend Bennet shared the management of the royal mistress. Clarendon complained that the pair were most devoted to the lady, and much dependent on her interest. He hoped the King's interest in her would not last:

> The King does not in his nature love a busy woman and has an aversion from speaking with any woman or hearing them speak of any business but to that purpose he thinks them all made for.[11]

Despite Charles's frequent protestations against any suggestion that he was governed by his mistress, Barbara clearly dominated him when at the height of her power in 1663. Bishop Burnet wrote that the King usually came from his mistress's lodgings to church, even on sacrament days, and all his ministers were making applications to his mistresses.[12] Pepys also recorded that Lady Castlemaine's interest at Court had increased and was more and greater than the Queen's. 'She hath brought in Sir H. Bennet and Sir Ch. Berkeley as the confidants of his pleasure'.[13]

Barbara proved an apt pupil in the arts of political chicanery and court intrigue, schooled by her cousin Buckingham, Charles's boyhood friend in exile. Buckingham was a man full of intrigue and guile, involved in one plot after another; one moment amusing the King with his extravagant conduct and the next clapped in the Tower for some outrage or other. Preferring married women to single, he made an art of adultery, and wrote that 'we choose our wives for posterity, our mistresses for ourselves'.[14]

For Charles, the core of government business lay in the work of the Privy Council over which he presided, and in the various committees (for naval and foreign affairs, intelligence, Tangier, and so forth) which reported to him. But outside formal council meetings, government business continued wherever the King was to be found, and here Barbara was able to use her influence:

> She was no political blue-stocking but a self-centred courtesan, a cultivated geisha and a woman accepted alone on terms of equality with mainly intelligent men. She promoted politics and personalities, affairs of state and patronage, as well as sexual provocation, in this series of after-supper conversations'.[15]

In an age when there was no such convention as collective ministerial responsibility, there were many such opportunities for unscrupulous politicians and ambitious ministers to intrigue, create factions, use and accept bribes, manipulate favourites and mistresses, and make a fortune or build a family power base. According to Burnet, ambition and enrichment, the pursuit of individual interest, actuated most men, not loyalty and principle. Charles would learn to make use of these ministers and their factions, sometimes influenced by them but always remaining his own master, as far as money and circumstances permitted. Bishop Burnet credited him:

> with a great deal of judgement, when he thinks fit to employ it . . . He thinks the world is governed wholly by interest and, indeed, he has known so much of the baseness of mankind that no wonder, if he has hard thoughts of them: but when he is satisfied that his interests are likewise become the interests of his ministers then he delivers himself up to them in all their humours and revenges – but he loves an intrigue![16]

Charles was certainly not the easy-going fool, who never said a foolish thing and never did a wise one, that many of his contemporaries believed.[17]

One of the most frequent criticisms of the King was that he was lazy and self-indulgent, minding nothing but pleasures and hating the very sight and thought of business.[18] This may have been true in the early years of his reign, but, in fact, the King rose at five almost every morning and worked for three hours on affairs of state before any of his ministers appeared. Laziness was not his problem, for he certainly worked harder at the business of government than his father had done and harder than many of his royal successors. Sir George Savile, Marquis of Halifax, knew the King well and wrote that he grew by age into a pretty exact distribution of his hours, for his business, pleasure and the exercise of his health.

With the frequent adjournments of Parliament, the work of the government was carried on by his ministers: Clarendon, his first Chancellor, a man of great experience and tireless industry who presided over the House of Lords and was prime minister in all but name; his Treasurer, the Earl of Southampton; and Ashley Cooper, Lord Shaftesbury, Chancellor of the Exchequer. Earlier the King had turned to a group of younger men, such as the Earl of Bristol (Lord Digby), Bennet, and the handsome, indolent young nobleman, Berkeley – young gallants, whose company, wit and familiarity he enjoyed. But apart from presiding over his councils and committees, and his out-of-committee activities, he handled much of his business personally. This was especially true of his dealings with France, which he controlled through correspondence, ambassadors, his sister Minette and, after 1670, Louise de Keroualle.

Business activities aside, he had many sporting interests – tennis, croquet and bowls, swimming and sailing his yacht on the Thames, riding, hunting and fishing. He skated on ice and walked regularly in St James's Park. (When his nephew, Prince George of Denmark, complained of a tendency to corpulence since his marriage, Charles gave him a few hints on fitness. 'Walk with me, hunt with my brother and do justice on my niece and you will not be fat.') He frequently attended horse-racing meetings at Newmarket, and was fond of the theatre. His scientific interests included mathematics and navigation, and he spent hours with his collections of watches and clocks and on experiments in his Whitehall laboratory. He was interested in architecture, building and landscaping, visiting his ships and naval fortifications and reviewing his troops. And he is still remembered as the founder of the Royal Society and the Royal Observatory at Greenwich, designed for him by Sir Christopher Wren.

The wedding of the year in 1663 was undoubtedly that of the Duke of Monmouth to 12-year-old Anne Scott, Duchess of Buccleuch, heiress of one of the largest fortunes in the land. It was arranged in the King's chamber by Charles, who brought forward the date to rescue the Duke from the attentions of the Duchess of Castlemaine.[19] In choosing Anne for his son's bride he gave him preference over Albemarle's son, Christopher, who was also seeking her hand in marriage. To contemporaries the wedding seemed less a religious service than an opportunity to show off the latest French fashions:

a veritable foam of lace petticoats and jewelled and ribboned ringlets, of streamers and fans, shoulder knots and diamond garter buckles.

Lady Castlemaine's numerous enemies commented gleefully that, for all her affected airs and load of jewellery, she looked pale and a little thin from the beginning of her third pregnancy.

The Duke of York was as amorous and lustful as his brother, although the women often offered themselves to their embraces, according to Sir John Reresby.[20] As heir to the throne this was not surprising, but the King thought James's choice and taste were deplorable and said his brother's mistresses were given him as penances by the priests.[21] Burnet wrote that he was perpetually in one amour or another; Gramont that his sole occupation was the seduction of the wives of the nobility and gentry (like Lady Anne Carnegie, wife of the Earl of Southesk, colonel of a militia foot regiment). Pepys noted that Lord Henry Brouncker was one of a number of pimps who brought James women 'through the Matted Gallery at Whitehall into his closet: nay the Duke hath come out of his wife's bed and gone to others laid in bed for him'.[22]

The Duke also became notorious for his affairs with maids of honour and ladies of the bedchamber, such as Goditha Price, daughter of the master of the King's household, and Mary, sister of Colonel Percy Kirke, who later transferred her affections to the Duke of Monmouth. Thanks to his amorous interest in Anne Ogle, her rich playboy brother Jack gained a commission in the Royal Horse Guards; while his affair with Margaret Brook, wife of the

King's elderly surveying architect Sir John Denham, caused a scandal. She agreed to become the Duke's mistress provided she were publicly owned and given a place in the Duchess of York's household, but she was not willing to go up and down the privy stairs like Goditha Price.[23] Even before her suspicious early death (see page 32), James had cooled towards her, because she troubled him with pillow talk and matters of state: Pepys noted that she was of Lord Bristol's anti-Clarendon faction.[24]

Lord Chesterfield, himself no mean cuckold-maker, had to hurry his wife Elizabeth (one of the loveliest women painted by Lely) off to his country estate at Bratby 'trussed up', to keep her out of James's clutches.[25] The Duke entered into a more permanent relationship with the 17-year-old maid of honour Arabella Churchill (see page 39); and later with another maid of honour young enough to be his daughter, Catherine Sedley, daughter of the wealthy baronet and dramatist Sir Charles Sedley. Catherine, an heiress, said she preferred life as a royal courtesan to the dull management of a servile house. The King meanwhile, commenting on his brother's amorous adventures, predicted 'he will lose his kingdom by his bigotry and his soul for a lot of trollops'.[26]

While frivolity reigned at a court filled with lovely women and brilliant men, Charles had sterner problems on his mind, not least of which was how to balance his budget. It was essential for constitutional harmony that crown and Parliament should agree as soon as possible on a just and workable financial settlement. In the early months, Charles was constantly asking Parliament for revenue to advance the public service and provide for the peace and security of the kingdom. If Parliament voted too little, there would be constant bickering; too much, and the crown would become independent of Parliament.

In the event, the House of Commons voted the King £1,200,000 a year, to pay not only for the upkeep of the royal estate, but also for the peacetime maintenance of the army and navy, and the salaries of judges and ambassadors. The figure was based on a totally inaccurate assessment of the annual yield from customs (£400,000) and excise (£300,000), supplemented by expedients such as stamp duty, revenue from the Post Office, a duty on wine, and the unpopular hearth tax. Even allowing for the very large sums he spent 'on his chargeable ladies about Court', the King's income throughout his reign always fell short of expenditure.

Moreover, his revenue was further reduced by wars and disasters, such as the Great Plague and the Fire of London. Charles never received the £500,000 he had spent paying his own and his father's debts, nor could Parliament have foreseen that an army would be needed and Tangier garrisoned at a minimum annual cost of £140,000. Even the Parliamentary grant for paying off the arrears of the navy and army, which MPs wanted to disband quickly, was £375,000 short of the required amount. By 1672, Charles's treasury would be almost bankrupt.[27]

The result was that Parliament used its financial powers to increase its constitutional authority over the monarch – a policy bitterly resented by the King, whose answer was to prorogue or dissolve Parliament. Charles relied instead on subsidies from Louis XIV, in return either for a pro-French policy or at least for non-interference with French interests on the Continent.

To try to make ends meet, Charles gave orders to halve expenditure on the navy and reduce his household costs and all other charges. He restricted the number of dishes per meal for his own and the Queen's consumption to 10; Prince Rupert was allowed six, and the maids of honour seven; with enough fire and candles for all, both above and below stairs.[28]

The army, despite its small size, made great demands on his income. London was its main base, and Charles had to restrict its peacetime duties to ceremonial connected with his person and the court, and to special tasks like riot and mob disorder. Much of its time was spent sitting idly in quarters or in the only barrack accommodation available – in the Tower of London, the Savoy (a royal almshouse and military hospital requisitioned as a barracks for the foot guards in 1679) or Scotland Yard, where two companies of guards were based for the King's special protection.

The foot regiment stationed nearest to the City supplied duty guards for the Tower, the palace at St James's and Whitehall. The Life Guards, based at Westminster and Whitehall, personally escorted the King wherever he went. Each of the three troops of Life Guards was divided into four squadrons, each squadron of 50 men. Two squadrons would perform one day's roster in every six, attending the families of both Charles and James. Two companies of Foot Guards were stationed in St James's Park and one troop of Royal Horse Guards was permanently quartered in Southwark. This arrangement gave the King sufficient troops near at hand to deal with London's frequent political riots or civil disturbances. 'They could be employed as police or thief-takers, patrolling the high roads, suppressing conventicles and keeping the peace at London playhouses.'[29]

On 4 July 1663 the King held a general review of his foot and horse guards in Hyde Park, witnessed by both Pepys and Evelyn. It was a splendid sight to see so many fine horses and men, the King and Duke on horseback, and the two Queens in the Queen Mother's coach. Lady Castlemaine was not there. The 4,000 troops, commanded by the Duke of Albemarle, consisted of gentlemen of quality and veteran soldiers, excellently clad and mounted.

Unfortunately, the army's conduct did not match its bearing. The Royal Guard, beholden to no one except the King, behaved with an insolence all too reminiscent of its predecessors. It quickly earned the hostility of Parliament and the hatred of the public, causing more trouble by way of riots and disorders than it ever helped to solve; frequently billeting itself on civilians under free quarter; and attracting some of the worst dregs of society into its ranks.

This behaviour created a legacy of resentment against the army which all its bravery in battle and patience in adversity would not overcome for the next two centuries.[30]

A typical foot regiment at this time was commanded by a colonel, often a member of the royal family or a distinguished general or nobleman. He owned the regiment, and was expected to make a profit out of its administration. It was his duty to see that his men were efficient, ready for service, and properly clothed and fed. Usually he had little to do with the running of the regiment, or even its command in action. This was left to the lieutenant-colonel, who had a major as his second in command; plus a staff of adjutant, chaplain, surgeon and mate, a quartermaster, and a marshal or sergeant major. The latter took offenders into custody, and ensured that camp followers, including women, kept to the rear on marches.

Regiments would have from eight to 12 companies, each company consisting of a captain, two subalterns, an ensign, two sergeants, three corporals, two drummers and 100 private soldiers. Frequently, the colonel, lieutenant-colonel and major also commanded companies, and drew the captain's pay in addition to their own. In peacetime, these establishments could be reduced both in the number of companies and/or in the number of men.[31]

Pepys went to Hyde Park a few weeks before the general review, having decided it might help his career to take part in a May Day parade in the coach ring. This was the rendezvous of fashion and beauty, where everyone who had either a pair of sparkling eyes or a splendid coach and horses assembled to see and be seen. He hoped to be noticed by the King or catch a glimpse of Lady Castlemaine – for him the loveliest of all the court ladies. For the occasion he hired new clothes, a pair of the latest fashion in gloves and a horse from the Chequer Inn in Charing Cross. Alas! His horse bolted, with Pepys clinging to its neck in fear for his life. He never did see his idols, but his career did not suffer: thanks to the favour of the Duke of York and the Earl of Sandwich, and his own application to work, he was to serve his King with great success, reorganising Admiralty affairs and helping to build his navy and command of the seas.

9

The Girl Most Fitted to Adorn a Court

The ascendancy of Barbara Castlemaine, both at court and over the King's affection, began to decline in 1663, although she would remain a prominent influence on both for some years longer. Charles began to tire of her constant infidelities, tantrums and imperious ways. Despite their strong mutual sexual attraction, neither was faithful to the other. She ran a whole stable of lovers – Charles Berkeley, Colonel James Hamilton, the dramatist Wycherley, an acrobat and tight-rope dancer called Jacob Hall, and John Churchill, to name but a few. As for Old Rowley, as one wag nicknamed the King after a well-known stallion in the royal stables, he was falling in love with a beautiful 16-year-old maid of honour who arrived from Paris at the beginning of 1663 to join the Queen's household and hasten Barbara's decline.

Frances Teresa Stuart was the daughter of Lord Blantyre, a Scottish Catholic and near kinsman of the Stuarts who had died fighting for Charles I. Frances was brought up at the court of Charles's mother, Henrietta Maria, in France, where Louis XIV noticed her elfin beauty and tried to induce her to stay at his court. But the Queen Mother brought her over to Whitehall, recommending 'this prettiest girl imaginable and the most fitted to adorn a court' for the coveted post of maid of honour to the Queen.[1]

Young and vain, Frances combined a perfection of face and figure with French coquetry and a Parisian flair for dress. Pepys wrote that it was, indeed, a glorious sight to see Mistress Stuart in black and white lace, her head and shoulders dressed with diamonds,[2] or wearing the male attire made fashionable by the Queen. This showed off Frances's supple figure and long legs, much admired by the King. Charles had her painted by the Dutchman Jacob Huysman, dressed in a buff doublet like a soldier, with a golden periwig and gold-hilted sword (see portrait plate 17). Later she was engraved as Britannia with helmet and trident, to show off her youth and beauty on British coinage for 300 years.[3] Soon even Pepys was changing his allegiance: 'She is the beautifullest creature I ever saw in my life – and doth exceed my Lady Castlemayne now.'[4] He fancied 'sporting with her with great pleasure'.

It was not just her beauty and coquetry which attracted Charles – there were already many beautiful women at his court. It was that rare commodity, her chastity, which intrigued him. But, flattered by the obvious admiration of the King, she flirted and allowed him to kiss and fondle her in public, in open sight of the Queen.

> He values not who sees him or stands by him, while he dallies with her open-ly and then privately in her chamber below, where the very sentries observe him going in and out.

She did all that was necessary to inflame the King's passions, wrote the Comte de Gramont, without exposing her virtue by granting him the ultimate favours. Barbara, recognising and fearing her rival, decided to take her under her wing. First, she adopted the same religion. The Queen was not amused. 'I fear,' she said, 'that my Lady Castlemaine's conversion was not prompted by con-science.' Barbara claimed she did it because otherwise she could not continue as the King's mistress and consequently mistress of State. The Queen asked Charles to prevent her going to Mass. Charles laughed and said: 'I never inter-fere with the souls of ladies, but only with their bodies, when they are civil enough to accept my attentions.'[5]

Barbara was having an affair with Henry Jermyn, nephew and heir of the Earl of St Albans and destined, as Earl of Dover, to become a privy councillor under James II and lieutenant-general of his bodyguard. One evening, as a frolic or to divert the King's attention from her affair, she invited Frances to sleep in her bed. Charles would find two tousled beauties to greet instead of one, when he paid his morning call. During the evening's sport, Pepys reports that it was decided:

> they two must be married and married they were, with ring and all other cer-emonies of church service and ribands and a sack posset in bed and flinging the stocking. Then my Lady Castlemayne, who was the bridegroom, rose and the King came and took her place with pretty mistress Stuart.

No doubt Barbara planned to make Frances the King's junior mistress under her control, realising she herself was now no more to the King than an occa-sional bedfellow ministering to his carnal appetites. But Frances did not fall for the bait! The incident, however, fuelled court speculation that she had suc-cumbed and become the King's mistress. 'Mrs Stuart, they say, is now a common mistress to the King, as my Lady Castlemayne is – which is a great pity', wrote Pepys.[6] Clarendon believed the King's regard for Mistress Stuart more nearly approximated to love than his other libertine attachments. Clarendon saw in her a welcome rival to Barbara, especially as Frances 'had not an idea of politics in her head'.[7]

Having spent the late summer of 1663 being carried from spa to spa in an attempt to cure her infertility, the Queen contracted a fever on her return to Whitehall. She became so ill that extreme unction was administered. The King was besotted with Frances Stuart, getting her into corners and staying with her for half-an-hour together, kissing her to the observation of all the world; Frances now stayed by herself and expected this, as Barbara Castlemaine used to do. Rumours spread in court that Charles would marry Frances if the Queen died. She was, after all, distantly connected with the royal line. 'But yet it is thought that this new wench is so subtle that she lets him not do anything more than is safe to her'. In order to make his visits more convenient, Charles allocated Frances apartments below his own in the palace.[8]

Despite her near-fatal illness, the Queen was constantly surrounded by her priests and Portuguese attendants, by physicians and visitors. She even received the French ambassador in her bedroom, for the luxury of privacy was never allowed to royal personages in those days. 'They were born in public, they dressed and undressed in public, surrounded by a crowd of princes, bishops, judges, cabinet ministers and foreign ambassadors watching their last agonies. For they were never allowed the comfort of a quiet room in sickness or a peaceful departure from this life.'[9] But the Queen did not die, and Pepys recorded on 4 January 1664 that she was very well again and the King lay with her on Saturday night last. Despite his many mistresses, Charles often made love to his wife, who had a number of miscarriages, as he continued to do his duty to beget the heir he so passionately wanted. To his sister, Minette, he wrote: 'I have been all this afternoon playing the good husband and I am very sleepy.'[10]

Prominent courtiers were anxious to use the new favourite to their advantage. Arlington, the Earl of Sandwich, and the Duke and Duchess of Buckingham were in a committee for the getting of Mistress Stuart for the King, wrote Pepys, but she proved a cunning slut. Their efforts were to no avail. She was advised at Somerset House by the Queen Mother and by her own mother, Mrs Walter Stuart; the plot was spoiled and the whole committee broken. The court debated whether Frances was a clever and virtuous virgin or a feather-brained innocent.[11] The Comte de Gramont gave as his opinion that it was hardly possible to have less wit or more beauty.

But ample evidence exists that, although she was gay and frivolous at 16, Frances grew up to be a shrewd, cautious, business-like woman. She liked the romance of love more than its reality, and frustrated the politicians by avoiding politics and declining to use her position to obtain money, titles or privileges

for herself or others. Thanks to Frances's lack of political interest, Barbara survived at court until the late 1660s – a remarkable achievement in an age when
women were said to be at their prime at 20, decayed at 24, old and insupport-
able at 30. Meanwhile, the King settled Barbara's debts of more than £30,000
and was heard to groan in lust and impatience that he wished Frances would
become 'old and willing'.[12] His passion even inspired his literary talent:

> I pass all my hours in a shady old grove,
> But I live not the day when I see not my love;
> While alone to myself I repeat all her charms,
> She I love may be locked in another man's arms.
> O then, 'tis O then, that I think there's no hell,
> Like loving too well.[13]

While the court speculated on Charles's success (or lack of it) with Frances,
Pepys plotted the course of the King's relentless siege during the next couple
of years with interest. He saw her having her portrait painted by Sir Peter Lely
(now in the Queen's collection), 'a lovely creature in dress and shape', surrounded by the King and courtiers. He noted the King visited her and Lady
Castlemaine every morning before eating his breakfast: the Queen would
pause before entering her dressing room until she knew whether the King was
there, for fear he should be with Frances, as she had sometimes found him.

> For certain, Mistress Stuart doth do everything now with the King that a
> mistress should do. The King doth follow Mistress Stuart wholly – and my
> Lady Castlemayne not above once a week.[14]

By early 1667 the King's wooing had become less patient, and Frances realised
she could not keep him at bay much longer. His unrequited passion was making him restless and moody. But she wanted marriage and a wedding ring, not
the bed of a royal harlot. Things might be very different in France, 'where
women are very coquettish before marriage and still more so afterwards',
according to Gramont. 'In England it is a miracle if a young lady yields to any
proposal but matrimony.' The King of France has his mistresses, but laughs at
the foolery of Charles, who makes his bastards princes and spends his revenue
upon them – and makes his mistresses his masters.

So Frances, still only 18, let it be known she would marry any honourable
gentleman worth £1,500 per annum. Evelyn applauded her decision, and Pepys
wrote that Mistress Stuart was as virtuous as any woman in the world. She
could no longer continue at court without prostituting herself to the King,
whom she had so long kept off, though he had more liberty to dally with her
than anyone else. She had no other way but to marry and leave court.[15] But the

courtiers stood aloof, afraid to enter the lists against the King – all except her cousin, Charles Stuart, fourth Duke of Richmond and sixth Duke of Lennox. At this time he possessed more debts than income, though because of his illustrious name and exalted position (hereditary Great Chamberlain, Great Admiral of Scotland, and a gentleman of the bedchamber), his credit was good.

Early in 1667 Richmond's second wife died, and within a fortnight the 26-year-old widower proposed to Frances. According to Gramont, the Duke came to her bedroom at midnight to make his proposal. Will Chiffinch, who had discovered that the Duke was paying serious court to Frances, informed Barbara and admitted her by the backstairs to the King's closet (a route not unfamiliar to her). The angry Barbara, jealous of her rival, told the King that Miss Stuart had doubtless dismissed him from her apartment on the grounds of affected indisposition or some pretended scruples of delicacy; but he had only to return to her chamber and he would find his happy rival, the Duke of Richmond, occupying his place. The King forced his way into the bedroom and found Frances in bed, with the Duke seated by her pillow. The King was furious, but, fearing to lose her, he offered to create her a duchess and promised 'to rearrange his seraglio'. Frances, knowing what the price would be, refused and the King stormed out, vowing never to see her again.[16]

A few days later, on a dark and stormy night, Frances eloped from her rooms in Whitehall, joined Richmond at the celebrated and ancient Beare Tavern by London Bridge, and fled with him to the Duke's country seat, Cobham Hall, near Gravesend. There the couple were privately married in March 1667. Frances begged the Queen's forgiveness for her affair with the King and sought her protection against his anger. She returned all the jewels Charles had given her. However, when the King learned of their marriage, he banished them both from court.[17]

Barbara was pregnant again, this time by the notorious rake Henry ('Harry') Jermyn, whose affair with Lady Falmouth drove Barbara into a jealous frenzy. She was determined Charles would acknowledge her child and have it christened in the Whitehall chapel, threatening to dash its brains out in front of the King. Charles declared the child was not his, since he had not lain with Barbara for the past months. So the farce continued, with the King on his knees begging her forgiveness and promising to offend her no more, while the whole court looked on in derision. Pepys commented:

> So they are all mad, and thus the Kingdom is governed. The King is as weary of her as is possible and would give anything to remove her: but he is so weak in his passion that he dare not do it. Her power over him is now not so much as a lover, for she scorns him, but as a tyrant to command him.[18]

On 29 July 1667, Pepys went to Westminster Hall to listen to the King address the House of Commons. Barbara and her faction had been urging Charles 'to rule by an Army or all would be lost', but Charles told Parliament that he had no intention of doing so. Suddenly a Quaker entered the Hall almost naked, 'only very civilly tied about the loins to avoid scandal', carrying a dish of fire and brimstone on his head, and crying 'Repent! Repent!'. The previous day Dr Robert Creighton, the royal chaplain, had preached before the King and a large congregation against the sins of the court and especially against adultery. He warned that, because of that single sin in David, the whole nation was undone. Pepys himself continued to call the court vicious, negligent and vain, and to attack its wantonness and vice. He compared it to Hell – 'no faith, no truth, no love, nor any agreement between man and wife, nor friends'.

Pamphleteers joined in the moral broadsides against the King, his court, and 'the royal whore' Barbara Castlemaine in particular. In March 1668, after the destruction of some City brothels during Lent by a mob of drunken and high-spirited London apprentices, 'sparing the great one in Whitehall', an ingenious libel was printed and distributed. It purported to come 'from the oppressed prostitutes of London, appealing for the protection of the nation's principal whore, Lady Castlemaine, the King's mistress'. It was entitled *The Poor Whores' Petition* and addressed to The most Splendid, Illustrious, Serene and Eminent Lady of Pleasure, the Countess of Castlemaine.

The Humble Petitioners were 'the undone company of poor, distressed whores, bawds, pimps and panders, long practised in a trade, wherein Your Ladyship hath great experience and for your diligence therein have arrived to a High and Eminent Advancement'. They pleaded for her help in catching the Ringleaders and Abettors of such outrages, 'before they come to your Honour's Palace and bring contempt upon your worshipping of Venus, the great Goddess, whom we all adore'. Barbara was a Famous Lady (By Special Grant), and had been:

> Serene and Illustrious ever since the Day that Mars was so instrumental to restore our Goddess Venus to her Temple and Worship and as a Reward of Devotion was soon created Countess of Castlemaine.

In giving her Gracious Answer, Barbara returned her thanks and those of her Sisterhood, in Dog and Bitch Yard, Moorfields etc., who give no Entertainment without Ready Money.

According to the ancient rules and customs of our Order (always without our Husband) we have satisfied ourselves with the delights of Venus; and in our Husband's absence we have had a Numerous Offspring (who are Bountifully and Nobly provided for).

Given at our Closet in Kingstreet, Westminster. *Die Veneris* April 24 1668.

No wonder the King was annoyed and the Lady horribly vexed![19] Another satire, attributed to Andrew Marvell, compared the King to one of these London apprentices who,

> Spends all his days
> In running to plays
> When in his shop he should be poring;
> And wastes all his nights
> In his constant delights
> Of revelling, drinking and whoring.

Meanwhile, the King relented towards Frances. She returned to court a few months later and was created lady of the Queen's bedchamber, attending Catherine to Calais to meet Charles's sister Minette in 1670. Her reappearance at court as a bride drew the attention of all eyes. It was clear the King's passion was unsubdued, but Frances conducted herself with the dignified decorum of a 'virtuous maiden, although rumour was, nevertheless, busy on the subject'.[20]

The Richmonds lived in great splendour at Somerset House, the dower-palace of the Queen Mother. Soon after their marriage the King sent the Duke to Scotland (some said to remove a jealous husband); then in early 1672 sent him as ambassador extraordinary to Denmark, where he died at Elsinore a few years later. On 19 May 1668, Pepys gossiped:

> the King is mighty hot upon the Duchess of Richmond . . . and one night, after he had ordered his guards and coach to be ready to carry him to the Park, he did, on a sudden, take a pair of oars or sculler and all alone, or but one with him, go to Somerset House and there, the garden door not being open, himself clambered over the walls to make her a visit.

Did the Duchess afford the King those favours as a wife which she had denied him as a maid? Frances continued for many years at court, enjoying the balls, fashionable supper parties, and the theatre. As a widow she moved into a new house in Whitehall's bowling green, overlooking the river on one side and St James's Park on the other. She attended James II's wife, Mary of Modena, during her accouchement in 1688. Charles made adequate financial provision for her widowhood, and she passed her final years in peaceful retirement in a house in St James's Square, where she died in 1702. She is buried in Westminster Abbey in the Duke of Richmond's vault in Henry VII's chapel.

Meanwhile, Barbara Castlemaine's lover Henry Jermyn was creating more than an illegitimate child. Since the Restoration, more and more of the landed aristocracy were abandoning their country estates, with the associated long months of loneliness and boredom, for the pleasures of London and court.

Here were to be found:

> rich wives, spruce mistresses, pleasant houses, good diet, rare wines, neat
> servants, fashionable furniture, pleasures and profits the best of all sorts.[21]

When they were not sitting in Parliament or frequenting the court seeking
office, favour or title, they could divert themselves with wife and family in the
theatres, coffee-houses and parks, or in the fashionable shops around
Whitehall. Others came for business, to settle legal matters in the four Inns of
Court and Westminster Hall, to invest in Bank of England stocks, or purchase
real estate. One such was Francis Russell, Earl of Bedford, whose development
of Covent Garden was the first planned layout in the expansion of London
beyond the City. In 1670 Charles gave him a charter to establish the famous
market for fruit and vegetables, and later flowers. Another property buyer
was the fourth Earl of Southampton, who carried out a similar development on
his Bloomsbury estate. Many of the streets and squares in central London
today commemorate their family names.

Freeholds were difficult to obtain and speculative building was forbidden, so
most of the nobility who came to London had to live with their families in rent-
ed accommodation, or in modest leased houses in Lincoln's Inn Fields, Covent
Garden or Drury Lane. All the great houses were more like country houses in
open fields than town houses suitable for courtiers. Berkeley House was built
by one of the most eminent Royalist officers of the Civil War, who married the
daughter of a rich East India Company merchant. Southampton House was
built by the lord high treasurer. There was Clarendon House in Piccadilly;
Goring House, on the site of Buckingham Palace and home of Arlington, secretary of state; and Montagu House in Bloomsbury, built by the ambassador to
Paris.

In August 1663, Henry Jermyn wrote to the King that the beauty of this great
town and the convenience of the court were defective in point of houses fit for
the dwellings of noblemen and other persons of quality. In 1661 the Queen
Mother had granted him the lease of meadows in St James's (or Pall Mall)
Fields; now he wanted to build a number of fashionable houses for noblemen
near the court. In 1665 the King granted Jermyn his freehold of over 11 acres.

Although building was delayed by the Great Plague and the Fire of London,
St James's Square soon became the centre of political and social eminence as
London began to expand westwards. Conveniently close to the court at St
James's Palace, it was for 50 years the most glamorous address in London and
its list of residents read like a court circular. Jermyn, by then the Earl of St
Albans, occupied his house in the south-east corner of St James's Square in
1667. The founder of the West End, remembered today in Jermyn Street, was
soon followed by his friends, Arlington, Halifax and Belasyse. Then came the

Earl of Oxford, Aubrey de Vere, colonel of the Blues, whose daughter Lady Diana, one of the great beauties of the age, married Charles's son by Nell Gwynn (Charles, Duke of St Albans, colonel of the future Eighth Hussars).

In St James's Square lived dukes and earls, ministers of state, the lieutenant of the King's bodyguard, his master general of ordnance, his lord steward of the household, the French ambassador, Honoré de Courtin, and Sir Thomas Clarges, brother of Albemarle's wife Nan. The royal mistresses Arabella Churchill, Catherine Sedley and Moll Davis were also residents of the square.

During the years 1667–70, turbulence reigned at Whitehall as the King, freed from Clarendon's influence and restraint, attempted to control his recalcitrant and bankrupt kingdom on his own. The euphoria of the Restoration had disappeared and Charles was at loggerheads with church and Parliament. He was subject to sudden changes of policy, deceptions and intrigues, at variance with his ministers and people. He was less secure, too, in his personal life: he quarrelled violently with his regular mistress, Lady Castlemaine, and began a series of socially outrageous liaisons, moving promiscuously from one woman to another, returning intermittently to Barbara's superior erotic charms as he slowly disengaged himself from her domination. Frances Stuart's rejection of him had a cataclysmic effect on his emotions, which only the advent of Louise de Keroualle would cure.[22]

10

War and a Growing Empire

In 1665, London was the centre of national life. It had a population of half a million (10 per cent of the country's total), and it produced more than half the country's wealth. Its inhabitants were crowded into a densely packed community along the north bank of the Thames between Wapping and Westminster. Officially, London was still a walled city; the City proper, bound by its seven ancient gates, locked at night – Ludgate and Newgate in the west, Aldgate in the east and Cripplegate, Aldersgate, Moorgate and Bishopsgate to the north. At the west stood St Paul's and at the east the Tower of London, the formidable fortress built nearly 600 years earlier, with its long and gruesome history as state prison and place of execution.

But the city's suburbs had long outgrown its medieval confines and were spreading out in all directions. Piccadilly (originally known as Portugal Street after Queen Catherine) was open country; Knightsbridge, Chelsea and Islington were rural villages. Apart from Southwark, there were few inhabitants south of London Bridge, still the only bridge crossing the Thames. It stood on its 18 arches, crowned by a double row of shops and houses: the turret of the southern end traditionally festooned with the heads of executed traitors, left to rot until they fell. Before the end of the century London's population would have doubled and its houses stretch from Blackwall to Chelsea.

The River Thames was London's High Street, a busy thoroughfare for the King's gilded barges, merchant ships bound for the Indies, colliers carrying Newcastle coal and boats loaded with the produce of Kent. Barges and ferries criss-crossed the river, linking the shipyards and royal arsenals lining the banks of the lower reaches to the farms and orchards stretching beyond the modern suburbs of Trafalgar Square and the Charing Cross Road.

Along the south side of the Strand were the palaces of the nobility – Somerset House, Northumberland House and the Savoy. Each had gardens running down to the river: each its own private landing stairs. Other large mansions, standing in parks and gardens, were scattered around the western outskirts. There were Bedford House and Burlington House (the only survivor of half a dozen great mansions built on the north side of Piccadilly in the 1660s) and Clarendon's vast palace in Piccadilly itself – demolished in 1683.

London was the seat of the court and of the fashion and pleasure surrounding it. Shops were becoming fashionable: ladies frequented the mercers, haberdashers and toy shops, gentlemen the armourers, goldsmiths and book-sellers. The rich shops in Covent Garden were kept by well-dressed women, busily employed but not without chances of flirtation and assignation with passers-by.[1] London was the centre of Parliament and the Courts of Law, of trade and commerce. Apart from its churches, London was not rich in public buildings: there were the Guildhall and the Royal Exchange, where merchants met for news and business, the Custom House, Westminster Hall, the Old Bailey, the Fleet and Marshalsea Prisons and the Halls of the City companies. But no other city could claim comparable theatres, places of amusement, clubs, coffee and eating houses. In the numerous taverns one could eat and drink, write letters, do business or, as Pepys so often did, meet friends or enjoy a little female company.

London attracted musicians and painters, writers and publishers; and for those with lower tastes there were such spectacles and entertainments as bull and bear baiting, the cockpit, the lunatics at Bedlam, the penitent prostitutes who beat hemp under the lash at Bridewell, gaming and commercialised sex. Brothels flourished in every part of the City (the highest class houses were in Covent Garden, the bankside 'stews' in Southwark) Actresses and courtesans were at the top of the market, for the exclusive use of their royal and aristo-cratic 'protectors'. Lower down came the streetwalkers, whom Pepys wisely avoided, seamstresses and barmaids, and the amateur shop girls, like Betty Martin, a linen draper's wife of Westminster Hall, whom he regularly patron-ised.[2]

London's narrow and crooked streets were crowded with the coaches of the nobility and tradesmen's carts, fighting for right of way, their wooden and iron wheels rumbling on the cobble stones. Rivers of filth ran down the centre of each street, passers-by grateful for the overhanging storeys as slop-pails were emptied out of upstairs windows. In summer London stank. There were no public conveniences: the polite entered an ale-house, others used the street wall. Mrs Pepys, taken ill at the theatre, went out into Lincoln's Inn Walks and 'there in a corner did her business'. Smallpox, fevers and, periodically, bubon-ic plague haunted the town and spread into the countryside. Smoke from the furnaces of the brewers, soap-boilers and dyers obscured the churches and palaces, fouled the clothes and corrupted the waters, turning into blankets of fog in winter and endangering the health of the King and his people.

In these badly lit and insanitary streets the bellman told the hour at night

and the state of the weather – 'Past one o'clock and a cold and frosty morning.'
The watch provided an inadequate police service. Latecomers on foot were
liable to be attacked by foot-pads or rogues with cudgels and men of rank provided themselves with armed escorts. Highwaymen infested the country lanes
around the city.[3] Inside London, the mobs were notoriously violent – in 1668,
for example, the apprentices systematically attacked the brothels. The population respected neither rank, sex nor person, and were prone to civil
disturbances, which the soldiers sent to quell often joined. There was public
disorder during the anti-Popish riots, and during Parliamentary elections in
Southwark and Westminster.

But London was not England. In the shires and counties, the old
squirearchy still flourished in what were largely agricultural communities,
with the hierarchy of nobility, gentry and peasantry seen as part of the natural order of things. Life proceeded at the pace of the plough, and poor roads
hindered the movement of goods and people. This led to local self-sufficiency
and people marrying within their own neighbourhoods. The squire hunted and
fished and sat in Parliament. His wife held the keys with responsibility for the
kitchen, brewery, buttery, storehouse and still-room, supervised the household staff and catered for the guests. Farming occupied half the population and
fields were being enclosed. Craftsmen worked in leather and pottery, ironware
and glass, hosiery and textiles.

Men and women in market towns and villages, unlike the London masses,
lived constantly among neighbours. Privacy hardly existed and some form of
authority (master or mistress, employer, clergy or parish officers) supervised
and regulated most aspects of their daily lives. Under the Poor Law paupers
were entitled to poor-relief in their place of birth, vagrants were punished in
houses of correction and workhouses were usually prisons under another
name. For the poor life was hard, with a cow, pig or vegetable patch as the
essential support for the family. Women's work was constantly interrupted by
child-bearing between the ages of 18 and 45, and mothers who survived were
old long before their time.

Only in London, especially in the shanty town areas of the east end, did people live in anonymous masses, with none to care for their welfare:

> uprooted immigrants, moving from one insanitary tenement to another at
> frequent intervals, encumbered by numbers of young children, of whom few
> survived to adulthood, largely dependent on casual labour, often in short sup-
> ply, living constantly on the edge of total destitution.[4]

Charles tried to improve conditions in the city. He imposed a rate to pay for
new sewers and drains, forbade the disposal of refuse and rubbish in the
streets, and required householders to show a candle in the windows during

winter nights 'upon pain to forfeit one shilling'. But he found the city's ancient rights an obstacle: London was governed by the Lord Mayor, who had the power to make his own ordinances and by-laws within the city limits.

London was also the centre of a growing colonial empire and the base for the great overseas trading companies like the East India Company, the Levant and Muscovy, African and South Sea Companies. Their early governors included the Duke of York, Prince Rupert and John Churchill. The King himself, Albemarle, Clarendon, Ashley Cooper and Sandwich were major shareholders. These companies were linked financially to the banking centres of Amsterdam, Frankfurt and Geneva and ministers, military officers and members of the Court took shares in their joint stock ventures. They ensured the companies received the help they needed to defend and extend their commercial enterprises. England, rich in harbours and with plentiful resources of coal, iron, lead, lime and timber, was ideally placed for world trade. The chief commodities were cotton and woollen products, but England also exported tin, pewter, brass, leather, glass and earthenware goods.

Each part of the empire, colonies and mother country, would have its allotted place in this trading policy, each contributing to the prosperity of all. In return for manufactured goods, English merchants brought home tobacco from the plantations of Virginia and Maryland; the fishing fleets of Devon took cod from Newfoundland to Spanish and Portuguese ports, where they traded it for wine and oil. Slave ships carried negroes to the West Indies and returned with sugar and rum from Jamaica and Barbados. Spices and silks from the Orient, naval stores, furs and rice from New York and Charleston, and the newly fashionable tea, indigo, saltpetre and calicoes from India were traded by the Levant and East India Companies for English-made products. Charles's dowry from his Portuguese Queen had brought trading rights in the Mediterranean and the Far East, which his merchants would exploit.

Most important of all, England's Navigation Acts of 1651 (during the Protectorate) and between 1660-63 under Charles II ensured that certain listed commodities, such as sugar, tobacco and cotton, could be carried to or from existing or future colonies in Africa, Asia or America only in English or colonial ships. It was decreed that these ships must be built in England, be English-owned, and three-quarters of the crew had to be English nationals. This fenced off English colonial trade from foreigners and eliminated the trade-competing Dutch as middlemen. The Acts also provided a reserve of trained seamen and sea-worthy vessels for the Royal Navy in time of war.

In order to take possession of Bombay, part of his wife's dowry, Charles sent a Royalist officer, Sir Abraham Shipman, to be the new governor. He sailed to India in April 1661, with a small force of 400 officers and men. The Portuguese governor, unaware of the marriage settlement, at first refused to surrender Bombay; during the protracted negotiations Shipman, most of his officers and one third of the men died of disease. The cost of maintaining Bombay, the unhealthy climate and poor commercial return persuaded Charles to offer it to the East India Company in 1668 for an annual rental of £10. Most of the original military force who still remained alive joined the Company, on the same rank and pay. They formed the nucleus of the Company's own army, which would help to expand its trade, territory and influence over vast areas in British India for the next 200 years.[5]

The restoration of Charles II began a new wave of expansion and settlement in the New World, with commercial profit and religious freedom as the two main motives. On his accession, Virginia was the only royal colony: New England belonged to the Puritans who had beheaded his father, and Maryland to the Catholic family of the Calverts (Lord Baltimore). By the end of his reign in 1685, a continuous line of English colonies would stretch along the Atlantic seaboard from Maine in the north to the border of Spanish Florida in the south.

The earliest colonists to leave the mother country, primarily for religious reasons, had been the Pilgrim Fathers, a group of about 100 'separatists' who refused to accept the authority of the Church of England. They set out from Plymouth, Devon, in 1620 on the *Mayflower* and settled under their leader, William Bradford, on the inhospitable Massachusetts shore. They called the place Plymouth Rock, and during the first year nearly half died of disease. But the settlers persevered, making peace treaties with the surrounding Indians. Their hard work soon enabled them to celebrate their first harvest Thanksgiving feast – the origin of the American tradition of Thanksgiving on the fourth Thursday of November. (See plate 19). In 1691 the Plymouth Rock colony was annexed to Massachusetts Bay.

The second group of religious dissenters, who were of far greater importance in the founding and growth of the Massachusetts colonies and the rest of New England, were the Puritans of Massachusetts Bay. Like the Pilgrim Fathers, these Puritan settlers sailed to America principally to free themselves from religious restraints, from the frivolity, extravagance and moral corruption of the Stuart court, and from gaming tables and playhouses. They wanted not only to separate from the established Anglican church but to 'purify' it, by simplifying the ritual, observing the Sabbath, and establishing their own way of life based on the Bible as they interpreted it. Under their lawyer governor, John Winthrop, 'the first great American', 1,000 men, women and children aimed to establish a self-governing commonwealth of purity and orthodoxy, in which all backsliders were subject to immediate correction in the stocks or expulsion from the colony. Family virtues were praised and adultery punished by death. Winthrop set the example with four wives and 16 children.

The settlers founded Boston and, as a result of their belief that everyone should be able to read and understand the Bible, education flourished; leading

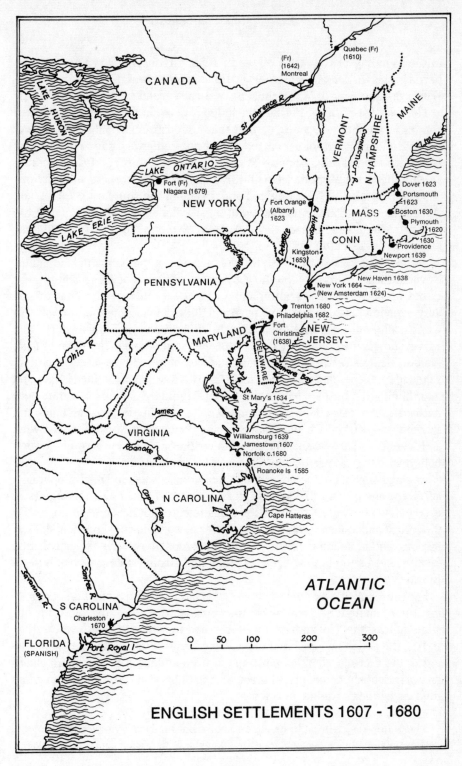

CANADA

Quebec (Fr)
(1610)

(Fr)
(1642)
Montreal

LAKE HURON

MAINE

VERMONT

N HAMPSHIRE

CONNECTICUT R.

LAKE ONTARIO

Fort (Fr)
Niagara (1679)

NEW YORK

Fort Orange
(Albany)
1623

Dover 1623
Portsmouth
1623
Boston 1630
Plymouth
1620
1630
Providence
Newport 1639

MASS

LAKE ERIE

R Hudson

R Delaware

Kingston
1653

CONN

R Susquehanna

New Haven 1638

PENNSYLVANIA

New York 1664
(New Amsterdam 1624)

Ohio R

Trenton 1680
Philadelphia 1682
Fort
Christina
(1638)

NEW
JERSEY

MARYLAND

DELAWARE

Delaware Bay

St Mary's 1634

James R

VIRGINIA

Williamsburg 1639
Jamestown 1607
Norfolk c.1680

Roanoke R

Roanoke Is 1585

N CAROLINA

Cape Fear R

Cape Hatteras

ATLANTIC
OCEAN

Savannah R.

Santee R.

S CAROLINA

Charleston
1670

FLORIDA
(SPANISH)

Port Royal I

0   50   100   200   300

ENGLISH SETTLEMENTS 1607 - 1680

to the founding of Harvard College in 1636. Sir George Downing (remembered today in Downing Street), whose mother was the sister of John Winthrop, governor of Massachusetts, was the second graduate of Harvard.

The iron fist of these Puritans included a belief in the English system of compulsory military services, namely that 'Free citizens should think it their truest Honour to be a soldier citizen'. Their non-conformist communities soon spread to other areas, such as Maine, New Hampshire, and Connecticut. During the Great Migration (1630–43), 20,000 hungry workers and religious dissenters settled in New England and 45,000 in the southern colonies and West Indies. In 1650 the population of these colonies was 52,000; during the next 50 years it would reach 250,000. After 1660 only the Dutch would challenge the English monopoly.[6]

As his empire expanded with the colonisation of the New England states, Newfoundland, Bermuda and the Caribbean, and parts of Africa and the Far East, Charles relied on sea power and maritime supremacy rather than on military expedition, which was expensive and difficult to organise and supply. He was a sailor himself, and encouraged ship-building at English ports like Newcastle, Hull, Portsmouth and Bristol, while the whole of the Thames from London Bridge to Blackwall became one vast ship-building yard. To protect England's colonies and trade sea lanes, Charles developed the Royal Navy and maintained its bases. Within the limits imposed by his revenue and Parliamentary restrictions on his supplies, he built up the royal arsenals and storehouses at Chatham and Rochester and the naval dockyards at Woolwich and Deptford. These seafaring pursuits would form the basis of his foreign policy, with the navy as the chief agent of his trade policy.

England's main competitor in trade and empire was the Dutch Republic – admired, envied and disliked by the commercial cities and merchants of England, who recognised the Dutch challenge to their maritime interests. By their thrift and industry, their religious tolerance and hospitality, their skills in banking and in building cheap and efficient ships, the Dutch had established for themselves the largest carrying trade and strongest commercial base in Europe.

For the English, war offered an attractive and alternative method of defeating their challenge. Parliament and most of the court had nothing but contempt for the 'Hollanders' and were 'mad for a Dutch War'.[7] In the East Indies, the Dutch had declared themselves Lords of the Southern Seas, denying traffic there to all ships but their own upon pain of confiscation, which enraged English merchants. Charles, writing to his sister Minette, summed up the Englishmen's warlike feelings:

The States keep a great bragging and noise but I believe when it comes to it, they will look twice before they leap. I never saw so great an appetite to a war as is, in both London and country, especially in the Parliamentary men, who, I am confident, would pawn their estates to maintain a war. And if I be forced to a war, I shall be ready with as good ships and men as ever was seen and leave the success to God.[8]

Charles wanted the Dutch to make the first step, but

the truth is the Dutch have no great need to provoke this nation, for, except myself, I believe there is scarce an Englishman that does not desire passionately a war with them.

His principal ministers – Clarendon, Southampton and Ormonde – shared the King's reluctance, but the war party had powerful friends like Albemarle among the courtiers and circles surrounding the Duke of York. Albemarle declared that reasons didn't matter: what the English wanted was more of the trade the Dutch now had.

During the winter of 1663–4, before war between England and Holland had been officially declared, fighting broke out in Africa. Charles had authorised an expedition under Sir Robert Holmes to attack Dutch possessions on the Guinea Coast and its profitable slave trade. In the Caribbean, a Dutch naval commander named de Ruyter bombarded Barbados and captured some English shipping. The governor of Barbados retaliated, with the help of the pirate Henry Morgan and his buccaneers, and virtually expelled the Dutch from the West Indies. (In 1671 Spain recognised England's right to Jamaica; Morgan, instead of being convicted of piracy, became a national hero. He would become the governor and commander-in-chief of Jamaica's forces.) But far from defending these islands with regular forces, the hard-pressed Charles had to rely on a civilian militia: in Barbados all eligible males were organised into militia regiments, the richer planters in the cavalry, the poorer settlers in the infantry.[9]

In March 1664, with hostilities clearly imminent, Charles took the provocative step of giving the Dutch New Netherlands in North America to his brother. He claimed that it was English soil from earlier discoverers, but in reality it was because the Dutch controlled the fur trade and allowed their goods to be brought into the colonies or into England in non-English ships in defiance of the Navigation Acts. The territorial grant to the Duke of York was the largest land grant ever made by any English sovereign. It included not only the future state of New York, but the entire region between Cape Cod and Delaware Bay – all the territory, in fact, occupied or claimed by the Dutch on the Atlantic seaboard. The grant included Long Island, Nantucket and part of the present state of Maine. In addition to this charter, Charles gave James £4,000 to conquer the territory.

The Duke of York needed these lands to produce a financial profit, and promptly appointed his groom of the bedchamber, Colonel Richard Nicolls, as lieutenant governor. Nicolls had served with the Duke in exile under the French Marshal Turenne. Instructed to take possession of the new territories, on 18 August 1664 he sailed with four ships and 300 soldiers into the harbour of New Amsterdam, which was protected by its fort and palisade (the site of the present Wall Street). Peter Stuyvesant, New Amsterdam's Dutch governor, was unable to rally the inhabitants to defend the town and surrendered without firing a shot. By the end of October, Nicolls had taken over not only New Amsterdam, which was renamed New York after his patron, but had also subdued Fort Orange (renamed Albany) up the Hudson River and Fort Casimir (Newcastle). Soon the seaboard of New England had been linked to the colonies of Virginia and Maryland. (The New Netherlands was officially ceded to England by the Treaty of Breda in 1667, confirmed by the Peace of Nymwegen in 1678. When the Duke of York became James II in 1685, New York became a royal colony.)[10]

Louis XIV, who had plans for extending his frontiers towards the Rhine, would have liked a *grande alliance* between England, Holland and France against his real enemy, Spain, who opposed his designs on the Spanish Netherlands. But he had long realised such an alliance was impossible, because of the commercial hatred between England and Holland. As an alternative, an alliance with England was preferred: Holland would oppose an attack on the Spanish Netherlands, which the Dutch regarded as a buffer between Holland and France.

Louis had made an earlier treaty with Holland promising to indemnify her from attack by any hostile force. But when he concluded this treaty, Louis never expected the Dutch to start hostilities with England; and now he certainly did not want to go to Holland's rescue against his cousin, Charles. This was a policy which could only benefit Spain and delay his advance on the Rhineland, so he made one last effort to maintain the status quo between Holland and England. He hurriedly sent his ambassador, Courtin, ('a man of pleasure', specially selected to fit into Charles's social life and study the court beauties) to Lady Castlemaine, as a well-tried means of gaining the ear of the King. But he also took the precaution of separately courting Frances Stuart, the prettiest girl on the English scene. 'She is the rising sun,' Courtin wrote on 9 July 1665, 'and, to tell the truth, she is incomparably more beautiful than the other.'[11]

Courtin found that the Spanish ambassador, just as keen as the French to get at the King through his womenfolk, had already won over the favour of the greedy and extravagant Lady Castlemaine. He therefore concentrated on Frances, flattering her to obtain invitations to the supper parties which she was in the habit of giving for the King and his friends. These parties became more frequent, and Courtin used them to meet the King on easy and familiar terms. Charles, however, was a past master at avoiding inconvenient political discussions, and Courtin gained little advantage from them, especially as Frances herself showed little interest in politics.[12] In any case, all his efforts were too late to prevent the declaration of war on 4 March 1665.

Charles believed the Dutch would concede his demands without fighting, or at least capitulate after their first defeat. The Duke of York, as admiral of the fleet, raised his flag at Portsmouth with orders from the King to fight, burn, smoke or destroy all Dutch warships and seize their merchantmen. A number of Dutch 'prizes' were captured in the Channel, and there were daily fights over herring shoals in the North Sea between the fishermen of both countries.

These and other pretexts were used as excuses for Charles to declare war on Holland on 4 March 1665. He told Parliament that, by borrowing very liberally from out of his own stores and with the assistance of the City of London, he had a fleet now at sea worthy of the English nation. In gratitude, Parliament voted him £2½ million for the prosecution of the war. To historians it is known as the Second Dutch War (1665–7), the First (1652–4) having taken place during the Commonwealth. Sir George Clark called it the clearest case in our history of a purely commercial war.[13]

At first, the English had 160 ships and some 25,000 men, including a regiment of English origin serving in Holland in Dutch pay and employment. This regiment traced its history to Elizabeth I, the London trained bands and Captain (later Colonel) Thomas Morgan, who was asked to raise a company of 300 men to help the Dutch against Spain. Soon the English contribution had risen to four regiments, joined by three Scottish regiments, all paid for as a permanent garrison by the Dutch, when they gained their independence from Spain in 1648.

When the Second Dutch War broke out, Charles ordered the Anglo-Dutch brigade to return to England. In Holland this regiment, together with two others, was faced with a resolution: they must either take the oath of allegiance to the Dutch, or be instantly cashiered, which meant ruin for the officers and want and misery for the men. Without hesitation, officers and men opted for disbandment. From those who returned home (thanks to money and passes provided by the English envoy at the Hague, Sir George Downing), the basis of the new Holland regiment (later known as the Third Foot, or the Buffs) was taken on the English establishment on 31 May 1665. Robert Sidney, 'the handsome lover of Lucy Walter', became its founding colonel.[14]

Others joined The Admiral's Regiment (The Duke of York and Albany's Maritime Regiment of Foot): raised on 28 October 1664 'for sea service' on board ship, under the command of Sir William Killigrew, it is today recognised as the birth of the Royal Marines. Under the regiment's colonel, the 1,200 men, dressed in yellow coats and red breeches and stockings,[15] were divided into six companies and served aboard the fleet during the Dutch Wars of 1669-1680. The Second and Third Dutch Wars were strictly naval affairs, but Charles raised 22 new regiments in 1665 and 1672, though only a small part of these were actively engaged, and then only as marines on board the ships. All were disbanded in 1674.

Leaving Albemarle ashore as his deputy, on 31 March 1665, the Duke of York as lord high admiral, with the veteran Admiral Sir William Penn and a crowd of volunteers 'of the first quality', went aboard the flagship, the *Royal Charles*. Two days later the King and his friends were having supper in Lady Castlemaine's apartment in Whitehall when Pepys, clerk of the King's ships and as such a member of the Navy Board, arrived to report that the English fleet had sighted the Dutch fleet sailing to attack them. All next day the thunder of guns from over 200 ships was heard in London in the first real engagement of the war. The Dutch were defeated in the Battle of Lowestoft by the Duke of York as commanding admiral, and Prince Rupert and the Earl of Sandwich as squadron commanders. Had the Duke followed up the victory, the battle might have been decisive. Nevertheless, Pepys recorded:

> They all fled: we have taken and sunk 24 of their best ships; killed and taken eight or ten thousand men: and lost, we think, not above seven hundred. A greater victory never known in the world.[16]

At the height of the battle, a cannon ball killed the King's friend Sir Charles Berkeley, recently created Duke of Falmouth, and Viscount Muskery. The shell missed the Duke himself, whose clothes were bespattered with their blood. The King wept openly at the death of his friend, which brought home to the court the less romantic side of war. As a result, the King ordered James, the heir presumptive, who had found a role for himself as a fighting admiral of the fleet, never again to risk his life in battle. He appointed the Earl of Sandwich to the command in his place.

Had Falmouth survived, loved and trusted by the King as he was, he would undoubtedly have been called upon to play an important part in the later negotiations for an alliance with France.[17] He had served the Duke of York in exile, had been knighted at the Restoration and became captain of the Duke's troop of Life Guards. The one true love of his life, if only for six months, was Mary Bagot, one of the loveliest of the Duchess of York's maids of honour. She became first his mistress, and later his wife. Charles showed his approval of the marriage by immediately appointing her a lady of the Queen's bedchamber.

The one grievous blot on an otherwise honourable career was his defamation of Anne Hyde. He told the King he was one of a number who had slept with her, in an attempt to prevent the Duke of York publicly acknowledging his secret marriage to her. Clarendon, her father, never forgave Falmouth, and called him a young man of a dissolute life and prone to all wickedness in the judgement of all sober men. It cannot be denied that he both condoned and assisted the love affairs of the royal brothers (hardly a crime for young men of the time), and he was a one-time lover of Barbara Castlemaine.

Louis XIV, in accordance with his treaty, had to join the Dutch against England, although acting chivalrously with his cousin Charles and giving as little help as possible to his allies. In June 1666, a year after the battle of Lowestoft, the Dutch commander Admiral de Ruyter avenged their defeat by inflicting some 8,000 casualties and destroying 20 ships of the English fleet.

Patronage was rife in the English navy; offices and advancement were bought and sold. As in the army, Charles gave naval commissions to courtiers, favourites and noblemen: Sir William Penn, for example, commanded a ship at 23, became a rear admiral at 27, and at 32 was a general-at-sea. Like the Duke of York, lord high admiral, Prince Rupert, Albemarle and Sandwich, Penn was both a practical seaman and an army commander, fighting naval battles using military principles gained on land battlefields (ie ship fought ship to effect a boarding, when pike, musket and cutlass could be used). Other officers, however, were experienced seamen who had risen from the lower decks of either the navy or merchant vessels.

Conditions in the navy were bad: the pay was poor and usually in arrears; food was short and often inedible; and the sailors were inadequate. Many were landsmen, often beggars or criminals, press-ganged into temporary service. After one naval engagement, some English sailors were found floating in the water dressed in their Sunday black, just as they had been when caught by the press-gang after church. Discipline was strict, with flogging by a rope's end or rattan cane inflicted for the slightest offence. Hanging was considered indispensable to man the fleet. In port, the ships were pestered by women: often there were as many petticoats as breeches on board, and that for weeks together. Ashore, sailors were a byword for drinking, rape, brawling and rioting. Morale in the fleet was so low that 3,000 English and Scottish soldiers actually volunteered for service with the Dutch.[18]

After the naval defeat by de Ruyter, Charles led his government in a great effort for vengeance. He called out the militia and commissioned three new foot regiments and 16 troops of cavalry to counter any invasion. He borrowed money from the City to repair the ships and hire more. On 19 July the navy put to sea once more, and gained a victory off the Suffolk coast. Rupert and Albemarle chased the enemy back to the Dutch coast and landed troops, who burned a town and an entire merchant fleet.

But despite this, 1666 saw another year's expenditure of energy, money, blood and misery achieving no final result.[19] Yet again, Charles had to ask for money to continue the war from a reluctant Parliament, which criticised the continuing dissipation of King and court. Pepys was told that in 1666 Charles had diverted £400,000 of war funds to private pleasures. 'Give the King the Countess of Castlemaine and he cares not what the nation suffers' was the cry of one member of Parliament. As for court matters, complained Pepys, the ladies lie longest in bed and govern all when they are up.[20]

Yet worse was to follow. Against Albemarle's strong advice, Charles moored his fleet and disbanded the crews, while he tried negotiations for peace. Short of money, the treasurer of the navy could afford to pay off less than a quarter of the seamen who had returned with Prince Rupert. During the winter months many of the remainder rioted in and around London, and Albemarle had to use his soldiers to quell the disturbances. A defiant Parliament voted a further £1,800,000 for the prosecution of the war. But this proved both inadequate and too late, especially as a trade depression, caused by war, plague and fire, delayed collection of the revenue.

The Dutch fleet was smaller in number than the English, but their ships were faster and more manoeuvrable in shallow waters. In June 1667 the daring Dutch admiral sailed into the Medway in a surprise attack, captured Sheerness Fort and bombarded Chatham, where the navy's ships were moored. With little loss to themselves, the Dutch inflicted a crippling blow on the English fleet – the worst humiliation in its naval history! Its flagship, the *Royal Charles*, which had carried the King back from exile, was captured and towed away. Only a desperate improvised defence, organised by Albemarle, saved the bulk of the navy's warships from annihilation. 'The night the Dutch burned our ships,' noted Pepys, 'the King did sup with My Lady Castlemaine at the Duchess of Monmouth's, and there were all mad in hunting of a poor moth,' while people talked of betrayal by Catholics and courtiers.[21]

Charles sued for peace, and signed the Treaty of Breda on 24 August 1667. This was a compromise by which New York and New Jersey, and Cape Coast Castle in Africa, were ceded to Britain; France kept Acadia and French Guiana; while the Dutch retained Dutch Guiana, their monopoly of the spice trade in the east, and remained as formidable as ever at sea. Pepys wrote:

> The War ended in disgrace. A peace was made only to preserve the King for a time in his lusts and ease, and to sacrifice trade and his kingdoms only to his own pleasures.[22]

The shock of defeat proved salutary. London did not soon forget the roar of the Dutch guns in the Thames. The over-confidence and the parsimony of the English Parliament had been matched by the courage and determination of the Dutch. England's defences were inadequate; garrison troops and dockyard workers had shown little stomach for the fight. The war had been mismanaged in every department. Corruption, speculation, waste and incompetence had been exposed at all levels both on land and at sea. The court was blamed for being too busy with its own pleasures to pay attention to public business: money was ill applied, and the King squandered enormous sums on mistresses and favourites.[23]

But from the rough schooling of the Dutch war, and improvements in administration made by the energy and ability of Pepys, who was often at his desk at four o'clock in the morning, a strong and efficient navy arose. Service in the Royal Navy would become a recognised profession. Ships were built and re-equipped with men and supplies; loans were raised to build defensive works on the Thames and Medway; garrisons were strengthened, and shore batteries built at Woolwich, Sheerness and Chatham. An army of 7,000 foot and 2,000 horse was commissioned and Charles mobilised the county militia. Monmouth went to Harwich and took with him, according to Pepys, a great many young Hectors, such as the Earl of Chesterfield, but to little purpose, except to debauch the countrywomen thereabouts.[24] But if war came again, it was hoped there would be a different ending.

Parliament, however, bayed for blood: the unpopular Clarendon, that old, pompous, proud vizier, was made the scapegoat, not only for the disasters of the war but also because of the huge cost of maintaining Tangier and the sale to the French of Dunkirk, 'won by Cromwell's redcoats and its sale an affront to national pride'. The people also blamed Clarendon for the lavish expenditure on his new house in Piccadilly (on the site of today's Albemarle and New Bond Streets, so named because Albemarle's son occupied Clarendon's house after the Chancellor's fall from grace). In June 1667 a mob cut down the trees and broke the windows of the palatial mansion; on the gates of Clarendon House, built from the stones of Old St Paul's, they painted a gibbet and wrote –

Three sights to be seen – Dunkirk, Tangier and a barren Queen.[25]

Clarendon disapproved of all the political, administrative and social innovations of Charles's reign: he was hopelessly lost in the raffish, cynical and competitive court of the King's early years.[26] He belonged to another age; the younger politicians intrigued against him and were resolved to see him go. Charles's Portuguese marriage had produced no heir to the throne, and it was alleged that Clarendon had known that Princess Catherine was barren and that he had allowed his daughter, already pregnant, to creep into the Duke of York's bridal bed in the hope that she would become Queen of England. The wedding had taken place at dead of night in the Chancellor's own house, though Clarendon knew nothing about it.[27] Parliament also believed that he and James were pressing the King to introduce military government and rule without Parliament, supported by French money. So strong was Parliament's fear of professional soldiers that this charge was placed first in the articles of treason impeaching Clarendon – a charge he vigorously denied.

Charles was losing patience with his old counsellor's dictatorial manner, growing weary of his schoolmaster moralising, and suspected him of frustrating his designs on Frances Stuart. But he recognised his unswerving loyalty, knew the imputations against his Chancellor were false, and had stoutly defended him from the charge of being a party to the marriage. This *mésalliance* between royalty and the Wiltshire squirearchy had infuriated the King's mother and had annoyed the King. Charles had stood by Clarendon against the allegations of his daughter's promiscuity, when even James had wavered in the face of courtiers who claimed to have dishonoured her.

But the unfortunate Chancellor was old and ill and his enemies were merciless and without scruples. He had enemies at court, wrote Evelyn, especially the buffoons and ladies of pleasure, because he thwarted some of them and stood in their way.[28] When Parliament impeached him, the King did not defend him. The only alternative to the Chancellor's dismissal was the dissolution of Parliament, and Charles needed money. The King asked him to resign rather than face the charges, but Clarendon refused and was dismissed in August 1667. He hung on until November, but rather than face a court packed with his enemies he fled the country. The following month a bill of perpetual banishment finally removed him from the English political scene.

In his autobiographical *History*, Clarendon blamed his increasing ineffectiveness and unpopularity on Charles's indolence, and the enmity of Lady Castlemaine and 'that wicked crew of ministers, who did him all the ill offices they could'. The enmity with Barbara Castlemaine was mutual, because he had refused to endorse with the Great Seal her patents of nobility and had consistently refused her the official and social recognition she desired. He would never acknowledge her power over the King.[29] Such refusals were bound to result in quarrels, tantrums, scenes and unpleasantness, such as had occurred over her appointment to the Queen's bedchamber, and Charles tried to avoid such scenes at all costs. Barbara's father had been Clarendon's close friend, but morally and politically he could not accept her. For him Church and King represented the ideals for which he had helped to restore the monarchy: she represented the enemy of those ideals, leading on the King in licence and immorality.

Thus did the lady whose charms were the boast and whose vices the disgrace of the nation dispose of the Chancellor. His downfall was certainly designed in Lady Castlemaine's chamber, wrote Pepys, [30] with Buckingham, Arlington, Coventry and the Berkeleys leading 'the wicked crew' in the call for his impeachment.

When Clarendon left the King on Monday morning, Lady Castlemaine was in bed, though about 12 o'clock, and ran out in her smock into her Aviary looking into Whitehall garden and thither her woman brought her her night-gown and stood jeering at the old man's going away (with great gaiety and triumph, which all people observed, wrote Clarendon,[31] and then added bitterly, 'But Madam, you too will grow old, if you live'.) 'And several of the gallants,' continued Pepys, 'did talk to her in her Bird-cage, telling her she was the Bird of Paradise.'

So ended a happy association of over 30 years for the old man, who had served his King well and faithfully. Whatever the power of Lady Castlemaine's sexual attraction, whatever the beauties of her person, she was a vindictive, greedy and peevish woman. Whatever Clarendon's faults, he did not deserve such a humiliation in front of his enemies.[32] Out of pity, Louis allowed him to settle at Rouen, where he spent his last years in completing a monumental *History of the Great Rebellion* and his autobiography, which are now his abiding claim to fame.

11

The Hand of God

Whilst the people were celebrating 20 June 1665 as a day of thanksgiving for the victory over the Dutch at the Battle of Lowestoft, and Barbara was sitting for Lely for her portrait as Bellona, goddess of war, the King was listening to Evelyn's account of the crowded naval hospitals. Suddenly there now appeared another enemy, much more formidable than the Dutch and more difficult to struggle against.[1] Pepys described the new enemy on 7 June 1665:

> This day, much against my will, I did in Drury Lane see two or three houses marked with a red cross upon the doors and 'Lord have mercy upon us' writ there – the first of that kind that to my remembrance I ever saw.

The Great Plague actually started during February and March in the worst of London's slums, the parish of St Giles in the Fields (where Tottenham Court Road and Oxford Street now meet). But soon Pepys was fearfully reporting the spread of the epidemic eastwards to the City, passing by way of the poor areas of Southwark, Whitechapel, Shoreditch and Finsbury. Not for nothing was the disease known as 'the Plague of the Poor'. During that warm summer it spread rapidly.

> The town grows very sickly and people to be afraid of it . . . In Whitehall, the Court was full of waggons and people ready to go out of town and at Somerset House, where all are packing up, too.[2]

As 'Death rode triumphant through every street',[3] clergymen abandoned their parishes, doctors their patients and the rich their servants: everybody who could fled the city. The wards of all the London hospitals became so full that visitors had to walk over the beds because there was no room to walk round them. New pest-houses to isolate patients were built in Marylebone, Soho

Fields and Stepney, as justices of the peace acquired land and accommodation to deal with the sick and dying. Soon the recognised graveyards were full, so mass graves or 'plague pits' were dug in Finsbury, Shoreditch and Tothill Fields and lined with quick-lime to dispose of the corpses. The air was filled with the stench of death.

Unemployed servants were recruited to drive the 'dead carts' and cry 'bring out your dead', until they themselves fell from their carts to join the bodies lying around. Gangs of looters roamed the deserted streets, plundering vacated houses and robbing any pedestrian who dared to venture abroad. The Lord Mayor ordered the killing of all cats and dogs, Pepys calculating that some 40,000 dogs and five times as many cats were destroyed within days – thus allowing the fleas carried by black rats, the real causes of the bubonic plague, to spread unhindered.

The King dissolved Parliament and on 26 July went by royal barge from Hampton Court to pay a last visit to Greenwich to inspect the new palace he was building there. This included today's Royal Naval College and the park designed by Le Nôtre, creator of the gardens of Versailles. Meanwhile Pepys noted that the sickness was everywhere, and began to think of setting things in order, both as to soul and body. The next day he watched the royal party, with Barbara Castlemaine and Frances Stuart, the Privy Council and the court, set off for Salisbury and Oxford. The young, pretty ladies sat astride their horses dressed like men, in velvet coats, plumed hats, lace, ruffled shirts and beribboned garters, as the bells tolled everywhere in the doomed city.[4]

The Duke of Albemarle was left behind to be responsible for central government, law and order, and the administration of London outside the city walls. 'The General is sent for to keep all quiet,' reported Pepys. 'It seems that the King holds him so necessary at this time, that he will keep him here.'[5] Albemarle had at his disposal the experienced General Craven (colonel of a number of Royalist regiments, including later the Coldstream Guards) and a strong force of soldiers. These he quartered in tents in Hyde Park to isolate them from infection, using them to guard the stricken city from internal or Dutch-fomented troubles. From his lodgings in the almost deserted palace, he sent his soldiers to search for former republican veterans, who were suspected of plotting a rising, and to arrest Quakers and other religious dissenters. Albemarle ordered taverns and ale and coffee houses to close at nine o'clock. All lodgers, visitors, guests and relatives had to leave the city – to die outside the city walls. Watchmen with sharpened halberds stood guard night and day to ensure that those diagnosed with plague were locked in their houses for 40 days, to die or recover as best they could.

Pepys moved to Woolwich with his wife, returning each day to the Navy Office to pursue the Dutch war. Despite the plague he worked hard to secure the requirements of the fleet, and Albemarle called him the right hand of the navy.[6] His doctor died, his servant became ill, but fear of the plague did not interfere with his amorous philanderings in the taverns and with his latest mistress, Mrs Elizabeth Burrows, the recently widowed wife of a naval lieutenant whom he seduced after she came to collect his arrears of pay. And at night his fear of death could be dissolved in dreams –

> last night, I dreamed – the best that ever I dreamed – that I had my Lady Castlemaine in my arms and was permitted to use all the dalliance I desired with her.[7]

A few weeks later, on 5 October, he went by water to Deptford to visit another of his mistresses, Mrs Bagwell, the pretty, young wife of a ship's carpenter (a warrant officer for whom he had found employment at sea), and noted that 'round about and next door on every side was the plague but I did not value it for there I did what I would with her'. One house would bear the legend 'Lord have mercy on us'; in the next there would be tippling and whoring, as the inhabitants chose a different way of passing the time till eternity.[8]

Pepys, with responsibilities for manning and supply at the Navy Board, often, as in the Bagwell affair, used his official position to obtain sexual favours as well as fees and commissions for his patronage. Such an arrangement was considered normal by both parties. Old Delkes, a waterman, brought his daughter, a young married woman, to Pepys's office and left her to be kissed and fondled 'to get her husband off, that he should not go to sea' (ie. be impressed into the navy). Betty and Doll Lane, seamen's wives, never found marriage any barrier to their long associations with Pepys. Betty married Samuel Martin in 1664; in August she told Pepys she was with child, and undone if Pepys did not get her husband a place. Before long she became his mistress, and Pepys found her husband a job as a purser on a number of ships. Pepys's long liaison with Mrs Bagwell began when she came to him to speak for her husband. Soon he broke down her resistance with seductive words and promises of getting her complacent husband a post. On 20 December 1665 young Mrs Daniel prayed him to speak for her husband, Samuel, to be a lieutenant. He agreed 'and had the opportunity of kissing her again and again, she being a pretty woman'. Pepys continued to look after both husbands' careers on the usual terms: one of his last acts, after the Revolution of 1688, was to recommend Bagwell for a vacancy in Chatham dockyard.[9]

During September, Evelyn walked through the City and suburbs to St James's,

> a dismal passage and dangerous to see so many coffins exposed in the streets and the streets thin of people, the shops shut up and all in a mournful silence, as not knowing whose turn might be next.

Grass grew in the now deserted streets around Whitehall, while all day the pest-carts trundled to the cries of their drivers to bring out the dead. Over 10,000 Londoners took to the Thames and lived on boats moored in mid-stream. As the plague spread beyond London to England's larger cities (Bristol, Gloucester, Leicester, Southampton and Dover), corpses rotted in the fields and country towns and villages. They had once welcomed refugees to fleece; now they posted guards to keep them out and pelted them with stones and manure to drive them away.

Suddenly, the plague slackened. On Christmas morning Pepys saw a wedding in church,

> which I have not seen many a day and the young people so merry one with another: and strange to see what delight we married people have to see these poor fools decoyed into our condition . . . Yet to our great joy, the town fills apace and shops begin to open again. I have never lived so merrily, as I have done this plague-time.[10]

The official total of deaths exceeded 68,000, but, since many deaths were not recorded, the actual figure may have been in excess of 100,000. Some blamed the debaucheries of the court for the plague, and God's desire to punish them, but Bishop Burnet thought otherwise, since the punishment fell heavily on the poor and was easily avoided by the rich.[11]

The King received a Christmas present from Barbara – a son, George, the future Duke of Northumberland, born at Merton College, Oxford, where she had lodged during the plague.[12] In neighbouring Christ Church, Frances Stuart beguiled her sovereign with French love songs and together they joined the court to dance the year away. The university was horrified at the disgrace of the birth and royal liaison. Several days after the delivery Barbara found a note pinned to her door stating that, had Barbara been the common whore she so well impersonated, rather than a great lady sinning under the protection of the royal mantle, the local authorities would have been obliged to have her tied on a ducking stool and ducked as the appropriate punishment. Barbara was furious: Charles offered £1,000 reward to anyone who would betray the culprit, while the courtiers enjoyed the jest.

Charles returned to Whitehall on 1 February 1666 to face yet another threat to his capital: the Great Fire. It started in the King's baker's shop in Pudding Lane shortly before two o'clock on Sunday morning, 2 September 1666, when an oven caught fire. Soon the house was ablaze; the baker and his family escaped but the maid, left behind, died in the flames. Aided by a strong wind and a dry summer, the fire spread to surrounding warehouses, cellars and wharves piled high with combustible materials – oil, tallow, hay, timber and coal – landed from the river. The fire would rage for five days and destroy the whole city between the Temple and the Tower of London. The Tower was saved from destruction by Admiral Penn and Pepys, who brought men from the royal dockyards to fight the flames.

Pepys, who lived less than a quarter of a mile from Pudding Lane, recorded the scene.[13] Everyone was trying to remove their goods, flinging them into the river or into lighters moored there; people staying in their houses as long as possible, 'till the very fire touched them'. Pepys, thoroughly alarmed, rushed to Whitehall to inform the King, the Duke of York and the court. He was ordered to instruct the Lord Mayor to demolish whatever houses were in the path of the fire, and to tell him that he would have all the soldiers he required to help.

Evelyn described how the whole city was in dreadful flames near the waterside. Over 10,000 houses were blazing in one huge conflagration. The noise was like an hideous storm: the cracking and thunder of impetuous flames, shrieking of women and children, hurrying people, falling towers, houses and churches. St Paul's was on fire, the sky was like the top of a burning oven, and night was turned into day for 10 miles around.[14]

Charles ordered in the Guards to aid the civil power, control the crowds, and help put out the fires. Officers were posted, 'watching at every quarter for outlandish men', for it was widely believed the fire had been started deliberately by foreign enemies, Papists, or both! Pepys met the Lord Mayor in Canning Street, exhausted with his efforts.

> What can I do? I am spent. The people will not obey me. I have been pulling down houses. But the fire overtakes us faster then we can do it.

Charles and the Duke of York came down from Whitehall in the royal barge to see the extent of the damage.

Next day, the fire was still spreading. Charles summoned the Privy Council and appointed his brother to take charge of the city. Albemarle was summoned from fighting the Dutch at sea to London, where his influence was of the greatest use in restoring order. The militia were called up from neighbouring counties, and seamen mobilised from Deptford and Woolwich to help with the demolitions. Charles, taking over from the exhausted Lord Mayor, was everywhere, consulting, giving orders, helping 'wherever remedies were required'. He rode round the streets escorted by his Guards, rewarding workmen with golden guineas for their efforts. Dismounting, he grabbed bucket and spade and manned the pumps, his face blackened, his clothes wet with perspiration. He laboured with the Duke of York, whom he put in charge of the fire-fighting operations to give an example to others.

The King, having ordered the buildings around Whitehall to be demolished, sent his personal goods, including his priceless printings, to Hampton Court for safety. The rich who lived in the Strand despatched their goods into the country by barge. Pepys hired a cart to move his money, plate 'and best things', and buried his wine and parmesan cheese in the garden. The nights were more terrible than the days, recorded Clarendon.[15] The light of the fire replaced that of the sun. All the fields were full of women and children – safe, but suffering from the intolerable heat and drought as if they had been in the middle of the fire.

On the fifth day the fire burnt itself out. The King ordered an immediate survey. Within the City 87 parish churches had been destroyed, 4,000 streets and 13,200 houses had been levelled, leaving only about one-fifth of the city standing. St Paul's, the Guildhall, the Royal Exchange and 52 Company Halls had either vanished or been badly damaged. Cheapside, the grandest thoroughfare in the old City, was totally engulfed. Evelyn walked from Whitehall to London Bridge, clambering over mountains of still smoking rubbish.

Some 100,000 people were made homeless: Charles despatched tents from the army, ordered wooden shelters to be erected for the homeless and set up food centres for the hungry. Yet it was not the unhealthy dwellings and insanitary streets in the slum areas of St Giles, Whitechapel and Lambeth, where the plague had prospered among the poor, that were destroyed. It was the lath and plaster medieval constructions, known to Chaucer and Shakespeare, which disappeared in the flames. The houses of the wealthy in the area between the Tower and the Temple, the residential and business quarters in the heart of the city, had vanished in the fire. Their merchants would rebuild those areas of London in brick and stone.

This rebuilding would be carried out to a definite plan, governed by a set of rules and regulations, at a pace which astonished the world. Streets, lanes and houses were classified according to importance and size. The heights of houses and the building materials were prescribed. The result was that the new houses were neat, healthier, built of brick or stone, fewer in number, better spaced, and with improvements in street-lighting, sanitation and water supply.

Much of this rebuilding was achieved through the energy and wisdom of the King, who ordered new sites for markets, government offices and the rehousing of the Royal Exchange. On 13 September 1666 he issued a proclamation governing the detailed regulations, which began, 'Since it hath pleased God to lay this heavy judgement upon us all, as an evidence of His displeasure for our sins', the King hoped to see God's blessing on the building 'of a much more beautiful city than is at this time consumed'.

His hope was exemplified by Sir Christopher Wren, whose genius would be stamped on the ecclesiastical architecture of the new London. St Paul's, his masterpiece and site of his burial, was rebuilt in white Portland stone, funded by a tax on coal entering the port of London. It would be completed in Queen Anne's reign, a dozen years before the death of the architect. His churches, some 23 of which, apart from St. Paul's, survive to this day, would dominate the future landscape of a London whose streets, squares and buildings would be considered elegant and spacious even by modern standards.

The Monument, designed by Wren to commemorate the Great Fire of London, still proclaims the guilt of the Dutch, the French, and especially of the Papists ('whoever said the contrary was suspected for a conspirator', noted Clarendon).[16] A council set up to investigate the causes, however, more realistically blamed 'The Hand of God, a great wind and the season so very dry'.

For Evelyn and the nation, the year 1666 had been a year of marvels: plague, war, fire, rain, tempest and comet; judgements 'highly deserved for our prodigious ingratitude, burning lusts, dissolute court and profane and abominable lives'.[17] It was also the year that Charles settled the order of precedence of his small army – 'the Regiment of Guards (Grenadiers) take place of all other Regiments and the Colonel as the first foot Colonel. All the regiments and Colonels to take place according to the date of their commission'. It was left to James II to give the cavalry precedence over the infantry.

12

Indecent Actresses and Decayed Soldiers

One of Charles's first acts on regaining his throne was to restore the theatres, banned under the Commonwealth and closed in London since 1642. The Puritans regarded the stage as sinful, so clandestine performances were interrupted by Cromwell's soldiers, actors were arrested and the spectators fined. Charles had a genuine love for the theatre and, stimulated by the French plays he had seen during his exile, he issued a warrant on 9 July 1660 giving two of his exile friends, Sir William Davenant and Thomas Killigrew, exclusive London rights 'to build theatres, present plays, make reasonable charges and to present actresses [for the first time] on the public stage'.

Killigrew, a dramatist himself and groom of the King's bedchamber, formed the King's Players, which included the experienced actors Major Michael Mohun and Charles Hart. He opened a new play-house, The Theatre Royal, in May 1663 in Drury Lane, on the site of the present Drury Lane Theatre.[1] It was a large building with two tiers of boxes, including a splendid royal box, an open gallery, and an apron stage jutting out into the pit, which was fitted with backless benches. There were two large changing rooms and the famous Green Room, where the cast waited for their cues and received visitors. As plays started at three o'clock in the afternoon, the theatre was partly lit by daylight and partly by candles. There was an orchestra and a regular company of 16 men and seven women. Admission prices were high – the cheapest one shilling, the highest four shillings, and oranges cost sixpence each.

Davenant, Shakespeare's godson, the author of plays staged before the Civil War and poet laureate under Charles I, formed the Duke of York's Servants from a group of younger men. They included Thomas Betterton, considered the finest actor of his time, and his wife Mary. The Duke's Theatre was established in the fashionable Lincoln's Inn Fields. The King's Players and the Duke's Theatre amalgamated at Drury Lane in 1682.[2]

Both theatres proved instant successes. Attracted to long-forbidden pleasures, elegant society crowded to the plays: the King, Queen, Duke and Duchess of York, the royal mistresses and aristocratic members of the court attended regularly. King and court, in fact, became the dominant influence on both the audience and the drama. Records show that the two playhouses drew their audiences from a small part of the population:

> the men and women of fashion who adorned the Court, army officers, lawyers from the Inns of Court, wits, critics, beaux and fops, sparks and bullies, kept mistresses and women of the town, the odd squire up from the country, together with some solid citizens, who went to see a play, especially at holiday time.[3]

There, too, came lackeys in attendance on their masters and mistresses, admitted free to join the noisier elements in the upper gallery.

The wealthy and cultured part of the professional and bureaucratic middle class liked to rub shoulders with the aristocracy and catch a glimpse of the King's favourites; the theatre thus became one of the main social centres of the age, as well as a regular form of entertainment. Samuel Pepys went there frequently, alone or with his wife. On 20 April 1661, for instance, he saw Beaumont and Fletcher's *The Humorous Lieutenant* performed before the King. His pleasure was great, he recorded, to see so many great beauties, but above all Barbara Palmer (Castlemaine), with whom the King did show a great deal of familiarity.

Comedy dominated the stage, which owed much in plot and dialogue to French influence, especially that of Molière and Corneille. The taste of Restoration play-goers generally was crude; the plays themselves reflected the moral laxity of the King and court, while the players were considered (perhaps a little harshly) as a 'Pimping, Spunging, Idle, Impious Race'.[4] The mood was anti-Puritan and anti-censorship, and notoriously permissive on sexual topics, although severe on political or religious subjects. The playwrights were nearly all Royalist courtiers: aristocrats like Buckingham, Rochester, Sedley and the Earl of Dorset wrote for this small audience. These men of fashion knew each other, had access to the King, and, together with the actors and dramatists, regarded the theatres almost as clubs attached to Whitehall.

There they would show themselves daily, meet their acquaintances, and carry on their intrigues. Sir George Etherege, with John Dryden the most important dramatist of the first decade, described in 1668 in his popular play *She Wou'd, if she Cou'd* the young sparks who were accustomed to stroll from one play-house to another, beribboned and bewigged, dressed in the French style. If they liked neither the play nor the women, they seldom stayed any longer than it took to comb their periwigs or whisper a word or two with a friend, then cocked their caps and strutted out again.

The ladies of the court, often masked to hide their identity or to spare their blushes, were as depraved and licentious as the men. They mixed with the courtesans and women of doubtful character who flocked to the theatre, conversing with the ladies of quality on equal terms. It was to meet these women, to make their assignations and carry on their amorous intrigues, that so many casual, flippant, bored and frequently intoxicated young men patronised the theatre, making it a magnet for the worse elements of fashionable society.

> One half of the play they spend in noise and brawl, sleep out the rest, then wake and damn it all.

Fatal quarrels were common in and around the playhouses; duels were fought upon the stage or in the pits, even while plays were in progress. Mr Scrope and Sir Thomas Armstrong quarrelled in the Duke's Theatre for the favours of Mrs Susanne Uphill, who entered the theatre masked. Armstrong challenged Scrope to a duel, and killed him at the first pass. During one performance at the same theatre, Henry Killigrew, son of Thomas, the theatrical manager, and one of the most disreputable of the court sparks, taunted the Duke of Buckingham, who had displaced him in the bed of the Countess of Shrewsbury. The enraged Buckingham drew his sword, leapt from his box and chased Killigrew over the benches and spectators in the pit. Killigrew fell and on his knees pleaded for his life. Buckingham, after giving him a couple of hefty blows, returned to his box, readjusted his wig and, bowing to the actors, graciously allowed them to continue.[5]

Not all playgoers treated the plays and actors in such a cavalier fashion, and Restoration comedy was not exclusively a matter of cuckolding and farce, but the noise from their activities often drowned the actors' lines, and their conduct contributed to much of the coarseness and childishness of the comedy and to the ranting and absurdity of much of its drama.

It was in such circumstances that the playwright William Wycherley, who was given a commission in the Duke of Buckingham's Regiment in 1672, met Barbara Castlemaine, later his mistress, while she was sitting in the King's box. They exchanged coarse jests and ribald commentary during the performance of his play *Love in a Wood*, which he dedicated to her. Through this play he gained a wife, the widow of the Earl of Drogheda, when they met in a shop in Epsom, where she had gone to purchase a copy. And it was for such audiences that he, Etherege, Dryden, Otway and Mrs Aphra Benn wrote their plays – bawdy, licentious and often plain vulgar, but full of wit and lively dialogue.

They aimed to mirror the morals and manners of the upper ranks of contemporary society, mocking and ridiculing religion, philosophy and marital fidelity.[6] 'Lord!' remarks one of Dryden's female characters, 'What a grievous thing for a she-citizen to be forced to have children by her own husband.' Characters were drawn from a narrow range of London society – citizens, aldermen, soldiers, clergymen, fops and beaux. Cynical rakes like Dorimant[7] were based on the most fashionable and promiscuous rake Rochester, the King's friend; other characters portrayed the bawds, thieves and ne'er-do-wells of low London society. The uncomplicated plots involved the stratagems of old roués, the tricks of coquettes, jealous husbands, wanton and shameless wives and the triumphs of swindlers – themes enjoyed by a cynical audience, which delighted in hearing women recite prologues of an astounding vulgarity.[8]

The great sensation of the Restoration theatre was undoubtedly the legalised employment of women on the professional stage. The King (with tongue in cheek) authorised them to prevent his subjects being corrupted by the sight of men dressed as women, and 'to be esteemed, not only as a harmless delight, but useful and instructive'. The actor, manager, producer and playwright Colley Cibber, who with Samuel Pepys provides us with the most vivid contemporary picture of the theatre, noted of the year 1660:

> Before the Restoration, no actress had ever been seen on the English stage and the advent of real, beautiful women could not but draw a proportion of new admirers to the theatre.[9]

Pepys saw women on the stage for the first time on 3 January 1661.[10] Previously, female roles had been played by men like Edward Kynaston, whom Pepys described as the loveliest lady that ever he saw in his life.[11] Cibber wrote that he was the darling of the ladies of quality, who after the performances would carry him in his female dress to Hyde Park in their coaches.[12]

Soon after the royal warrant actresses replaced 'padded boys' in female roles, and young women with good looks but no dowry quickly discovered the possibility of a theatrical career as a springboard to matrimony or to the life and status of a courtesan. Male spectators, from the King down to the court gallants, looked upon the actresses as little better than prostitutes, while the actresses themselves were never slow in encouraging promising lovers or 'protectors'. The gallants were permitted behind the scenes on payment of a small fee, and the audiences were given broad hints in prologue and epilogue that the ladies of the theatre were not to be petitioned in vain.[13]

Evelyn, who considered the theatre 'foul and indecent' and who had the same low opinion of actresses, wrote that 'inflaming several young noblemen and gallants, they became their whores and to some their wives'.[14] Taking their cue from the royal brothers, it became fashionable for courtiers to take actresses as kept women, with their own house and financial settlement. The King, for instance, 'first spoiled Mrs Elizabeth Weaver' (c1660), an actress in the Theatre Royal. Mrs Hester Davenport, an actress in the Duke's Company, was owned by Oxford, wrote Pepys,[15] despite the fact that her husband boarded his principal actresses at his own house adjoining the theatre. Mrs Long, renowned for her elegant appearances in men's clothes, was taken from the Duke's Theatre by the dissolute young Duke of Richmond, future husband of Frances Stuart; Mrs Johnson by the Earl of Peterborough; and Peg Hughes (an actress in the King's Theatre and mistress of Sir Charles Sedley) by Prince Rupert, who installed her in a substantial house in Hammersmith, where she bore him a daughter, Ruperta, in 1673.

'There was another greater person than any of these,' continued Evelyn, 'who fell into their snares, to the reproach of their noble families and the ruin of both body and soul.' The King had his actresses (Nell Gwynn and Mary Davis), while Buckingham had Frances Davenport. Elizabeth Barry, daughter of a Cavalier barrister, was introduced to the stage by her lover, the Earl of Rochester, who shared her with the dramatist Etherege. Even Pepys would have his Mistress Elizabeth Knepp, an actress, singer and dancer in the King's Company. The satirist Thomas Brown commented:

> It was as hard for a pretty woman to keep herself honest in a Theatre as 'tis for an Apothecary to keep his treacle from the Flies in hot weather: for every Libertine in the Audience will be buzzing about her Honey-pot . . . and when once she has a Maggot in her Tail, all the Pepper and Salt in the Kingdom will scarce keep her Reputation from stinking.[16]

One actress who sought to legitimise her relationship was the Earl of Oxford's Hester Elizabeth Davenport. She rejected his passionate advances, demanding marriage, which was accordingly solemnised with all due ceremony and before witnesses. But the priest was one of the colonel's trumpeters and the witness his kettle drummer – both of whom rapidly vanished back to their regiment after the ceremony. The colonel's second wife was the promiscuous beauty Diana Kirke.

On stage feminine costumes were designed to be provocative, bared bosoms and flowing tresses became popular, and prologues and epilogues were often given by favourite actresses in male clothes to titillate the audience. When an actress masqueraded in 'breeches' parts, she submitted her body for inspection; when she danced in petticoats, she tantalised the spectators with glimpses of 'a neat silk leg and a pair of Holland thighs'.[17] Elegantly-dressed beaux would invade the stage and the 'tiring rooms', paying to ogle the actresses, 'to towse and mouse them' or, if the gallants preferred, to sit among 'the naughty women' in the audience or haggle loudly with the orange-girls about their wares'.[18]

One such orange-girl, who would rise like Cinderella from rags to riches and become, in the words of the poet Richard Flecknoe, the pride of the stage and darling of the court, was Ellen Gwynn. She was born in 1650, probably near Covent Garden,[19] of an ancient Welsh family. Her father was a captain in the Royalist army, who fell on hard times like so many others after the defeat of Charles I. He married much beneath himself and died, it is believed, in a debtor's gaol at Oxford. Before long his widow, Mrs Eleanor Gwynn, was installed in Coal Yard Lane, a squalid slum off Drury Lane, with her two daughters, Rose and Nell. In 1663 Rose was imprisoned in Newgate for debt; in 1672 she married a captain in the Duke of Monmouth's guards. In the same year she received a pension from the King of £100 a year, paid out of the Irish revenue – the usual source of funds granted to the King's mistresses and favourites. Records show that a kinsman of hers, William Chomley, was granted a commission on 17 October 1678 as ensign in Colonel John Russell's Regiment of Foot Guards (Coldstream), and promoted to captain three years later.[20]

According to her own story, Nell was 'brought up in a brothel to fill strong water to the gentlemen'.[21] Her nubile beauty and gift for repartee ensured her graduation to the King's Theatre as an orange-girl – one of the precocious young wenches who nightly sold their wares to Killigrew's theatre-goers. Soon she became the mistress of the manager, Charles Hart, a fine actor and great-nephew of William Shakespeare. Hart had Nell trained for the stage and later played opposite her in lead roles.[22] John Lacy, one of Charles II's favourite actors, who gave up a lieutenant's commission in the army to join the King's Theatre, taught her to dance. Before long she became one of the most popular comic and character actresses of the period, playing saucy wenches to perfection. Richard Flecknoe, poet and dramatist, whose verses were mostly of the kind which chiefly pleased the author, wrote of her –

> She is pretty, and she knows it:
> She is witty and she shows it.
> She has a hundred other parts,
> For to take and conquer hearts.[23]

Pepys saw her at the King's Theatre on 3 April 1665, with the King and Lady Castlemaine in attendance. Two years later Pepys went with his actress friend, Mrs Elizabeth Knepp, to Nell's 'tiring rooms, 'where Nell was dressing herself and was all unready: and is very pretty, prettier than I thought'.[24]

When 19 years old, Nell was seen by the poet and handsome court rake Charles Sackville, Lord Buckhurst. Buckhurst had served with conspicuous gallantry as a naval volunteer against the Dutch in 1665, and wrote the well-loved poem *To all you ladies now on land* the night before a naval engagement. 'He was inflamed by her shapely thighs' as she rolled from side to side of the stage in the role of Mirida in *All Mistaken*.[25] She became his mistress and he her Charles the Second. Nell left the stage for a few summer weeks 'to keep a merry house' at Epsom, then a fashionable spa, with Buckhurst and his boon companion, Sir Charles Sedley (wit, libertine and dramatist, and father of James II's mistress, Catherine Sedley, the Countess of Dorchester). When the lovers quarrelled, she returned to the London stage, 'very poor, having lost her great friend, Lady Castlemaine, Hart, her Charles the First, and neglected by them all'.[26]

It was at the Duke's Theatre during the winter of 1667–8 that the King met and fell in love with Nell. According to Bishop Burnet,[27] she was introduced to him by the Duke of Buckingham in an attempt to replace Lady Castlemaine in the King's favour because of her hold over the King and her influence at court.

For the same reasons, Buckingham had already introduced to the King's bed Jane Roberts, a clergyman's daughter 'with brawny limbs, a supple conscience and loose principles' (three excellent qualifications for a lady of pleasure); and Moll Davis,[28] the natural daughter of Colonel Thomas Howard, first Earl of Berkshire, an actress in Davenant's troupe at Lincoln's Inn Fields and known as a sweet singer and the loveliest dancer in the world.[29] Pepys called her an impertinent slut and Queen Catherine, normally so tolerant of her husband's 'pretty little fools', stalked out of the theatre in the palace of Whitehall when Moll came on stage to dance her jig.[30] But Mary Davis proved a great source of pleasure to the King, who took her off the stage and set her up in a richly-furnished house in Suffolk Street, and later in St James's Square.[31] Charles also gave her a handsome pension and other gifts, including a £700 ring, 'which she shows to everybody and owns that the King did give it to her.' In return she presented him with a daughter, Mary Tudor, who in due course married the Earl of Derwentwater. Their son, James, the third Earl, was beheaded for high treason.

Nell's relationship with the King (whom she called her Charles the Third) was more enduring: for almost 17 years to the end of his life, Nell would maintain her position at court. Gilbert Burnet, Bishop of Salisbury, wrote that her wild humour and mocking wit was such a constant diversion to the King that even a new mistress could not drive her away.[32] She was the most indiscreet and wildest creature ever in a court, yet she continued to the end of the King's life in great favour and was maintained at vast expense. But he never treated her with the decencies of a mistress, but rather with the lewdness of a prostitute – as she had been indeed to a great many. This was a rather harsh judgement, which hardly summed up their relationship accurately!

Pepys noted on 11 January 1668 that the King sent several times for Nelly and she was more than willing to grant him her favours. At first the affair was hushed up at court, and Nell's previous lover Buckhurst was sent to France on a complimentary mission to get him out of the way. Nell did not give up the stage until pregnancy (a burden borne by almost all the ladies who had any intimate relationship with the virile Charles, and a most inconvenient state for an actress) forced her to do so. Their son, Charles Beauclerk, later first Duke of St Albans, was born in May 1670. In gratitude, Charles set her up in a fine house at 79 Pall Mall (now the premises of the Eagle Star Insurance Company) and gave her the freehold. It became her London home for the rest of her life. Her other house in Chelsea was reached by the King's Road – supposedly named because Charles used it so frequently to visit her.

Pepys saw Nell a number of times on the stage and in her dressing-room. He frequently praised her prettiness, but complained of the base company of men who visited her and how lewdly they talked. He admired her particularly when she appeared like a young gallant and had the motions and carriage of a spark.

> Nell in her boy's clothes mighty pretty, but Lord, their confidence, and how many men do hover about them, as soon as they come off the stage.

This fashion of women dressing in men's clothes suited Nell's figure admirably, for she was not one of the typical Stuart beauties. Below medium height, her rounded figure, long legs and chestnut hair falling over her shoulders appealed to Charles, who at the height of his desire for her paid frequent visits to Lely's studio when he was painting her naked. A number of such paintings exist in the National Portrait Gallery, the British Museum and in private collections. Fashionable ladies also wore clothes which made them look like men for riding. Pepys came across the maids of honour in the galleries at Whitehall wearing velvet coats and doublets, and the Duchess of Portsmouth wore a coat of pigeon-breast with silver brocade and breeches having slashed seams at the thighs to show red and silver lace.[33]

Nell was popular with the general public. Lord Rochester called her the labouring lover of the King and the darling strumpet of the crowd. The people often cheered 'the Protestant Whore', in contrast to the Catholic ones, when she appeared in her coach and horses. But in court circles she was regarded as an upstart. Evelyn complained that her low origins, bad reputation and uncouth language brought no credit to the monarchy. He called her an impudent comedian and a lady of pleasure. Walking on 2 March 1671 with the King near her house in Pall Mall, next door to St James's Palace, Evelyn was shocked to hear 'a very familiar discourse' between Charles and his mistress, who often talked to her lover from a terrace behind her garden wall (See plate 16). For much of 1669 to 1671 she was his favourite bed-mate, and their second son, James (called after Charles's brother), was born on Christmas Day 1671. Their elder son, Charles, Duke of St Albans, was appointed colonel of Princess Anne of Denmark's regiment of cavalry (the Eighth Horse); their younger son would die at the tender age of nine.

But Charles never remained faithful to his mistresses for long, especially in the years after his rejection by Frances Stuart. By Christmas 1671 Nell had already been eclipsed by the French beauty Louise de Keroualle; prior to Louise, 'the Merry Monarch had been restlessly rolling about from whore to whore'.[34] To the long list of attractive women of easy virtue remunerated by the King should be added Eleanor Gordon, married at the age of 11 to Baron Byron; Mrs Mary Knight, an actress and singer with a lovely voice: the widow of his dead favourite, the Earl of Falmouth, on whom Charles squandered a small fortune and who remarried to Charles Buckhurst, sixth Earl of Dorset; and Elizabeth, Countess of Kildare, daughter of the Earl of Ranelagh.[35] To quote Antonia Fraser, one should include 'the nocturnal visitors introduced up the Privy Stairs by William Chiffinch, a page of His Majesty's Bedchamber and Keeper of the King's Private Closet. Their numbers, like their identities, are unknown to history.'[36] Perhaps Chiffinch performed a great and honourable service to the Stuarts by not writing his memoirs.[37]

Colley Cibber, manager of Drury Lane Theatre, stoutly defended Nell's reputation and character. Considering all the disadvantages of her rank and education, she had less to be laid to her charge than any other ladies in the same state of preferment. She never meddled in matters of serious moment, nor was the tool of working politicians. She never broke into the amorous infidelities of which others were accused, but was as visibly distinguished by her particular personal inclination to the King as her rivals were by their titles and grandeur.[38] Nelly put it more simply –

> If these be ladies of quality, why do they demean themselves to be courtesans? They ought to die for shame. As for me, it is my profession. I do not pretend to be anything better.[39]

As Cibber states, although Charles gave her a pension, Nell Gwynn did not receive the wealth or noble titles of her illustrious rivals for the King's affection. Unlike Barbara Castlemaine and Louise de Keroualle, she did not interfere in politics, although she occasionally used her influence with the King on behalf of some of his courtiers, like Buckingham and Monmouth, when they fell out of favour.

The years of her rise to fame coincided with those of Lady Castlemaine's decline. In 1670 Barbara was created Duchess of Cleveland 'as the ornament and prize of virtue',[40] and lived in splendour at Berkshire House in St James's, later known as Cleveland House. The grounds included today's Green Park. Charles also gave her the Palace of Nonsuch near Cheam, together with large gifts of money, plate and grants from customs and excise. She obtained dukedoms for her three sons – Charles, Duke of Southampton, Henry, Duke of Grafton and George, Duke of Northumberland – and rich husbands for her two daughters.

Anne married the Earl of Sussex, and Charlotte the first Earl of Lichfield.

Charles, it is believed, intended to confer on Nell the title of Countess of Greenwich, but died before he could bestow the honour. He did reward their son, Charles Beauclerk, with the dukedom of St Albans. Nell never married, repelling her various suitors, however rich, with the jest: 'she was no such sportsman, as to lay the dog, where the deer should lie.'[41] She died, aged 37, at her home in Pall Mall and was buried at St Martin's in the Fields, her parish church. Her vicar, Thomas Tenison, later to become Archbishop of Canterbury, preached her funeral sermon and took as his text the words of St Luke: 'Joy shall be in heaven over one sinner that repenteth, more than over ninety and nine just persons, which need no repentance.'

History does not tell us whether Nell repented or not. She certainly enjoyed her good fortune while it lasted, and knew both poverty and success. Debt was commonplace in her family, and in her will she provided money to release parishioners of St Martin's in the Fields and St James's, Piccadilly, from debtors' prisons. Tradition has it that, influenced by the fact that her father and cousin were soldiers who had fallen on evil days, she may have provided help for disabled and elderly soldiers in the foundation of the Royal Hospital, Chelsea, but there is no evidence to support such a story.

Towards the end of Charles's reign, public attention was attracted to the distressed condition of soldiers, discharged because of age, wounds or infirmity, begging or starving in towns and villages, especially in Ireland. The daily discharges of these men from the army only added to the numbers of aged veterans of the Civil War. There were no pensions available for other ranks, although some men were retained on the muster roll without being required to perform any duties. Lump sums were paid to the dependants of those killed in the service, and on 1 January 1685 Charles issued a royal warrant to redefine the 'King's Bounty' as 11 months' pay for the widow of any person slain in fighting and one third of that for each orphan unmarried at the time of the father's death.[42]

Officers, on the other hand, were eligible for a pension from a contingency fund, included in every army establishment between 1661 and 1685. They could go on 'half-pay' – a form of retainer – whilst unemployed following a reduction of the establishment or disbandment. In Paris, Louis XIV had opened Les Invalides in 1674 for the support and succour of his soldiers, aged, wounded or disabled in war. This foundation greatly impressed Charles and his son, the Duke of Monmouth, who inspected the buildings on behalf of his father in 1672 and again five years later.

On 27 October 1679 Charles issued a royal warrant to the lord lieutenant of Ireland, the Duke of Ormonde, for the erection of

an Hospital for such aged and maimed officers and soldiers as might have to be discharged as unserviceable; and to make a deduction of six pence in the pound from all military pay towards that object.[43]

Charles gave 64 acres in Phoenix Park, Kilmainham, near Dublin, as the site for this building, the first stone of which was laid on 29 April 1680 by the Duke of Ormonde, who was largely responsible for the scheme. The Hospital of King Charles the Second, Kilmainham, admitted its first pensioners – 10 officers and 100 soldiers – in March 1684. From 1698 out-pensioners were given 18 pence a week instead of their maintenance in the Hospital. Thus Ireland, having been first to provide permanent barracks for its garrison companies, now became first to build a hospital for its old soldiers.

Charles wanted a similar scheme for his worn-out soldiers on the English establishment but lacked the money to carry it out, since in 1679 Parliament had declared all military forces to be illegal. As a result Charles dissolved Parliament two years later, for the last time, still refusing him the necessary supplies for his army. Popular folklore, reinforced by the Chelsea Pensioners themselves, gives Nell Gwynn the credit for persuading the King to build the Hospital at Chelsea. Her own military recollections and her compassion are said to have been aroused by the pitiful sight of a maimed soldier who one day approached her coach to beg. Old traditions die hard in the army: the old pensioners of Chelsea, a neighbourhood well-known to Nell's mother, who lived and was drowned there, used to drink their first toast to Nell 'their founder'.

Whatever the inspiration for the Hospital, the truth is that on 8 September 1681 Charles instructed Sir Stephen Fox to build an institution for the English army. In 1640, at the age of 13, Stephen Fox had been appointed closet-keeper to Prince Charles and followed him into exile. His humble, diligent, industrious and prudent service was rewarded in 1661 by his appointment as the first Paymaster to the Forces, followed by a knighthood four years later. With Albemarle's help, he reformed the army's pay system by the punctual payment on a weekly basis, instead of the usual arrears of pay. He took 12 per cent interest against his private credit, the King repaying him at the end of every four months. This system proved popular with both King and army.

Fox's honesty and business acumen also found the means to finance the King's project for the Chelsea Hospital. As he explained to Evelyn on 27 January 1682, the King was resolved to build a Royal Hospital on the Royal Society's ground at Chelsea for 400 men, in the form of a college or monastic community for 'olde, lame or infirm soldiers in ye service of the Crown'. It is possible that Charles had promised this piece of land to Nell, who surrendered it in exchange for 79 Pall Mall, which Charles built for her with the freehold. She was certainly one of the Hospital's early benefactors. Additional land – the meadows between the Chelsea College and the river – were purchased from Lord Cheyne and Sir Thomas Grosvenor,[44] whose marriage to the 13-year-old heiress Mary Davies laid the foundation for this family fortune and estates in Belgravia, Pimlico and Park Lane, including Grosvenor Square where the American Embassy stands.

Charles laid the foundation stone in the spring of 1682 and he, with Fox, generously endowed the Hospital. It was supported by a tax of 10 per cent on the purchase price of officer commissions and a five per cent deduction on all military pay. Three months later, on 17 June 1684, a further deduction of one day's pay per annum was levied on the army by royal warrant. The handsome building, with its 50 acres of grounds, was designed by Sir Christopher Wren and not completed until 1690. The first group of in-pensioners – 99 men severely disabled by wounds and old age – were admitted on 4 February 1692. A few days later a request was made to the clerk of works for

coffins, crutches, wooden legs and ashen stumps, feather pillows, leather girdles and all sorts of trusses for lame and bursten (broken) men.[45]

Soon the remaining 377 pensioners moved in. Living outside the Hospital were enrolled pensioners – four companies of Invalids, armed and quartered as garrison troops at Windsor, Hampton Court, Teignmouth and Chester.

Charles never lived to see his Hospital finished (although he visited the incomplete buildings a few days before his death); but he would have loved the place and the company of his old soldiers, whose bawdy language and hard drinking he would have appreciated. In the chapel hang numerous trophies representing 'the hideous carnage, the noble self-sacrifice, the manly daring, the death, the glory and the heroism of England's triumphs', epitomised by the veterans in their long red coats and three-cornered hats. They are still a popular sight on the London scene, 300 years after their foundation.[46]

13

The Standing Army: From Ensign to Colonel

The design is, and the Duke of York is hot for it, to have a land army and so to make the government like that of France', wrote Pepys on 12 July 1667. But it is doubtful if Charles ever seriously intended to use his army to help him govern the country. Certainly he liked his troops, reviewing them and visiting them on manoeuvres, and was determined to maintain the nucleus of a standing force to protect his person and ensure his crown. He had seen his father lose his throne for want of an army, and had witnessed at first hand the power of Cromwell backed by his soldiers. He had no intention of being forced into exile again.

Since the earliest days kings of England had raised armies in times of war, but the concept of a force which was not disbanded on the conclusion of hostilities was a radical departure. 1661 saw the introduction of a new type of standing army: a non-political body concerned solely with the execution of civil authority in the preservation of law and order and in national defence. The army assisted in sea and land battles against the Dutch; overseas, it garrisoned Tangier; but, despite the fears of Parliament that it posed a Catholic threat, no such threat ever materialised. Throughout Charles's reign the military remained subordinate to civil authority, establishing a precedent for following centuries.

The right to raise and use an army was, and had been from the earliest times, a royal prerogative. By the terms of the Militia Act of 1661, Charles was given the legal right to command 'all forces by land and sea and all forts and places of strength', but no mention was made of a standing army in peacetime. No serious objections were offered by Parliament when the King established a small army in 1661: England was still politically unstable, plots abounded, and it was agreed that the restored monarch needed security. Provided the King paid for his troops or hired them out to various European monarchs, who maintained them so long as they stayed in their service, Parliament was happy that the troops should remain a department of the royal household under the authority and patronage of the king and his nominees.[1]

But gradually Parliament used the standing army as an emotional issue to attack the King's prerogative, arguing that it was a threat to constitutional government. In peace there was nothing for an army to subdue but the Magna Carta, argued Colonel Titus in the House of Commons,[2] and numerous examples of tyrants who had used the military to enslave their subjects were cited in support. A standing army caused many nuisances for the whole country, and public funds were used to keep 'a large number of idle hands to lord it over the rest of the subjects', causing annoyance to industrious and hard-working citizens.[3]

The soldiers were coarse, rough and badly behaved; their officers were often oppressive, cruel and fractious. Frequent quarrels, murders and robberies were committed by the soldiers; townsmen claimed that the soldiers oppressed them; a military camp was said to debauch a whole neighbourhood. The public disliked having soldiers quartered upon them, the use of press-gangs, the non-payment of debts, and

> the insolence of officers and the debaucheries that are committed by them and their soldiers in all the towns they enter, to the ruin of multitudes of women, dishonour of their families and the bad example to others.[4]

Apart from financial restrictions, Charles was his own master in military affairs and generally used his small army in pursuit of national interests. On three occasions – during the Dutch Wars of 1665–7 and 1672–4, and for a projected French war in 1678 – Charles increased his army and gave Parliament real fears he might use it to overthrow the constitution and establish his own arbitrary government. Furthermore, he loaned a number of regiments to Louis XIV during 1674–8 against the entreaties of the House of Commons, and used the army as his ultimate political weapon during the Exclusion Crisis and at Oxford in 1681, when he dissolved Parliament. Fears were kept alive by the Popish Plot but, whatever the occasion or pretext, Charles avoided the trap of absolute rule supported by the military.

Whatever the rights and wrongs of the arguments, the King's army offered career prospects for both officers and men. There were few recruiting problems for home service during the peaceful years of Charles's reign, although press-gangs had to be used to fill the mass levies during the national emergencies of 1673 and 1678. In the early years there were enough disbanded veterans of Cromwell's troops to fill regimental vacancies and those required for service in Tangier, Portugal and Bombay. Overseas service was loathed, however, and whenever possible expendable Irish and Scots were used in preference to native-born Englishmen.

In peacetime, too, the army was small and compact, with few casualties to cause vacancies; but in war, as from the mid-1670s, military authorities were faced with the problem of manning the army for the colonies and overseas service, and the use of press-gangs was necessary. To reinforce Tangier in 1672, for example, 200 men were pressed into service in the west country; but they were of very poor quality –

> whereof there were two women that had entered themselves for soldiers in men's apparel . . . some of them were old men and most very poor creatures.[5]

The easiest method of recruiting in wartime was to obtain volunteers from the militia, who could be disbanded on the conclusion of the campaign. Parliament preferred the militia to the standing army, setting aside large sums for its upkeep. Despite its inefficiency, it belonged to them and not to the King. Many members of Parliament who attacked the army served as deputy lieutenants or officers in their county militia, which gave them social standing and influence in their localities. Parliament in 1679 resolved 'that the continuing of any standing forces in this nation, other than the Militia, is illegal: and a great Grievance and Vexation to the People',[6] despite the poor performance of the militia against the Dutch. The militia was riddled with inefficiency: it could hardly march, let alone fight, and lacked the necessary mobility and training of professional troops for war. By the 1670s some county militia had not been mustered for four years. The Suffolk militia, for example, needed on the exposed eastern coastline during the Third Dutch War, was short of officers because of 'death, sulking and fear'.[7]

Because of its inefficiency and static organisation, Parliament had raised from the militia (for the Second Dutch War in 1666) a select mobile force of three regiments of cavalry, an infantry regiment and 17 independent troops of horse. This was more successful, so in the following year when the Dutch raided Chatham this special force was expanded to 12,000 foot and 3,200 horse. It was more mobile and better trained than the ordinary militia troops, but Parliament lacked the money to perpetuate it and the special force was disbanded. There were fears that this force smacked of a standing army, a charge for which Clarendon was impeached in the same year on the grounds that 'he designed a Standing Army to be raised and to govern the Kingdom thereby'.[8] Parliament argued that the militia was for home defence only, not for making external war. It should not be regarded as a vehicle for recruiting for the royal army. Correlli Barnett justly remarked that the militia ceased to be politically acceptable the moment it became militarily effective.[9]

To obtain volunteers for the enlarged armies during the 1670s, recruiting by 'beat of drum' was employed. Regiments sent a captain, sergeant and corporal with a drummer and two private soldiers to suitable villages, where the captain's flag would be planted and the villagers summoned by the drummer.

The captain or sergeant would mount an improvised rostrum, often a cart in the market place, and harangue the assembled crowd. In suitable flowery language, he would entice them to enlist for a bounty of five shillings and visions of future booty.

> What think you now, gentlemen, of a purse full of gold out of a Frenchman's pocket, after you have dashed out his brains with the butt of your firelock, eh? asked Captain Plume, a recruiting officer.[10]

George Farquhar, a recruiting officer who married a rich heiress hoping to pay off his debts, was forced to become an actor when he found she had deceived him financially. He describes such a recruiting scene in his famous play *The Recruiting Officer* (1706), in which soldiers talk frankly of their military life, casual affairs and bastard children, while the rascally recruiter Sergeant Kite addresses the crowd in Shrewsbury market place –

> If any gentleman, soldiers or others, have a mind to serve Her Majesty (Queen Anne), and pull down the French King: if any 'prentices have severe masters, any children have undutiful parents: if any servants have little wages, or any husband too much wife, let them repair to the noble Sergeant Kite, at the Sign of the Raven in the good town of Shrewsbury, and they shall receive present relief and entertainment.

Encouraged to have a drink in the local bar and accept the 'King's Shilling' (often surreptitiously placed at the bottom of the tankard), the gullible farmer's lad would be offered visions of a brighter future –

> Over the hills and far away
> To Flanders, Portugal or Spain.
> We shall lead more happy lives,
> By getting rid of Brats and Wives,
> That scold and bawl both night and day,
> Over the hills and far away.

By the end of the play the resourceful recruiter has decided to quit the 'Recruiting trade' and serve his monarch and country at home:

> With some regret I quit the active field,
> And with my fair spouse to stay,
> And raise recruits the matrimonial way.

Almost without exception, the foot soldier was recruited from the lower social orders, usually from rural areas, with a large number from Scotland and Ireland. Some would be volunteers who craved excitement and adventure, loot and rape; others were discontented agricultural workers, unemployed apprentices, vagrants and paupers, for whom the army offered a haven from debt and crime. The Life Guards and Royal Horse Guards enlisted a superior type of soldier – younger sons of poorer gentry, who hoped their experience in the ranks would fit them eventually for a commission.

But army life was tough, pay uncertain, and fraud and embezzlement rife. Dishonest officers misappropriated supplies, drew up false muster rolls, defrauded the soldiers, and were in turn defrauded by the government.[11] In Farquhar's play the recruiting officer enters his new-born illegitimate son in the lists – 'Enter him a grenadier by the name of Francis Kite, absent upon furlough. I'll allow you a man's pay for his subsistence.' The foot soldier's pay of eight pence per day[12] was subject to deductions for food and accommodation (subsistence), and for clothing, personal equipment, hospitals and medicines, and any other stoppage from these 'off-reckonings' which unscrupulous colonels and auditors could invent. The government, for its part, delayed paying regiments for years, while the sale of appointments and commissions, worthless clothing and equipment were some of the frauds practised. In fact, the whole of the public service at that time was regarded as a medium for extortion and personal enrichment. The military offered no exception to the general corruption which prevailed.

Such malpractices had a profound effect on the standing of the military in British society. The officer tended to become a corrupt tradesman or a rich play-boy, instead of a salaried state servant or a respected person earning a respectable wage.[13] 'The devil take all officers', shouted Farquhar, 'they do the nation more harm by debauching us at home than they do good by defending us abroad.' Only a couple of years after the birth of the standing army, an officer wrote of the guard at Sandown Castle:

> a company of Foot was sent from Dover to help guard the place, pitiful weak fellows, half-starved and eaten up with vermin, whom the Governor of Dover cheated of half their pay and the other half they spent in drink.[14]

Another colonel asked for additional provisions, because it was very hard for poor men that had no pay nor means of their own to live upon bread alone and do duty.[15]

Years later, the Duke of Schomberg would say of William III's English troops in Ireland that the regiments were mobs of undisciplined boys; the officers were ignorant, negligent and useless. The officers would neither instruct their men in the art of war nor provide against sickness by looking after their men's bodily needs.

Only single men were enlisted, as an order of Charles II dated 1663, drafted on the advice of the Duke of Albemarle, makes clear:

> No muster master shall knowingly muster a private soldier in any troop or company that is married. Nevertheless, if any soldier desires leave to marry, it shall not be denied to him but at the same time to be discharged and another unmarried to be entertained in his place.[16]

The army provided an opportunity for a man to escape from the responsibilities of a wife and family (but not from an unfinished apprenticeship) by a false attestation. Since the army was constantly on the move, the soldier would pick up his 'woman' from wherever he happened to be stationed, at home or abroad: some soldiers would marry their women, most cohabited or sought temporary liaisons. Some women would be the usual camp followers of all armies down the ages.

The army's attitude to marriage was to discourage it. An order of the Coldstream Guards dated 3 November 1671 stated that no soldier should marry without the previous consent of his captain, on pain of being cashiered or losing the pay that was due to him. In 1685 that order was applied to the whole army, and remained army policy for the next 200 years.

But the army needed some women to do simple domestic chores, especially washing the men's underwear, so it allowed six men per 100 soldiers to marry. Their wives (or 'women', as Army regulations specified) received six pence per day (about 2.5d) for washing for the men of their barracks. These 'recognised' women 'on the strength of the company' were given privileges (such as half a man's rations and a quarter for each child born in wedlock) denied to their less fortunate sisters.

Once enlisted, normally for life, the soldier was provided with the bare necessities, such as a coat or shirt, breeches, stockings and shoes, by the colonel of the regiment.[17] The soldier was usually billeted in an inn or ale-house, since barracks were non-existent and billeting in private houses was illegal. An Act of 1677 expressly stated that no soldier could be quartered on any subject or inhabitant of the realm, of any degree, quality or profession whatever, without his consent.[18] By billeting soldiers in an inn, men of the same regiment could be kept together and assembled quickly to meet an emergency. The captain gave four pence of the soldier's subsistence money to the inn-keeper for accommodation, usually in the attic or outhouses, food, small beer and candles. This frequently left mine host out of pocket, unpaid and resentful of having soldiers quartered upon him.

For his part, the soldier's idea of paradise in the seventeenth century was to live in somebody else's house, call for the best, have coal to give warmth, make the owner perform the office of a servant, eat, drink, sleep and make

'The Very Familiar Discours between Charles II and Mistress Nellie'.
(Evelyn). Painting by E M Ward. *(Courtesy of the Board of Trustees of the
Victoria and Albert Museum)*

Frances Stuart 'in Buff Doublet like a Soldier'. Jacob Huysman 1664.
(By gracious permission of Her Majesty the Queen)

Frances Stuart (1648–1702) 'the prettiest girl in the world', as Pallas Athene, the warrior goddess beloved of Zeus. Sir Peter Lely.
(The Mansell Collection Ltd)

American settlers celebrate the First Thanksgiving with the Indians. Painting by Ferris. The Bettman Archive. *(Syndication International, London)*

Louise de Kéroualle, Duchess of Portsmouth
(1649–1734). Henri Gascar. Christie's Images.
(By courtesy of the National Portrait Gallery, London)

Catherine Sedley, Countess of Dorchester (1657–1717).
Studio of Sir Peter Lely. *(By courtesy of the National
Portrait Gallery, London)*

Henry, 1st Duke of Grafton (second son of Charles II and Barbara
Castlemaine) (1663–90). Colonel of the Grenadier Guards. Thomas Hawker.
(Reproduced by kind permission of the Duke of Grafton)

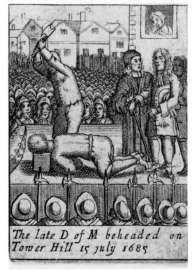

Top Duke of Monmouth (1649–85). Studio of Sir Godfrey Kneller c 1678. *(By courtesy of the National Portrait Gallery, London)*

Below Contemporary playing cards to celebrate the defeat of Monmouth Rebellion. *(By permission of The Trustees of The British Museum)*

Battle of the Boyne 1 July 1690. Contemporary engraving by Theodore Maas.
(By permission of The Trustees of the British Museum)

love, and have nothing to pay. He would take his revenge for any lack by making free with the inn-keeper's property, victuals and wife, threatening to knock his teeth down his throat with a sword-hilt or to thrash him with a pike-staff, if he objected.

> To enjoy all the sweetness of stolen goods without any fear of the penalties – that is the meaning of free quarters and the *summum bonum* of military bliss to the British soldier![19]

At the birth of Charles's small army most officers were either old royalists or officers of the New Model Army who had chosen to follow Albemarle. Some of the former were Catholics who had escaped the 'purges' (the oaths of allegiance and supremacy) which Parliament had enacted but which the King ensured were ineffectively applied. Many of those purged sought commissions with Louis XIV or German princes. During the Third Dutch War, Charles kept his Catholic soldiers at sea, where they were beyond the Parliamentary 'tests'. But in 1678, because of the Popish Plot, Charles had no option but to dismiss many of them.

The officers of Charles's small army were men of wealth, good family and position. For many of them soldiering was a hobby, pay no consideration. Military experience was not a necessary qualification for commissions, which were court appointments usually awarded for services to the crown. Charles's army also offered a career, mainly for the younger sons of gentry and peerage who looked for alternatives to careers in the navy, the law or the church. Under the primogeniture principle, the first son inherited the family titles and wealth; other sons had to marry well, usually within their own class, or secure a sinecure like an army commission, to avoid becoming a family liability or even to restore its fortunes. Since it was no longer possible for an officer to live on his pay, as in Cromwell's army, and because almost all commissions had to be purchased, most officers needed private means. As military duty did not occupy much time, a personal income allowed an officer to enjoy life as a country gentleman or live up to the standard of regimental expectations. Competition was thus fierce for the small number of officer vacancies, which amounted to some 350 in 1665, rising to about 600 in 1684.[20]

Advancement at home depended on royalist connections or links with the twin centres of military patronage – the Duke of Albemarle, until his death in 1670, and the Duke of York. Those without such influence or an inheritance, or who came from the poorer families of the upper class, had to find alternatives. They might seek a post abroad, where they could offer their professional services to a foreign power such as France or Portugal. Or they might take a commission in an English regiment on campaign, or in a garrison overseas, hoping to share the booty or prize money or fill a promotion vacancy caused by battle or climate. Sir Palmes Fairborne, Percy Kirke and the Churchill brothers all served in Tangier for such reasons.

Commissions and promotions were expensive to purchase. Although the sale of commissions was illegal throughout Charles's reign, and promotion was supposed to be on merit taken from a list of deserving candidates kept at Whitehall, the King turned a blind eye. He paid John Russell £5,100 for the colonelcy of the Grenadier Guards in 1681 for the 19-year-old Duke of Grafton – Barbara's son Henry Fitzroy. He purchased command of the Life Guards for another son, the Duke of Monmouth, for £10,000. 'Nepotism or avarice secured the promotion of many a man out of his turn and without any reference to his comparative merits. When an officer sought for promotion, he whipped up all his influential friends – the mention of a few big names carried greater weight than any record of the officer's services.'[21]

The career of the nobly-born but impoverished John Churchill, the future Duke of Marlborough, provides a good illustration of these practices. His father, Winston Churchill, had fought for the King as a captain of horse during the Civil War and his mother (née Elizabeth Drake) was descended from the Elizabethan hero Sir Francis Drake. In recognition of his father's loyalty and his family's sufferings in the Stuart cause, at the age of 15 Churchill was found a place as a page in the household of the Duke of York. Two years later (14 September 1667) the Duke obtained for him an ensign's commission in the Grenadier Guards, in the place of John Howard, who, as a Catholic, was forced to resign his commission. Scandalmongers of the period said Churchill owed his commission to the fact that his eldest sister, Arabella, one of the Duchess of York's maids of honour, was the Duke's mistress. 'How fortunate then for England and Europe that the Duke found her person so agreeable'.[22]

Churchill's good looks and handsome figure soon attracted the notice of court beauties, and even awakened a passion in Barbara Castlemaine, nine years his senior. She was insatiable in her physical appetites; he a lusty young man sowing wild oats and flattered that the King's favourite mistress desired him. They enjoyed a wanton relationship. Impatient, however, to distinguish himself in his military career and improve his finances, he left her seductions to embark in 1668 as a volunteer in the Tangier garrison. There he served in the Governor's Regiment (the Queen's Royal West Surrey Regiment).

> But all agreed that a man, who was the lover of the King's mistress and brother to the Duke of York's favourite, was in a good position to get preferment and could not fail to make his fortune.[23]

Churchill returned from Tangier in 1671, bronzed by African sunshine, to the pleasures of the court and to the arms of Barbara.[24] Charles discovered them in bed together and, knowing his Barbara, said to Churchill: 'I forgive you, for you do it to get your bread.' To remove this dangerous rival in the Duchess of Castlemaine's unsteady affections, the King sent him, with his company of the Guards, aboard the Duke of York's flagship to fight the Dutch in May 1672. In the engagement which followed, Churchill's good service earned him promotion to a captaincy in the Lord High Admiral's Regiment. A lieutenant in the King's Company, senior to Churchill, complained that for all his 12 years of service he had been passed over, and that Churchill's promotion was not unjustly attributed to court favour.[25]

A captain at 22, Churchill next joined a contingent of 6,000 men under the Duke of Monmouth sent by Charles II to serve Louis XIV against the Dutch. At the siege of Nymwegen, Churchill attracted the attention of Marshal Turenne, who predicted a great future for 'le Bel Anglais'. The following year (1673) at the siege of Maestricht, in company with the Duke of Monmouth, Lord Arlington and D'Artagnan and his musketeers, Churchill held an advanced fortification in a desperate fight before the arrival of reinforcements. The hero of Dumas' *The Three Musketeers* was killed in the engagement, but Churchill survived and was thanked by the French King at the head of the army for his exploits, which included saving the life of the Duke of Monmouth.

He returned to England to become gentleman of the bedchamber and master of the robes, with promotion to lieutenant-colonel in the Admiral's Regiment at the early age of 23. From Barbara, who frequently gave presents to her lovers, he received £5,000 for his favours. With this gift he purchased an annuity of £500, a modest but useful beginning to the financial fortune he was soon to amass.[26]

Cavalier officers did not consider their duties included any training for war in times of peace. When not actually fighting they believed they were free to enjoy themselves; so for the next two or three years Churchill plunged into the vortex of dissipation at court, the idol of beauty and fashion. Courtin, the French ambassador, reporting to his master in 1676, observed that Churchill had a reputation in the debauched court circles in which he mixed for trading on his fine figure and handsome face. That sort of vice was common at the French court, where pretty fellows of high birth and light purses received money, jewels and even estates from women of wealth and quality. 'The ladies of the palace vied for his homage and nobles of the land cultivated his society', continued Courtin. When Churchill applied for a colonelcy with the French army, Louis, briefed on his amorous adventures at court, replied haughtily:

> Monsieur Churchill is too fond of pleasure to discharge well the duties of a colonel in the army of the King of France. He would give more satisfaction to a rich and faded mistress than to a monarch, who did not want carpet knights in his armies.[27]

The French King would pay dearly in the very near future for such a remark!

But the libertine in Churchill died when he first set eyes on the 15-year-old Sarah Jennings, who frequented the court with her elder sister Frances ('La Belle Jennings'). Frances was one of the attractive maids of honour with whom the Duchess of York surrounded herself. Sarah came from modest country stock and, like Churchill, found the court offered the only source of advancement for the poor and gentle-born, whether able or beautiful-bodied. When the first Duchess of York died and James married Mary of Modena (1673), the 15-year-old bride chose Sarah as one of her maids of honour.

Seducing these nubile young virgins from respectable families was the fashionable sport of the court. Courtiers looked upon maids of honour, commented Gramont,[28] only as amusements, placed expressly at court for their own entertainment. But Sarah considered herself above falling to a lecher and certainly not to Barbara Castlemaine's lover, however handsome and gallant a soldier he might be. Her sister Frances, 12 years older, had scorned the amorous advances of the Duke of York; she preferred marriage to Captain Sir George Hamilton of the King's Guards, who had to resign his commission because of his faith and became a general in the French service.

Sarah, too, wanted a wedding ring, not to become just another 'great belly' at court. Churchill's family opposed the match. They wanted him to marry another maid of honour, the rich but plain heiress Catherine Sedley, the only child of the rake Sir Charles Sedley. So the lovers married in secret, while Catherine Sedley replaced Arabella Churchill as the Duke of York's mistress. As his famous descendant Sir Winston Churchill commented, 'It was the only time Marlborough was ever forced to surrender and then only to a chit of 17.'[29]

They started their married life in 1678, with little money but bright hopes for the future. It was a love match at a time when such marriages were unfashionable, especially at court. Their love would last for the rest of their days, despite the frequent partings associated with army life – he campaigning abroad, she on duty with the Duchess of York. It was Sarah, through her close friendship with Princess Anne, who built up the family fortune by shrewd investments in land and property, obtaining 'the broad acres' needed for social status and political power. She ensured their daughters married into the ranks of the highest and wealthiest in the land – the Blandfords and Godolphins, the Spencers and Montagus. For children, too, were a form of investment for upper class families. Titles could be traded for marriage settlements, and intermarriage gain wealth, power, privilege and high places. Breeding was a wifely duty – pleasure in sex and lust could be left to courtesans and mistresses.

The beauties of Charles II's court, whether wife or mistress, founded a number of army families, some of which continue to this day. Arabella Churchill's son by the Duke of York became the famous Marshal de Berwick, one of the greatest soldiers of the eighteenth century. Her daughter, Lady Henrietta, married the first Earl of Waldegrave, whose son followed in the footsteps of her uncle, the Duke of Marlborough. Frances Jennings's second husband was the Earl of Tyrconnel, who commanded James II's forces in Ireland. Three of their daughters married viscounts, and a son commanded the Fifth Foot. Nell Gwynn's elder son by Charles, the Duke of St Albans, became colonel of the Eighth Horse; while two of Barbara's sons, Henry and George, were colonels of the Grenadier and Horse Guards respectively. Barbara's line, the Buckinghams, whose blood is in the present Queen Elizabeth and in a number of aristocratic families, has produced no less than 13 prime ministers and has a long tradition of military service to the crown.

14

Petticoat Diplomacy

On 3 January 1670 General George Monck, Duke of Albemarle, died, standing almost upright in his chair like a Roman general, with all his officers about him. It was almost exactly 10 years since he had left Coldstream on his historic march south to restore the King. During his later years, although remaining close to the decision-making of the country, he had gradually dropped out of the more intimate counsels of his sovereign, who nevertheless continued to consult him on important matters. He had become a great lord and courtier, respected, if not loved, by all. The King trusted him, the common people idolised him and even Pepys, who joined Clarendon in not liking him, wrote that Albemarle had strange luck to be loved, though he was the heaviest (dullest) man in the world, but stout and honest to his country.[1]

Albemarle's wife died a few weeks later, while his body was lying in state in Somerset House; both were buried in Westminster Abbey. It was thought she had lost all taste for living. Pepys called her 'dirty Bess' and 'a plain homely dowdy', echoing Clarendon's opinion that she was a woman of the least wit and less beauty. Others, on the contrary, have suggested she was neither unattractive nor ill bred. Despite her low origins, Albemarle had always been devoted to her and acknowledged the help she gave him in his career and in the restoration of the King. Both had a passion for money: she was frequently accused of selling offices in her husband's department, and of even worse methods of extortion. Perhaps one can sympathise with them, for both had known extreme poverty.[2]

The London Gazette of 30 April 1670 reported a state funeral of almost royal splendour given to Albemarle, paid for by the King. The procession set off from Somerset House, where hundreds of people had paid their last respects. The Strand was lined with two regiments of the City militia. First marched the Duke of York's troop of Horse Guards; next, the King's troop commanded by the Duke of Monmouth, followed by the regiment of Foot Guards (the

Grenadiers) and Albemarle's own regiment of Coldstreamers, led by his friend the Earl of Craven – 'all of them in excellent funeral order'. The chief mourner was Albemarle's only surviving child, Christopher. Then followed a host of nobility, courtiers, officers of state (including the Duke of Ormonde, the Earl of Sandwich and Lords Arlington, Shaftesbury and Clifford) and officers of the army (including ensign John Churchill) and a host of common people. Towards the end of the procession came the Duke's favourite horse and his grooms. His body was received by the clergy and laid to rest in Westminster Abbey, near to those of kings, in Henry VII's chapel at the feet of Queen Elizabeth I.

Such was the royal tribute paid to a man who was called the father of his country and of the British army. It should not be forgotten that he was also a distinguished admiral, and had shown his personal courage at Nantwich and Dunbar, at sea against the Dutch, and in London during the plague and the Great Fire. His experience and knowledge of military science led to his recall to take charge of every national emergency. He had no political ambitions, but by his example demonstrated that a politically-wise soldier was necessary and helpful at the centre of government. Like many loyal regular officers today, he believed in order, discipline and political stability, and hated anarchy. He showed his loyalty to established authority, whether that of Cromwell, Parliament or King, so long as that authority was clearly identifiable. In the same way he expected loyalty from his own officers, and punished those who fomented unrest among his troops for political reasons. Like all good officers he was concerned for the well-being of his men: he attended to their pay, beer and clothing, and cared for the wounded, the widows and disbanded soldiers.[3]

A few days before he died he achieved one of his most cherished ambitions. His son, Christopher, was married to the 15-year-old Lady Elizabeth Cavendish, daughter of the Earl of Ogle, second Duke of Newcastle. Her grandfather had been the Royalist commanding general in the north during the Civil War. Albemarle left his only surviving son a vast fortune and estates in a dozen English counties, in Ireland, and overseas in Carolina and the West Indies. In 1674 the young couple bought Clarendon's great palace and grounds in Piccadilly.[4] Christopher was knighted by the King and became, like his father, a regimental commander, replacing Monmouth in command of the King's Horse Guards. As lord lieutenant of Devon, in 1685 he raised the Devonshire and Cornwall militia to oppose Monmouth when he landed at Lyme. He became chancellor of Cambridge University and governor general of Jamaica. He died of a tropical disease in 1688, aged 35, a month before William of Orange landed at Torbay. With his widow (who on his death married Ralph Montagu, ambassador to France), he is buried in the family vault in Westminster Abbey.

Charles did not appoint a successor to Albemarle as captain general and commander-in-chief of the standing army – a post considered by the King to carry too great a power and trust, as matters stood, to be put in any one person's hand. Nor was there a military officer whom Charles thought to be politically safe for the secret negotiations he was currently planning with France. The country was at peace, and the small size of the army did not require the full-time attention of a soldier for command and administration. The Duke of York coveted the appointment to add to his post of lord high admiral, but Charles decided to leave it vacant until his natural son, the Duke of Monmouth, was mature enough to be given the post. Thus for eight years the appointment was held in abeyance, until Monmouth achieved the title and powers in 1678. It is interesting to note that, although he was given the title of captain-general (or lord general) of the army in England and Scotland, the title of commander-in-chief was dropped.[5]

In 1670 Monmouth was certainly not mature enough to command the royal army. In his early twenties, he was busy sowing his wild oats as the leader in fashion and extravagant behaviour for young men about town. When the Third Dutch War broke out (1672–4) and a rebellion at home seemed a possibility, Charles nominated a committee under the Duke of York to 'consider all military matters' and take charge of army administration. Its members included Monmouth, and three experienced officers who had served with Albemarle during the early years of the Restoration – Prince Rupert, the Earl of Oxford and the Earl of Craven. But day-to-day and detailed army administration was left to a civilian, albeit a former army officer during the Civil War, Henry Bennet.

Some time before the death of Albemarle, Charles decided to seek an alliance with his cousin Louis XIV, although he realised that such an alliance would be difficult for Parliament and people to accept. As early as 26 October 1662 he had written to his sister Minette: 'I consider nothing of greater value than the intimate friendship between the King, my brother, and myself.'[6] Now he hoped to seal that friendship with an alliance. Henry Bennet, Earl of Arlington, a politician and diplomat 'who had risen to power by court intrigue and the favour of a royal mistress',[7] was also a Catholic whom Charles could trust in his negotiations with France. As secretary at war, Arlington wielded the power which subjected the army to civil control – a process, which would be confirmed in the 1688 Settlement and the Mutiny Act.[8]

In 1667, on the death of Philip IV of Spain, Louis had invaded the Spanish Low Countries, claiming that the rights of Spain in those territories had passed to his wife, Philip's eldest daughter. Louis took the opportunity to protect France's exposed eastern frontier by building a series of fortresses under the great French military engineer, Vauban, and to annex a string of Flemish towns (Charleroi, Armentières, Tournoi, Douai and Lille) captured by Marshal Turenne. France retains these towns to this day.

But the invasion of the Spanish Netherlands had one consequence not fore-seen by Louis. It alarmed the Dutch, and the treaty of Breda which ended the Second Dutch War was followed a few months later (May 1668) by a triple alliance between England, Holland and Sweden, aimed at curbing the power of France. Louis knew he could buy off Sweden and England with the gold they needed, but he decided the Dutch had to be conquered.

It is doubtful if Charles had given up his commercial antagonism to the Dutch, but a Protestant alliance against Catholic France suited Parliament, and Charles needed money. In February 1668 he asked Parliament to provide this money: 'I lie under great debts contracted in the last war. Fortifications have to be repaired and I must build more great ships.'[9] But Charles was well aware of the possibility of French gold, which would free him from the hopeless financial and religious fetters with which the parsimony and intolerance of the House of Commons imprisoned him.

Moreover, Charles's natural sympathies were with France. Charles was the grandson of Henri IV and his sister, Henrietta, was married to Louis XIV's brother, the Duke of Orléans. Apart from blood ties, Charles had enjoyed French hospitality during his exile and huge French subsidies in the past to avoid calling Parliament. He admired the splendour of the French court, the autocracy of their King, and Louis's Catholic religion – to which Charles was possibly a secret, and his brother James an open, convert. French troops could, if his sovereignty were challenged, defend his throne. Charles had little objection to the French being predominant on the Continent, provided Louis left England master of the seas, and Charles had no moral scruples about breaking an alliance with a friend, if it suited his purpose. He was accustomed to lies and treachery himself, and was surrounded by ministers, peers and commoners ready to take substantial bribes from either or both sides to fur-ther their interests; Charles was a skilful diplomat, however underrated by his 'brother' in France.

Nor did women deceive him any longer, despite what they and others might think. He saw them as venal or pleasure-loving, useful but to be used – like his ministers. In his letter of 26 October 1662, he had established 'a private chan-nel' of communication with Louis through his sister, which he knew would never be suspected. In September 1668 he asked her to use her diplomatic skills to remove the greatest obstacle between the two nations – Louis's scheme to create a great fleet and extend French commerce, 'which was a great hindrance to an entire friendship'.[10]

To understand the complex inner life of Charles's court, especially in the later years of his reign, one must also have regard to the activities of half-a-dozen able and charming French ambassadors at Whitehall, and the constant stream of correspondence which passed between them and Louis XIV's ministers at Versailles, not only on political matters but on all the scandal of the hour, however petty and ephemeral.[11] Louis knew his cousin was at the mercy of heretics and corrupt legislators, and saw Charles's ladies of pleasure ('enemies of our nation', as the virtuous Evelyn called them) as potential agents. Successive French ambassadors in London[12] had told him that since his accession Charles had abandoned himself to a wild pursuit of women, and Louis decided to use these women to further French interests.

In August 1668 he replaced his ambassador in London with Colbert de Croissy, the brother of Louis's great foreign Minister and treasurer, Jean Baptiste Colbert. He gave them orders to break up the triple alliance and send detailed reports of all that went on in the English court, particularly in the privy part. Colbert wrote to his brother in London:

> I think it would please the King if you would send him gossiping letters about everything that happens in the private life of the King of England and in what is known as the inner circle of his Court.[13]

De Croissy replied that he would keep his brother informed about the squabbles of these ladies, which were often as much a cause of deep concern to the King of England as the most serious business, and of those little affairs on which great events so often hinged. This diplomatic activity and system of bribes and pensions would reach a peak under the French ambassador Barrillon and the Duchess of Portsmouth.

De Croissy set to work on Lady Castlemaine, whom he believed was ready to accept overtures (and gifts) from France. He told his master that Charles had confided to her that Lord Arlington would not hear of an alliance with France, and that Lady Castlemaine had become a Catholic convert. Louis sent his congratulations and a handsome present of jewellery. 'Ladies are fond of such keepsakes, whatever may be their breeding or disposition: and a nice little present can, in any case, do no harm.'[14]

A few days later, on 3 April 1669, de Croissy wrote that Charles set great store on the counsel of Barbara, who could put more pressure on the King to achieve an alliance than any other person. Colbert replied that the King of France read with pleasure the curious details about the intrigues of the English court, and of the ladies 'who are the chief personages there.'[15] On 25 May, de Croissy wrote to Louis:

> I can assure your Majesty that Lady Castlemaine will do everything possible to carry the King towards the speedy conclusion of a favourable alliance with Your Majesty because she thinks it is very advantageous to the King and consequently to herself.

But Barbara was not the kind of secret agent the King of France wanted. She could not be trusted with state secrets. She certainly loved 'little presents' and was constantly in need of money: the court was amazed at the fineness of her cambric shifts, at her smocks and linen petticoats trimmed with the richest lace, at her costly furniture and plate. But de Croissy knew that an ambassador could not rely on her discretion because she surrendered herself completely to the passion of the moment, be it love affair or quarrel. She could betray secrets in a drunken bout to the actor or dancer who followed the King into her bed. Her greed for money to pay her lovers made her vulnerable, while her violent tempers and infidelities wearied the King.[16]

De Croissy recognised, however, that her quarrels with the beauties of easy virtue who surrounded Charles were as much (if not more) the object of deep concern to the King of France as the military evolutions of his generals, Turenne and Condé. 'A war with England depended on the humour of an actress or a bedchamber woman.'[17] So he persevered, despite the cost and low return:

> I have given away all that I brought from France, not excepting the skirts and smocks made up for my wife, and I have not money enough to go on at this rate. Nor do I see the use of going to much expense in satisfying the women here for rich keepsakes.

He advised Louis to give Madame Castlemaine only such trifling tokens as a pair of French gloves, ribands, a Parisian undress gown, or some little object of finery.[18]

Historians today doubt Barbara's influence with Charles, who told de Croissy that the only woman who had a real hold on him was his sister, the Duchess of Orléans. But contemporaries certainly believed in Barbara's power over the King. In the event the alliance took two years to shape, and Barbara deserted the enterprise before she could claim any credit in it. She preferred to sell Berkshire House and lands, to build Cleveland House, and to squabble over the ownership of a house and grounds in Phoenix Park, Dublin. Nevertheless, she was not a cipher during the political negotiations preceding the French alliance.[19]

15

The Grand Design

The most important of the instructions given by Louis to Colbert de Croissy was to conduct secret negotiations for a treaty of alliance between England and France. Both agreed that the mutual love of Charles and Henrietta should be utilised in these negotiations, so the young, pretty, intelligent and very pro-English Henrietta assumed the leading role in the plot. Born in Exeter in 1644 and smuggled out of that city during its siege to France, she had married the effeminate brother of Louis XIV, the Duke of Orléans. He was a buffoon and a homosexual transvestite, who both neglected and dominated his wife.

Henrietta Anne was a Catholic and passionately wanted to unite France and England. She proved a perfect negotiator for the two kings, able to dangle the advantages of a French alliance before her brother – the elimination of Dutch commercial competition, the destruction of the Dutch navy, and the partition of Holland between France and England. There was the possibility of stationing a royal army of mercenaries in the Netherlands, if necessary, for Charles to use against his rebellious Parliament. Finally, and most importantly for Henrietta, the Catholic religion could be restored to its old place of authority in England. In September 1668 she wrote enthusiastically, and realistically, to Charles of England becoming supreme in commerce, 'which is what your people most passionately desire and what will probably never occur, so long as the Republic of Holland exists'.[1]

It is very doubtful if Charles ever seriously intended to introduce Roman Catholicism by force or to rule by means of military power. Such a policy was impracticable. But he warned his sister in January 1669 of the need for absolute secrecy, 'otherwise, we shall never compass the end we aim at'. If Protestant London, for instance, learned his true object, before the plans of the grand design between England and France were ready, a revolution in England would have been almost inevitable. Quietly, Charles placed the forts and arsenals in the hands of officers he could trust: Plymouth was put under the command of Colonel Sir John Grenville, the Earl of Bath; Hull under General John Belasyse, for example. He also sought to improve the morale of his small army.

In December 1669, Charles produced a draft treaty which demanded £200,000 in return for his declaration of Catholicism, with the promise of more cash and military aid in the event of a rebellion in England. A further £600,000 was to be the price of Charles's help against the Dutch, with Ostend, Minorca and the Spanish American possessions as a booty.[2] This draft was more than Louis was prepared to accept, and reinforced his belief that Henrietta should go to England to effect a compromise. He judged that her visit would achieve more than weeks of protracted diplomacy.

Through his foreign minister Colbert, Louis showered presents on her – jewels, perfumes, gloves, diamond garters (the latest fashion) and 20 purses of gold. He placed a room next to his own apartments in the Louvre at her disposal, so they could work together on the project. The only problem to the visit was her husband, who hated his wife and angrily refused to let her go. It was even reported that this notorious homosexual made her perform her marital duty several times a day

> since he has known about this business, in order that she may become pregnant, which condition would prevent her from exposing herself to so long and dangerous a journey.[3]

Eventually, Louis persuaded his brother to agree to his wife going as far as Dover, at first for only three days, although the visit was later extended.

Riding in a glass coach with the Queen and his two mistresses, Louise de la Vallière and the Marquise de Montespan beside him, Louis went with his Court and an army corps escort to Dunkirk to see Henrietta on her way. He gave her 200,000 crowns towards her expenses and personally chose her suite, which included the Count de Gramont and his English wife, the former 'Belle Hamilton'. 'All the ladies in France that think themselves fit to be seen have offered themselves to wait on her', wrote the English ambassador, Ralph Montagu, to Charles. Owing to the lack of accommodation at Dover Castle, her household had to be limited to 237 persons, for the grandees of France were accustomed to travel in great state. Dover was little more than a village at this time and many of the illustrious visitors, both English and French, as well as the household officers, ladies in waiting, chaplains, grooms and manual servants had to seek accommodation in the local cottages.[4]

Leaving Nell with her two-week-old son, Charles set off to meet his beloved sister. They met at Dover on 16 May 1670, greeting each other ecstatically after a nine year separation. The Duke of York saw little of his sister, having to return hastily to London to take command of the troops in case of disorder caused by threats of a Presbyterian uprising in the capital. Dover Castle, where Henrietta lodged, was decorated like an enchanted palace, and, away from the dictatorial Louis and her obsessive husband, she became young again.

Charles celebrated his fortieth birthday during her visit, and arranged a varied programme of entertainments for her – concerts, balls, feasts, ballets, sea trips along the Kentish coast, and a visit to Canterbury to see a comedy performed by the Duke of York's troupe, followed by a banquet in the hall of St Augustine's Abbey. The Queen and the Duchess of York were there, and Frances Stuart, Madame's old friend, now the Duchess of Richmond and in attendance on the Queen as one of her ladies of the bedchamber. The Duke of Monmouth flirted with Henrietta, while Charles began to show more than a little interest in the prettiest of her maids of honour, Louise de Keroualle, elder daughter of an ancient and noble Breton family, whom Henrietta had brought over with her.

Masked by all the merrymaking, the secret political talks went on, with Louise present at all the private negotiations – she knew the provisions of the treaty better than most of Charles's ministers. The treaty was finally signed on 1 June 1670. It is sometimes known as the *Traité de Madame* because of the part Henrietta played in the negotiations, especially in the highly secret sections concerning Charles's resolution to become a Roman Catholic. She thus negotiated the compromise under cover of a state visit as Duchess of Orléans and sister-in-law of the French King.

The official Treaty of Dover was signed – for the consumption of Parliament – by the five members of the Cabal (so called from the initials of Charles's ministers, Clifford, Arlington, Buckingham, Ashley and Lauderdale). It provided for another war against Holland in support of France, both countries agreeing to attack simultaneously and not make a separate truce. England would conduct the war by sea, France by land, with Charles providing 6,000 soldiers. The secret treaty was signed only by the Catholic ministers, Clifford and Arlington, who were in the King's confidence (the others were carefully and successfully kept in ignorance). It bound the two kings together in perpetual alliance, with a clause by which Charles agreed to declare himself publicly a Catholic 'when the affairs of his kingdom permitted'. In return for implementing this clause, Charles would receive about £160,000 and the services of 6,000 French troops for the suppression of any disorders which might follow the declaration. Naturally, this clause was to remain unknown to Charles's Protestant ministers and to Parliament. For waging war on Holland, Charles was to receive three million livres per annum and the spoils of Walcheren, Sluys and the island of Cadsand. The exact timing of the war with Holland was to be left to Louis.

In the event, war against Holland was declared on 14 March 1672, but Charles only declared himself a Catholic on his deathbed 15 years later – for the rest of his life he remained outwardly head of the Anglican church. He made an attempt in 1672 to introduce religious freedom by his Declaration of Indulgence, which suspended all penal laws against Protestant dissenters and Popish recusants, but he was forced to withdraw it the following year. In 1673 Parliament replied by passing the famous Test Act, not repealed until 1828, which required all holders of public office, civil or military, to take the sacrament of the Church of England. But Charles never tried to introduce Catholicism into England – a very wise decision, considering his brother's fate in 1688!

The eve of Minette's departure arrived after a 15-day idyll. Charles had given his sister magnificent jewels, 6,000 pistoles for her expenses, and 2,000 crowns to build the Queen Mother a monument at Chaillot. When Henrietta sent her maid of honour Louise for her jewel case, and asked her brother to choose the jewel he most wanted, he took the young girl by the hand and with the charm of a practised seducer said: 'This is the only jewel I covet and want to keep beside me'.[5] Henrietta politely refused to leave Louise behind, since her parents had placed the girl under her protection. But she promised that, if Charles had Louise named as maid of honour to Queen Catherine and if her parents agreed, she would not stand in Louise's way.

Next day, after protracted farewells, Henrietta and her retinue sailed back to France, where Louis XIV and his court gave her a triumphant welcome. The Comtesse de la Fayette wrote that Madame had achieved a considerable success in diplomatic terms, and found herself at the age of 26 the intermediary between the two kings of the century. The Treaty of Dover owed much to her political skill and persuasiveness, her fanaticism for the Anglo-French alliance, and her grasp of every detail involved in negotiations carried out over many months.[6] 'As for me,' Henrietta wrote on her return, 'I have accomplished more than I ever hoped to do.'[7]

But within a few weeks Henrietta was dead. She died on 30 June 1670 at St Cloud, in the presence of Louis XIV and the grieving court. Her last thoughts were of her brother – 'my only regret in dying is leaving him'. Charles was in despair, angrily believing her final agonies were due to poison; modern medical opinion suggests it was acute peritonitis. Louis was stunned, fearing the Treaty of Dover might be in jeopardy. In a final tribute, Henrietta was entombed in the basilica of Saint Denis among France's greatest Kings and Queens. The great French divine, Abbé Bossuet, was commanded by Louis to pronounce her funeral oration – a masterpiece of French literature.

Among the influential politicians now hostile to the French alliance was the scheming and ambitious George Villiers, second Duke of Buckingham and boon companion of the King in exile. He had married the daughter of Cromwell's leading general, Fairfax, at the time betrothed to the Earl of Chesterfield (who had already declined Cromwell's offer of one of his daughters in marriage and a command in his army). Cromwell, well aware of Buckingham's debaucheries and political instability, broke up their honeymoon, regarding the marriage as a Presbyterian plot. Buckingham was arrested and clapped in the Tower, and would almost certainly have been executed if Cromwell had not died. Charles made Buckingham a gentleman of the bedchamber and later a Privy Councillor.

Although the King indulged, and was amused by, Buckingham's often outrageous extravagances, he did not trust him – and certainly not with the secret clauses of the Treaty of Dover. His character was accurately summed up in Dryden's famous lines –

> Stiff in opinions, always in the wrong;
> Was everything by starts and nothing long.[8]

Charles sent Buckingham to France to represent him at his sister's funeral. Buckingham had noticed the King's ardent looks towards Louise, and saw in her another opportunity of using a woman's charms to influence the King for his own ends and supplant his cousin, Barbara, at court and in the King's favour. He carried with him Charles's offer to Louise of a place as maid of honour to the Queen – an indispensable condition for Louis XIV's consent.

Louis honoured and fêted Buckingham at Versailles, and to gain his goodwill gave a yearly pension of £10,000 to his latest mistress, the Countess of Shrewsbury. Buckingham had killed her jealous husband in a duel whilst she, dressed in page's costume, held the bridle of her lover's horse.[9] To Louise, Buckingham talked eloquently about the attractions of the English court and the opportunities as a maid of honour of consoling the King over the loss of his sister. He hinted that, as the Queen was sickly, Charles might even take a new wife. By agreeing to the proposal, Louise would also be able to serve Louis and France. The young girl, uncertain of her future and with no desire to enter a convent – the fate of many an aristocratic French girl without a dowry – agreed, after obtaining her parents' consent. Louis, well briefed by Colbert on Charles's infatuation, saw in Louise an opportunity to place a French agent in the English court and a potential mistress in the King's bed.

So the plot was laid. Louise's father, a count and soldier by profession and distantly related to the French royal family, despite his family's poor circumstances, provided Louise with a useful wardrobe. He hoped his daughter would find in England the rich husband her proud lineage warranted, but which was denied her in France. Buckingham put his coach at her disposal. He promised to meet her at Dieppe and escort her to Whitehall in the royal yacht, which Charles had provided. She set off in October and arrived in Dieppe, only to discover to her bitter humiliation that the Duke had found other distractions and forgotten his promise. Left without news of his whereabouts, her pride hurt, and penniless, she never forgave him. The English ambassador in France, Ralph Montagu, came to her assistance and arranged an escort, money and the yacht to convey her to Dover.

The King sent the Duke of Arlington to meet her: he had been a member of Charles's court in exile and his agent in Madrid, and was a fluent linguist. Evelyn considered him the most cultured of all Charles's intimate circle, 'having the Latin, French and Spanish languages in perfection: has much travelled and is the best bred and Courtly person his Majesty has about him'.[10] Arlington was a friend of Barbara, now Duchess of Cleveland (created in 1670); a friendship which would be cemented in August 1671 by the marriage of his only daughter, Isabella, at the age of five to Henry, Earl of Euston and Duke of Grafton, son of Barbara and the King. (Diana Frances, the present Princess of Wales, is a direct descendant of this union of Henry and Isabella.)

Barbara persuaded the King to grant Arlington an earldom and create him a Knight of the Garter. Arlington, in return, agreed that all his property, including Euston Hall with its 2,000 acre deer park, should descend to Henry's heirs. Buckingham and Arlington were political rivals, and in abandoning Louise at Dieppe Buckingham did himself a great deal of harm:

> the Duke of Buckingham lost the merit he might have gained and brought over a mistress, whom his own strange conduct threw into the hands of his enemies.[11]

Arlington took over her sponsorship from Buckingham, and was to prove as ready to assist his master's pleasures as Clarendon had been to disapprove of them.

Thus the stage was set and the players in position for the next act of the Stuart drama.

16

The French Whore Will Do Her Duty

In September 1670 the Marquis de Saint Maurice, ambassador of the Duke of Savoy to Louis XIV, wrote to his master:

> No one yet knows anything of what the Duke of Buckingham has negotiated: he has taken Mlle. de Keroualle to serve the Queen of England: she is a beautiful girl and it is believed the plan is to make her the mistress of the King of Great Britain: the Duke would like to supplant his enemy Madame Castlemaine and King Louis would not be displeased to see one of his subjects in that lady's role, for women, it is remarked, have great power over the mind of the said King of England.[1]

Louise arrived in London poor, lonely and very vulnerable to court intrigues, but proud of being related to both Louis XIV and Charles II. From the first she was disliked and distrusted by the English at large as a foreign adventuress. The court and Lady Castlemaine recognised and feared a rival, but Arlington made much of her. He played upon her anger towards Buckingham, and hoped by pandering to the King's sexual urges to influence him through her, were she to become his mistress.

Charles wept when he saw her, associating her with the loss of his beloved sister. Now aged 40, he was much attracted to the young French beauty, 19 years younger than himself, with her feminine ways, cultured background, soft voice and the languishing looks of a Parisian coquette. Already physically in love with her, he wanted her for his mistress. Before long he had installed her in a suite of rooms near the Stone Gallery, close to his own. But he found, as he had with Frances Stuart, that she was going to be no easy conquest. Her Ursuline convent upbringing, the value she placed on her chastity as a potential bride, and her lack of a dowry strengthened her resolve. Courtiers of both sexes analysed her charms, calculated the pleasures the King would get from her favours, and laid bets with one another on how long she could hold out against the King's obviously growing passion.

De Croissy reported to the French king that Charles went to her rooms every morning at nine o'clock, never staying for less than an hour and often until 11 o'clock. He returned after dinner, shared all her stakes and losses at cards and never let her want for anything.[2] All the ministers sought her friendship; Lord Arlington told de Croissy how pleased he was at this new attachment of the King and that, although he never communicated state affairs to ladies, they could still render ill services to statesmen and defeat their plans. Arlington said it was well for the King's ministers that Charles should have a fancy for Mademoiselle de Keroualle, who was not of an evil disposition and was a lady. It was better to have dealings with her than with lewd and bouncing orange-girls and actresses, of whom no man of quality could take the measure.

Unlike Lady Castlemaine, who was always hectoring the King to do whatever she wanted, Louise, said Forneron, was no termagent or scold. When the King was with her, persons of breeding could, without loss of dignity, go to her rooms and pay him and her their court.[3] The Queen, resigned to her husband's infidelities, found that Louise served her with a deference which had been lacking in Lady Castlemaine.

Barbara still dominated the court, however, and Louise realised she was disliked by his other mistresses – Nell Gwynn and Frances Stuart, the Duchess of Richmond. Throughout the autumn of 1670 and into 1671, Louise flirted and teased the King, but steadfastly refused to yield to his advances. Colbert de Croissy, aware that Charles might tire of her stubbornness, urged her to surrender herself for the sake of France. Louis and his ministers asked 'how long will the resistance of this childish-looking girl be carried on?'.[4]

On 21 September 1671 de Croissy wrote to his master that, while Lady Castlemaine was losing favour, the King of England's fancy for Mademoiselle de Keroualle grew stronger. The attacks of nausea she had suffered when dining with him made him hope he would find in her a useful ally.[5] But her indisposition was only a chill, and de Croissy's brother, the French foreign minister, continued to ask on behalf of Louis the terms on which Mademoiselle de Keroualle and the King had come to stand mutually. Lord Arlington told the ambassador he hoped de Croissy would advise Louise to cultivate the King's good graces, not speak to him of affairs of state, and ensure that Charles would find peace, enjoyment and contentment at her lodgings. Lady Isabella Arlington, his Dutch wife, a crafty and lewd woman, daughter of Louis of Nassau of the House of Orange, bluntly urged the new favourite either to give herself unreservedly to the King or retire to a French convent.

Among Louise's friends in London was the Seigneur de Saint Evremond, who, despite a distinguished army career, had been exiled by Louis XIV.

Aware of her religious scruples, he dissuaded her from entering a convent and from doing penance, before she had done anything to repent:

> I have seen prudes, regretting their virtue, yearning for the delights they dare not enjoy. Happy the woman, who can discreetly manage her affairs, without denying her desires. Do not repulse temptation too severely![6]

Faced with such cynical advice to put the sweets of temptation before her pride, it is hardly surprising that de Croissy was at last reporting: 'She will do her duty to serve His Majesty'.[7]

It was the Arlingtons, with the help of the French ambassador, who finally settled the matter. Each year in spring and autumn the King went with his closest friends to the races at Newmarket. The Arlingtons owned nearby Euston Castle: a perfect fairyland with its 200 rooms, some of them private suites 'propitious for love intrigues, beautifully furnished, set in a park with musicians hidden behind bushes to serenade lovers'.[8] The Arlingtons, with de Croissy to chaperone Louise and keep Louis informed, devised a plot to invite Charles and Louise to be their guests at the October race meeting. Plenty of wine and a good bed would do the trick.

The house was filled with at least 200 lords, ladies and gallants of the court, including the Earl and Countess of Sunderland, and the Duke of Buckingham with his mistress, the Countess of Shrewsbury. The King came over every second day, sometimes with the Duke of Monmouth, and stayed the night. During the mornings the guests passed their time hunting and hawking, then played dice and cards at night.

Under the pretext of enlivening the hours of a long October evening in a country house (or possibly to salve Louise's conscience) the two countesses arranged a mock wedding, with Louise as bride and Charles as bridegroom, for Louise never regarded herself as an ordinary mistress.[9] As tradition demanded, Louise was laid out in the bed, her garters loosened with customary ribaldry from those standing around, and sack-posset drunk – the sack to make the groom lusty, and the sugar to make him kind. Then Charles slipped into bed and took Louise in his arms in a night of passion. Nine months later (19 July 1672) their son, Charles Lennox, was born. He would take the title of the Duke of Richmond, left vacant by the death of Frances Stuart's husband. He would become ADC to William III and sire a line of high-ranking and distinguished military officers.

The night's seduction was the talk of the court. Evelyn, who was a house guest at the time but too much of a prude to take part in the ceremony, recorded the occasion for posterity:

> It was universally reported that the fair lady was bedded one of these nights,

and the stocking flung, after the manner of a married bride. She was for the most part in her undress all day and there was fondness and toying with that young wanton. It was confidently believed she was first made *a Miss,* as they call these unhappy creatures, with solemnity at this time.[10]

De Croissy reported to the delighted Louis that he had made Louise joyful in assuring her of the pleasure with which the French King had learned of her brilliant conquest. There was every prospect that she would long hold what she had conquered. To show his delight, Louis XIV sent the chief procuress, Lady Arlington, a valuable diamond necklace and £10,000 for her part in the seduction. Saint Evremond predicted that the silk ribbon which girded the waist of Louise de Keroualle had bound England to France. Thus two monarchs, an ambassador and a great minister of state combined with two scheming women to push a reluctant virgin into a royal bed.[11]

Soon Louise was recognised as the *maîtresse en titre,* and the two kings would heap titles and riches on her. Charles was beginning a special relationship which only ended on his death-bed: 'I have always loved her,' he was to whisper, 'and I die loving her.'[12] He loved her for her beauty, her ruffled curls, her languorous eyes, and the exhausted pout of her lips after a night of passion. She studied to please and observe him in everything, so he passed the rest of his life in a great fondness for her, wrote Burnet.[13]

Although she would remain first in his affections, that did not mean he would be faithful to her. Charles found it was as hard to discard old mistresses as it was easy to acquire a new one. In addition to his old favourites, Barbara Castlemaine, Nell Gwynn and Frances Stuart, Louise would have to learn to compete with other rivals. This was especially true of the redoubtable Hortense Mancini, youngest of the nieces of France's Cardinal Mazarin, acclaimed the most beautiful woman of her age. Louise discovered that her languid grace, her airs of weakness and her French refinement were not enough to disarm the crafty statesmen, jealous favourites and lascivious women about the King.[14]

'Poor Castlemaine is turned off,' wrote Madame de Sévigny to her daughter on 30 March 1674. 'Such is the fate of mistresses in that kingdom.' The contrast between the Duchess of Cleveland and the new favourite was striking. Barbara was a nymphomaniac, used to giving pleasure to her lovers, openly unfaithful and of a fiery temper. Her appeal was sensual and physical. Louise, on the other hand, learned to understand the King and his moods, and his need for a happy, uncomplicated domestic life. Her mental abilities, refinement and love of the beautiful in art and music appealed to Charles as much as her considerable physical charms and the exciting bed and excellent table she provided for him. She could not participate in his interest in the theatre – partly because of her poor knowledge of English, but also because she was revolted by the indelicacy and coarseness of the stage.

Both Barbara and Louise shared one thing in common, though – their insatiable ambition to acquire riches and honours. Louise proved even more costly to maintain than Barbara. She would receive grants and bribes from ministers, like Shaftesbury and Danby, as well as from ambassadors anxious to use her influence with the King. She had income from revenue, annuities from excise duties, and enormous sums from the King. In 1681, for instance, £136,000 passed through her hands. The sums spent by the King upon other women, though vast, were comparatively meagre, wrote Burnet.[15] Evelyn, in 1675, noted that her splendid apartments in Whitehall, which increasingly became for the King a quiet meeting place for his friends and himself to relax, were ten times more luxuriously furnished than the Queen's at Somerset House (where she lived from 1675). They were the wages of a wanton, according to Forneron.[16]

As the King's ardour increased, so did Louise's confidence in her political skills. She proved a born political schemer, intelligent and charming, for she had been well-schooled at the court of the Duchess of Orleans in the arts of patience, endurance and dissimulation. Those who had dangled this nubile beauty before the susceptible King had hoped to use her to their political advantage. But this most absolute of all the King's mistresses found Charles was his own master, while all around her valets turned into traitors, chaperones into procuresses, statesmen into fools or brutes.[17]

Louise had to live against a backcloth of deceit, bribery and intrigue. Arlington was soon complaining to the French ambassador of her ingratitude to him for the many obligations he had conferred on her. Shaftesbury tried to bribe her to get Charles to declare Monmouth his heir. Louise would herself claim that it was she who made Halifax an earl, and that Sunderland and Judge Jeffreys owed their rapid promotions to her recommendations to the King. Lord Latimer, Danby's eldest son, was admitted to the royal bedchamber through her influence. 'Nobody shall come to Court or to any preferment but those who will be my creatures,' she claimed. 'The King of England has promised to support me and I am allied to most of the sovereign princes abroad.'[18]

Louis XIV early tried to capitalise on Louise's influence with Charles, and was kept well informed by his ambassadors of her activities. He realised she was well placed to help France's interests in three political areas – an alliance against Holland, a profession of the Catholic faith by Charles, and a marriage between the Duke of York (whose wife, Anne Hyde, had recently died) and a princess of Louis XIV's choice. She would play a part in these affairs and be rewarded by Louis with gifts of money, land and titles in France. He corresponded with her as *'Ma chère Cousine'*.

But increasingly self-interest and the interests of her royal lover outweighed her patriotism, and she acted less as an intermediary between the two monarchs. As for Charles, he ceased to interview his ministers, the French ambassador and the leading courtiers in the Queen's suite, using Louise's apartments instead. As Halifax put it, her chamber was the true Cabinet Council.[19] There she organised little supper parties, followed by 'a gay and unconfined revel, when tongues were loosened and gossip flowed'. She flattered Charles through his love of luxury and music and, in these comfortable surroundings, she observed the schemes and motives of those who attended him.

She was deeply unpopular in England because she was French and a Catholic, planted in Charles's bed, the people believed, as a covert spy to ensnare the King and to subjugate their country to French interests.[20] Despite her aristocratic birth and refined manners, she was constantly reminded by the populace and Nell Gwynn that she was 'nothing but a whore'. Lady Sunderland, who had helped to undress her for the mock wedding, called her an abominable harlot. One of her enemies pinned a note to her bedroom door –

> Within this place a bed's appointed
> For a French bitch and God's anointed.

Nell and Louise shared the King's favours and were rivals at court. The King divided his care, his time and his health between these two, wrote the Marchioness de Sévigny in 1675. The actress was as haughty as Mademoiselle: she insulted her, she attacked her, she frequently stole the King from her, and boasted whenever he gave her the preference.[21] Nell told the King that Parliament had recently passed an Act to ban useless foreign commodities prejudicial to the expansion of British trade, and that its provisions to condemn and burn such commodities should be applied to the latest French importation!

The poet Andrew Marvell, son of a Yorkshire clergyman and a great favourite of Charles, also attacked the King and his court and blamed their excesses on Louise -

> But his fair soul, transformed by that French dame,
> Had lost all sense of honour, justice, fame.
> Like a tame spider in his web he sits,
> Besieged by whores, buffoons and bastard chits.
> Lulled in security, rolling in lust,
> Resigns his crown to Angel Carwell's trust.[22]

[The English could not pronounce Keroualle, so they called her Madame Carwell.]

Pamphleteers had a field day: one sent a humble address to the King's Ladies of Pleasure from their Lowly Sisters -

> We, your Majesty's most loyal and dutiful subjects, the Ladies of Pleasure in the several seraglios of Moorfields etc and the various stews in and about the virtuous Palace of Westminster and the Cities of London and Westminster, thank the King for the many blessings they had reaped, under his easy government, from the playhouses, masques, balls, Hyde Park and St James's night revels, publicly recommended and honoured by your Majesty's presence, and for the great licence and privilege we have enjoyed under your Majesty's Justices of the Peace, no ways inferior to those of the ladies of Rome or Venice.

They assured the King they did not resent the honours and great titles given to some of their profession, but humbly requested him to accept their zeal, which they would continue to express 'as long as we are able to wag our tails from the hands of our chiefs, Louise de Keroualle and Nell Gwynn . . . whom we have prevailed with to present this address.'[23]

In 1671, while Charles was engaged in seducing Louise, Anne Hyde, the Duke of York's wife, died of cancer without producing a male heir to survive infancy. James's partiality for extra-marital affairs did not discourage him from wanting to marry again. There was now little possibility that Queen Catherine would produce an heir, and James's only surviving children were Mary and Anne, so the choice of a new bride was of vital importance to the royal line.

While a search was being made for a suitable candidate among the German, French and Italians proposed, he fell in love with Lady Susan Belasyse, a vivacious but scheming 17-year-old widow, to whom he promised marriage. This time Charles would have none of it. 'It was too much that he had played the fool once: that was not to be done a second time and at such an age,' recorded Bishop Burnet.[24] James sighed as a lover and promised the King to obey as a subject. All the belles of the court dressed themselves in their precious stones and other finery to make a conquest of the heir presumptive to the throne. The beauty and wealth of Elizabeth, Duchess of Northumberland, made her a worthy competitor; while Lady Falmouth, another fashionable widow, was highly commended.

De Croissy reported to his master that the Duke would rather take a French princess, to whom Louis might give a dowry. Louis replied that if the Duke of York wanted a wife who was almost certain to bear him children, he could not do better than take Madame de Guise (a widow related to Louis), who had laid in three times in two years, and whose birth, wealth and hopes of fecundity should make up for her want of beauty.[25]

Louise, like the French king, had her own candidates: either of the two

French daughters of the Duchess d'Elbeuf, an old friend of hers at the court of the Duchess of Orléans. If her candidate were successful, the new English Queen would thus be under an obligation to her. But the two girls, nieces of Turenne, were only 14 and 15 years old; the Duke of York (surprisingly, considering his final choice) found them too immature. Louise then suggested either of the two Italian princesses of Modena. The 15-year-old Mary Beatrice had been considered as second wife for the King of France's brother Philip, Duke of Orléans, on the death of Henrietta; or there was her 30-year-old aunt, Leonora d'Este.[26]

The 42-year-old Duke of York, who, whatever he looked for in his mistresses, was determined to have beauty in his second wife, hesitated, for both had their attractions. Charles gave as his advice that 'beauty contributes nothing to, and takes nothing from, the happiness of a marriage'. Eventually he chose the younger Mary – not just because of her beauty, slender figure and tender age, said James, but because she was likely to be the more fruitful. Charles agreed with Louise's Italian choice, but Louis XIV, who finally gave his approval and a marriage dowry of £90,000, was furious at Louise's ill-disposition to the service of France, largely to heighten her own credit. The bride-to-be wept, and asked to be allowed to enter a convent in Modena rather than marry a man 27 years older than herself, but eventually submitted 'to her noble task'. She was married by proxy on 30 September 1673, before coming to England some months later. Henry Mordaunt, the Earl of Peterborough, who had helped to negotiate the marriage, stood as James's proxy.

Parliament, naturally, wanted to stop this marriage to a 'daughter of the Pope'[27] before it could be consummated, while others argued that England did not lack beautiful girls. James's mistresses, who were generally Protestants, were tolerated without much fuss: it was his marriages which caused controversy. All blamed this 'Carwell', who must have seduced the King by devil's wiles. When the child-bride arrived in Dover, in tears, James claimed she was married and bedded that same night. When he introduced their new stepmother to his daughters, Mary and Anne, there was less than four years between the two Marys, and he said, 'I have brought you a new playmate'.[28]

Despite the prejudices against her religion, Mary's sweetness and courtesy soon won all hearts at court. She grew up into a strikingly beautiful woman, one of England's more beautiful Queens. Tall and with an exquisite figure, she would prove very loyal and, unusual in those times, faithful to her husband despite his continuing infidelities.[29] The new Duchess of York knew of her husband's attachment to Arabella Churchill (and would know even better her successor, Catherine Sedley), who gave birth to yet another healthy child. Mary, despite a number of pregnancies, was destined not to produce a male successor.[30] She would prove a strong supporter of her husband's Catholic policies and become the centre of an inner group of Catholic and Francophile ministers. Her love and companionship would be a great comfort to James in the tribulations which lay ahead.

Another worry at this time was the King's health. He had lately suffered three apoplectic fits and people blamed his over-indulgence in sex. Even Louise had to beg her lover to refrain from visiting her at night for the time being.

Louise still pursued her own personal ambitions with him. As long as she had no title, her enemies could sneer at her and her son's bastardy. She felt affronted that Barbara Castlemaine should be given precedence over her, considering her as nothing but a royal courtesan. In August 1673, at Louis XIV's request, she was naturalised as an English subject, so that Charles could create her Duchess of Portsmouth. He also appointed her lady of the bedchamber to the Queen, granted her an annuity of £10,000 out of wine licences, and endowed her younger sister, Henrietta, on her marriage to the seventh Earl of Pembroke.

This period saw a great expansion of honours awarded to the 'unofficial' royal family. In 1674 the King created his third son by Barbara, George Fitzroy, Earl of Northumberland (Duke in 1678); Charles Fitzcharles, his son by Catherine Pegge (wife of the baronet Sir Edward Green) and known as Don Carlos, became the Earl of Plymouth. A year later, yielding to the importunities of Louise and Barbara, Charles raised his son by the former (Charles Lennox) and his first two sons by the latter (Charles and Henry Fitzroy) to equal rank with the Duke of Monmouth: they became the Dukes of Richmond, Southampton and Grafton respectively. In 1676 the elder of Nell's two sons was made Duke of St Albans and the younger Lord Beauclerck.

Nor were the royal daughters forgotten. The wedding of the year 1674 was that of Anne Fitzroy, Barbara's first-born, to Lord Dacre at Hampton Court, where the guests feasted and strolled amongst the newly completed gardens, fountains and cascades. The bride received £20,000 and the groom was made Earl of Sussex. Barbara's other daughter, Charlotte, married the Earl of Lichfield; while Mary Tudor, the daughter of Moll Davis, married the Earl of Derwentwater. Altogether, Charles created six dukedoms and one earldom for his illegitimate sons and four of his daughters became countesses.

In return for Louise's services as an agent of France, Louis XIV, who looked upon her as a vital link in the chain binding the two countries together, ennobled her Duchess of Aubigny with estates in France – despite her failure to persuade Charles to declare himself a Catholic. Charles decided this was not the right time – a decision Louise dutifully passed on to de Croissy. But there still remained the third of Louis XIV's objectives to be pursued – war with Holland!

17

Men and Women At War

The last 10 years of Charles's reign is the story of the King's struggle to resist the flood of suspicion and hostility which his dream of a French alliance, culminating in the secret Treaty of Dover, had released against him. For the first four years this flood grew, until it burst its banks and almost overwhelmed the monarchy in the torrent of hatred and terror, called the Popish Plot. Then Charles, with consummate skill, fought against the pent-up waves of angry national feeling to find himself, during the final years of his reign, at peace with his people and wielding a power possessed by no other Stuart.[1]

Following the Treaty of Dover, Holland had been successfully isolated; but before England dare declare war against the Dutch, it had to solve its bankruptcy problems. When the Cabal of ministers met on 2 January 1672, it faced a government indebtedness to its bankers of nearly £2,500,000, with the coming year's revenue already assigned to them. Money was urgently needed to muster, arm and supply the fleet, but since the Restoration expenditure had exceeded income annually by over £400,000. An additional £660,000 over three years had been voted to the King by Parliament, but this had failed to bridge the gap. The Cabal therefore suspended all payments to bankers for a year, hoping to liquidate the debt in better times. It also negotiated an interest rate of six per cent on new loans, instead of the usurious rates previously in force.

The result was that £750,000 was made available for the fleet, and Charles could fulfil his promise to Louis to make war on Holland. Before the end of the month a dozen waggons, guarded by a troop of cavalry, were winding their way through the narrow streets of Rye bound for London, loaded with the first instalment of the promised French war subsidy. Within days Charles officially declared war on Holland (17 March 1672), and Louis XIV followed suit a month later. The overt part of the Treaty of Dover had been fulfilled. The declaration of war was popular in England for its attack on Dutch commercial wealth. But all Protestant hearts trembled at the sight of a Catholic king setting

out with a force of over 100,000 to attack Flanders and the heavily outnumbered army (some 30,000) of the leader of Protestantism in Europe.[2]

With Louis's money in the Navy Board's coffers to secure the country's first
line of defence, Charles was able to station two men-of-war as colonial guard-
ships in the Chesapeake Bay throughout the Anglo–Dutch conflict of 1672–4.
The tobacco fleet could be met as far south-west as the Azores, and given full
protection until it made port in England. Escorts could be provided for the
spring fishing fleet of up to 500 craft outward bound for the Grand Banks of
Newfoundland and more escorts for their autumn return, with the fleet's holds
crammed with salted cod for the Catholic countries of Europe.[3]

'War is a series of surprises,' wrote Fisher.[4] By the laws of probability, the
navies of England and armies of France should have made short work of the
small Dutch republic; but the expected did not happen. The Dutch, faced by
Europe's finest army, commanded by the century's greatest generals, appointed William of Orange to command their forces, and opened their dykes to
flood the land in front of their invaders, compelling them to withdraw.

Charles had been left by Louis to fight the war at sea, for which he raised a
special marine regiment solely for service at sea and placed it under the command of Prince Rupert. This unit would supplement the Admiral's Regiment
(The Duke of York and Albany's) and the companies customarily drawn from
infantry regiments to man the fleet. The Dutch proved successful in prevent-
ing the English force from landing; Pepys's old patron, Edward Mountagu, the
Earl of Sandwich, was killed on his flagship, the *Royal James*, in the opening
battle in Sole Bay. The King rewarded his admiral of the fleet, who had
brought him back from exile, with a similar state funeral to that received by
Albemarle.

The Third Dutch War, which dragged on from 1672 to 1680, proved incon-
clusive. In 1674 public opinion, largely Protestant and anti-French, together
with both Houses of Parliament (won over by Dutch bribes and the intrigues
of William of Orange) forced Charles to make a separate peace by the Treaty
of Westminster. Louis XIV, angry with Charles for having broken his Dover
obligations, was left to carry on the war against Holland alone – which proved
much to England's maritime advantage.

Charles, an accomplished diplomat, was quick to seize the advantage. He
had concluded the triple alliance with Holland and Sweden in 1668 while
secretly negotiating the Treaty of Dover. Now he excused his duplicity by
blandly assuring his French ally that he had been forced to sue for a separate
peace only because of lack of money. He offered to act as a neutral mediator
between France and Holland; but showed his partiality by allowing his English
troops to remain in French service, and permitting Louis to recruit in Scotland
and Ireland. He constantly furnished Louis with ammunition, while refusing
these same facilities to William. Thus, concludes Burnet,[5] Charles got out of

the war with very little to his credit at home or abroad. England emerged without loss of territory, but the gains were hardly worth the expenditure of £6,000,000 and the sacrifice of thousands of lives. Within a year Charles had completed another secret alliance with Louis in return for more French subsidies; but between 1674 and 1677 the country became increasingly pro-Dutch.

Charles's finances were, in truth, in their usual state of disarray, and it needed a strong Lord High Treasurer to put them on a sound footing. Fortunately, the King found such a man in Thomas Osborne, Earl of Danby (later Duke of Leeds), whom he promoted to the post. Danby's father had been lieutenant-general of the Royalist forces raised in York during the Civil War, and Danby himself was a Yorkshireman: hard, efficient and a capable financial administrator. In keeping with the moral standards of the times, he sought to control Parliament by bribery and to increase his own wealth by a private trade in offices.[6] Charles never liked him very much, but recognised and used his ability. Danby, unaware of the secret provisions of the Treaty of Dover, pursued a pro-Anglican, pro-Dutch policy, and gradually replaced Arlington in the King's confidence. (Danby married off his daughter to the Earl of Plymouth in 1678, thus following the precedents of Clarendon and Arlington in attaching his family to the royal house.)

Helped by favourable trade balances, Danby was able to raise the royal revenues considerably. He made budget savings by disbanding the new regiments in an army which in February 1674 numbered some 19,000 officers and men, reducing it to its peacetime establishment of 6,000 men. Naval expenditure was similarly cut, and he reduced the profits of contractors supplying services to the forces. Above all, he managed to reduce the expenditure of the royal household and privy purse, despite the large sums Charles continued to spend on his mistresses and their children – Portsmouth, Cleveland, Nell Gwynn and later Hortense Mancini – bolstered by large grants from France paid into the secret service account (the source of much of the money lavished on his ladies).[7]

Burnet also mentions the revenue from Ireland, which was paid into the King's private purse, as a source of funds for the King's favourites. Phoenix Park, Dublin, for example, was only saved from becoming a gift by Charles to the Duchess of Cleveland (Barbara Castlemaine) because alternative estates were found to bestow on her. The jewels of the Duchess of Northumberland, coveted by Louise de Keroualle and purchased for her by Charles at a cost of £4,000, were paid for by the King from the Irish exchequer.[8]

Danby, despite his anti-French sympathies, was wise enough to cultivate the friendship of the reigning mistress, the Duchess of Portsmouth, and she became his close ally. But even he could not prevent the King from spending large sums of money on his building projects at Windsor, his palace at Greenwich, and St Paul's Cathedral. While Danby and Parliament pressed

Charles to declare war on France, the King was able to continue pleading lack of money, especially for his navy, and so remain neutral, with the help of French subsidies, thus allowing France to pursue its war on Holland.

Meanwhile, Charles was faced with problems on the other side of the Atlantic. In 1675 an insurrection broke out in Virginia, the first serious rebellion in North American history. The oldest (and once considered the most loyal and English) of the Plantations, Virginia was founded in 1607 by a group of stock-holders hoping to convert Indians, locate gold and discover the North-West Passage to Cathay. In addition, they hoped to produce all the commodities of Europe, Africa and Asia. Instead, as Indian massacres and disease took their toll, it declined into a place of poverty and discontent, and disappointed its patrons commercially for the first 20 years. The Jamestown settlement failed to prosper, despite the faith and military discipline of the men, who 'twice a day were marched into the fields by beat of drum or into the forests to cut wood, and twice a day marched back to Jamestown to eat and pray.'[9]

The colony was saved by tobacco, which, despite James I's condemnation of smoking as 'a custome lothsome to the eye, hatefull to the Nose, harmfull to the braine, dangerous to the lungs and in the blacke stinking fume thereof, nearest resembling the horrible Stigian smoke of the pit that is bottomlesse', became popular in Europe. It also helped to provide the colony with 'young and uncorrupted maids', and women from Newgate and Bridewell 'as many as can be spared' who were recruited and shipped out by the company to Jamestown, where a planter who wanted a wife paid the company 150 pounds of best tobacco leaf for a girl. Every lass promptly found a husband and every married couple had the right to build a house for themselves, while the bach-elors continued to bunk in barracks.

The early colonists were joined by volunteers, discontented with their lot at home. Poor men even undertook years of servitude to pay for their passage, hoping to be rewarded with free land. To supplement the volunteers, trans-portation was developed as a means of disposing of vagrants, felons and even unwanted children. Directions for justices of the peace published in 1664 state that 'such prisoners as are reprieved to be transported be not sent away as per-petual slaves but upon indentures for a term of seven or fourteen years.' Defoe's Moll Flanders was one such victim.[10]

In 1668 tobacco prices dropped to rock bottom. The governor of Virginia, Sir William Berkeley, had been reappointed by Charles II after being forced to resign during the Commonwealth for having offered asylum in the colony to gentlemen of the Royalist side.[11] Now he had to face the anger of the planters, burdened with a succession of bad crops and high taxes and frightened by Indian attacks on their farms. They chose Nathaniel Bacon, a young English lawyer from Gray's Inn, whose estates were especially exposed to Indian raids, to co-ordinate their resistance. Elected their general, he led a military force of rebel volunteers against a peaceful Indian tribe, slaughtered them, and captured Jamestown. Unable to garrison it, he burnt it to the ground. Berkeley called out the loyal militia, and civil war began.

As there were no regular soldiers in the colony, Charles sent out a fleet with an armed force from England to support the governor. The Foot Guards between them provided a nucleus of 425 officers and men, with additional contingents from the Lord Admiral's Regiment (Marines), the Buffs (Third Foot) and the King's Regiment. Commanding the force was Colonel Herbert Jeffreys of the First Foot Guards (the Grenadiers), an experienced professional officer who had vigourously suppressed a number of civil upheavals in Portsmouth, York, Leeds and London. By the time the force arrived in January 1677, Bacon had died, the rebellion had collapsed, and Berkeley had summarily executed 23 of the leaders for treason. The English force promptly returned to Deal, having lost half their number from disease, since Parliament believed the colonies should finance their own protection. They had to rely on locally enlisted militia, which prior to 1680 consisted of adult male colonists between the ages of 17 and 60 serving on a part-time basis.

In any case the colonies were a royal responsibility and for Charles, in his usual financial difficulties, military expeditions, even in emergencies, were costly and the achievements hardly commensurate with the expenditure. Military administration was inept and bungling; in the midst stood the common soldier, who fell between King and Parliament, and received no pay, no clothes, and little or no food. But through 25 years of colonial service under Charles the soldiers did not mutiny or rebel, but simply accepted their lot.[12]

At the end of 1675, Louise had to withstand one more emotional onslaught in a grave threat to her position as the King's official mistress. Hortense Mancini burst on the London scene, one of the most beautiful and intelligent women of the era. She was the loveliest of a famous constellation of five beautiful nieces of the great cardinal Mazarin, and was related to James's new wife, Mary of Modena. Hortense rode into Whitehall on horseback, dressed as a man of fashion, accompanied by five male servants and a little blackamoor, who ate at her table.[13] She had been invited by Ralph Montagu, the English ambassador in France, who had been plotting with Buckingham and Arlington during the winter of 1675-6 to engineer the downfall of Danby and the French favourite. It was intended that Hortense should supplant Louise in the King's affections.

During his exile Charles had fallen passionately in love with Hortense and had asked for her hand in marriage. Cardinal Mazarin (who practically governed France while Louis XIV was a minor) had little faith in Charles's ability to regain his throne, so the 16-year-old heiress to his vast fortune was married off instead to the Grand Master of Louis's artillery, whom the cardinal ordered to adopt his name.

Duke Mazarin, twice the age of Hortense, was a prude and religious bigot who became increasingly jealous of everybody around his beautiful wife. He removed her from court, kept her travelling around Europe regardless of her health, and locked her up in a convent for the good of her soul. Between frequent journeys around her husband's numerous estates, court balls and forced penances in convent retreats, she bore him four children in the seven years she lived with him. In his prudery, he forbade the women on his estates to milk cows lest they succumbed to indecent thoughts, and defaced his priceless paintings by Titian and Corregio because they contained naked figures.[14]

Hortense, growing tired of his eccentricities and treatment of her, escaped from his clutches. Her subsequent escapades became legendary, as she rode across Europe dressed in masculine garb, snapping her fingers at king, judge and church amid the complaints of deceived wives, the curses of unpaid innkeepers and the amorous attention of both men and women.[15] 'Each sex provides its lovers for Hortense', wrote her friend and adviser Saint Evremond[16] (who had settled in London with a pension from Charles as governor of the ducks in St James's Park). The English court greeted her with warm curiosity – the men with admiration for her beauty, the women with jealousy of her romantic and adventurous past, but all with uneasiness, wrote the current French ambassador and distinguished soldier, Ruvigny, when alerting his master to the new situation.[17]

No one was more uneasy than Louise, now heavily pregnant and aware that her enemies were already rejoicing at her imminent downfall after a reign of six years. Nell Gwynn went into mourning in memory of the Duchess of Portsmouth, 'now dead to the Court', and the Duchess of Cleveland departed for Paris, leaving the field clear. The Duchess of York welcomed her cousin, Hortense, to Whitehall and lodged her in her apartments, where Charles was able to spend hours with Hortense under the pretext of visiting his sister-in-law during her confinement.

In 1676 Louis XIV replaced Henri de Ruvigny (son of the 1667 ambassador) as ambassador with Antoine de Courtin, who was far more suited by nature to deal with petticoat diplomacy.[18] He was instructed to treat Louise with the utmost respect, given £80,000 for bribes, and asked to find out the intentions of the Duchess Mazarin, 'who may use against France the credit, which her beauty gives her with the King of England'. The key was money, according to Courtin: if Louis did not force the deserted Duke Mazarin to send Hortense's jewels to her and increase her allowance, she would be obliged to procure money in England. She would resent this, and thus probably act against French interests if she became Charles's acknowledged mistress – which seemed a strong possibility.[19]

At 30, Hortense was a good deal older than Charles's usual concubines when they first made his acquaintance, but to the attractions of her Junoesque figure she added the allure of a passionate and reckless nature, and sexual expertise gained from lovers of both sexes. She had associated with many of the brightest intellects of France and Italy. Soon Charles had lodged her at St James's Palace, and most nights he would go through the official ceremony of retiring in the bedchamber and then steal across the park to spend the rest of the night with Hortense.[20]

All this gossip amused the King of France, but he was alarmed at the prospect of Louise being superseded. She was the chain by which he had bound the volatile Charles to him, and her downfall would inevitably mean those opposed to France coming into power.[21] Despite his military successes Louis had grown tired of waging war on Holland by himself, and was attempting to negotiate peace terms at the Congress of Nymwegen: at all costs the Dutch plenipotentiaries must not be deterred from concluding peace with France. He instructed his representatives at the congress to keep up the pretence that the Duchess of Portsmouth was in the best of health, and still the reigning mistress, with the ability to support French policies with the King of England. Soon, improved in health after a visit to the hot springs at Bath, Louise resumed her former role at court, entertained widely, and put on a brave front, despite her tears in private.

Charles hated domestic storms, preferring instead a gay but uncomplicated love life. With Courtin's help, Louise and Hortense called a truce to their rivalries, and were soon meeting and dining together to form a harmonious group around the King.[22] By 1677, Hortense was receiving large sums of money from both France and Charles; Charles, for instance, granted her a pension of £4,000 a year, causing an outburst from Andrew Marvell:

> That the King should send for another French whore
> When one already had made him so poor.

Although her physical charms appealed to Charles enormously, he told Courtin that he would not allow politicians to work on him through women like Hortense. But the opinions of his mistresses certainly carried some weight for all this, particularly at times when his mind was divided. As for Hortense herself, she was devoid of political ambition, and uninterested in the buying and selling of honours and offices at which Louise was so adept. She was not the material from which successful mistresses are made: she stayed on at court for some while, available to Charles from time to time, but she was merely a butterfly, beneath the notice of ministers and ambassadors, and no longer of interest to French diplomacy.

Finally, after creating a scandal by her passionate friendship with the youthful Anne, Countess of Sussex (one of Charles's two daughters by Barbara Castlemaine, married to a brutal husband), and a prolonged and public flirtation with the handsome Prince of Monaco, Hortense disappeared from the English scene to seek pastures new. Much to the fury of Nell, the 'weeping willow' Louise became the favourite concubine again. Her influence was needed by both Charles and Louis XIV, as Buckingham and Arlington deserted the French cause and joined Shaftesbury's faction, which was hostile to the King and court. Anti-French feeling was growing: war with France seemed increasingly inevitable, and Charles's throne itself looked in danger of toppling.

18

The Champion of Protestant Europe

On 14 February 1677 Charles opened the fifteenth session of the Cavalier Parliament with his customary appeal for money for ships, and an offer to pass Bills to secure religion, liberty and property. French successes on the Continent had alarmed both Houses: the people hated France and all things French. Led by Danby, the nation was drifting to war with France. Only Charles hesitated.

At the same time Courtin was complaining to Louis:

> England hates us more and more. The soldier, the sailor and the civilian but particularly the middle and lower classes are imbued with hatred for France, despite the Court and the courtiers following the fashions of Paris and Versailles.[1]

The following month (March 1677) he wrote that if Parliament were as tractable as the ladies, whose hate nevertheless was usually implacable enough in this country, he would not despair of winning England over. Courtin distributed bribes in the House of Lords, but told Louis that similar methods in the House of Commons were a useless waste and very unwise, because in these people hatred of France had almost reached a state of rage. They did not want the King of France to rule over the Low Countries. He asked instead for cases of champagne and liqueurs.

> When a session of Parliament ends, people go to dine at each other's houses and a few bottles of wine sent at the right moment smooth the temper. That is when factions are formed.[2]

Unknown to Parliament, Louis and Charles had signed a secret treaty on 16 February 1676, agreeing not to conclude separate peace treaties with the

Netherlands. MPs presented an address to Charles pointing out the danger to England from the growing power of France, and the need to strengthen England's position by suitable alliances to bring help to the Low Countries. Charles promptly adjourned Parliament, claiming they were attacking his royal prerogative to make peace or war as he thought fit. He told Courtin:

> I am compromising myself with my own people because of my love of the King, your master. I am resolved to keep my pledged word but I urge him to help me a little and to make peace before the winter.

Charles desperately needed money though, and seriously thought of recalling his hostile Parliament. Louise recruited Lauderdale and Sunderland to encourage him to hold out against Parliament, and tried to stiffen his resolve by reminding him of Louis's past kindnesses and his quarterly payments of French gold. Lauderdale, responsible for Scottish affairs, was the only minister privy to the King's secret treaty with France and was high in Charles's favour; Sunderland was one of the rising generation, who would dominate the political scene in the last years of the King's life.

In August 1677, Louis showed his appreciation of Charles's stand by agreeing to pay a £40,000 subsidy, and then £80,000 per annum, in exchange for England's neutrality. This left France free to lay waste to Holland and impoverish herself by war, while English ships gradually monopolised world sea trade. The Low Countries never recovered from the blow.[3]

In May 1677, Paul Barrillon, Marquis de Branges, replaced Antoine Courtin as French ambassador and would continue as such until the end of Charles's reign.[4] Barrillon, who came from a legal family, was a master in the art of corrupting men while showing a smiling face to those whom he ruined.[5] He lacked the finesse and courtesy of Courtin. Louis instructed him to support Louise's role in the English court and make use of her friendly relations with Danby in the interests of France. But Barrillon made Louise feel herself under compulsion to receive him at almost any hour of the day and night, in the service of the French King; she felt that he revealed every detail of her private life to the French court, and used her as a mere instrument for his own ends.

Above all, Barrillon displayed the talents of an accountant, discussing with Chiffinch and other go-betweens the amounts of bribes to be distributed among politicians. He made valuations of consciences and drew up price-lists of men.[6] Many prominent politicians were on his payroll: the short Parliamentary session of February 1677, for instance, cost him £3,000 in bribes alone. Chiffinch drew the sums from the French embassy to pay the recipients, leaving his wife to pay 'occasional mistresses and lesser concubines' the sum of £50 each for mounting the backstairs at Whitehall.[7]

Treasury records show that during this period Louise received a total of £36,000 in royal gifts, and Nell £8,000. The amounts probably reflected the difference in their formal status, for Louise was now a Duchess and Nell, born a commoner, went untitled (although it was rumoured that Charles intended to create her a countess). It has been estimated that Louise, the most expensive of Charles's mistresses, cost the nation about £40,000 per year with her pension and presents – apart from the large sums of money she received from France.

By providing large credits to Barrillon, Louis hoped to ward off his most pressing danger – an Anglo–Dutch alliance based upon the marriage of William of Orange to James's elder daughter, Mary. William, now 27, had long desired to split England from France. He arrived in London unexpectedly in October 1677 and, while staying with his uncles at Newmarket, formally asked for the hand of princess Mary, an attractive girl of only 15. He settled down to talks with Charles and the Duke of York, and with Lord Danby and Sir William Temple, the English ambassador at the Hague, who both favoured the match. After much haggling over the peace terms, William got his way. Charles's advisers persuaded him that if William left without a satisfactory peace settlement, the King would lose his role as mediator between France and Holland, and with it Parliamentary support. The people greeted William with enthusiasm as their possible next sovereign, and the incarnation of Protestant resistance to Catholicism and French domination of Europe.[8]

Neither Charles nor James felt strong enough to withstand the nation's outbreak of patriotic and religious fervour. Charles told his brother he wanted the marriage immediately: James reluctantly agreed, and Mary wept for 18 hours. Barrillon alerted his master to the danger, telling him that the only friends of France in England were Charles and the Duke of York. Barrillon suggested that it might be the wisest course to accept the inevitable and congratulate William on the success of his suit. But already it was too late.

The Privy Council, English and Scottish people received the news with enthusiasm and the usual bonfires and ringing of bells. The wedding was celebrated on Mary's birthday on 4 November in her bedchamber in St James's Palace. As Charles closed the curtains of the bridal bed, he exhorted his nephew to get to work – for England and St George! Louis was not amused. He considered Charles's exhortation a poor return for his many subsidies.

Louise, to whom the Prince of Orange had paid careful respect on his return to Whitehall, felt, through her keen political instinct, that William would achieve what he wanted and supported him. Once again she acted in her own interests and not those of Louis XIV. Louis was naturally angry with Charles and the Duke of York, who had now given his daughter to the greatest enemy Louis had in the world, and stopped Charles's subsidy.[9] He continued to support Louise as his agent, despite her lapse, Barrillon reporting that 'the leading courtiers keep close to the Duchess of Portsmouth'. Louis's anger fell instead on Danby, whom he blamed as the architect of the plan.

The Dutch and the English hurriedly concluded a treaty on 31 December 1677, and Charles made preparations for war against France. Louis launched a new campaign and successively invested Ypres, Brussels, Namur, Luxembourg and Ghent. Ostend was granted to England as an advance base for an expeditionary force of 11,000 foot and 1,000 horse to fight alongside the Dutch and Spanish, and protect the Low Countries from French depredations.[10]

Whereas the Dutch wars had been largely naval, Charles now needed a much bigger army for a land war against France. Danby had given a large number of army commissions to MPs to ensure the army subsidies were passed, so in February 1678 the House of Commons voted him an estimated £1 million to pursue the war. Charles immediately commissioned 15 new regiments of foot, four of cavalry and three of dragoons; within weeks 25,000 men were under arms, with a fleet of 90 ships at sea.[11] Under Monmouth as commander in chief, 14 of these regiments were rushed to Flanders to support the Prince of Orange. But before they were engaged in action, the peace treaty allowed them to return home.

In May Parliament refused the King any more money to maintain the army and Charles, on the brink of war with Louis and no longer neutral, lost his subsidy from France. Not for the last time in English history would a Parliamentary opposition clamour for war while parsimoniously denying the government the means to wage it! The Third Dutch War, which had promised to be so short in 1672, had dragged on for six years. France had captured a chain of towns to secure its north-eastern frontier, and London feared invasion. On 31 July 1678 the Dutch made a separate peace at Nymwegen, which saw France at the height of its power, Spain weak, Germany divided and England left abandoned.

To the English people the rivalry with Protestant Holland seemed less formidable than the new military and commercial power of Catholic France. Absorbed at home in religious and political strife, England's interests overseas were concerned with extending her maritime empire and possessions in the New World. Charles now became increasingly on the defensive to save his throne and his brother's succession, while Parliament demanded the reduction of the army to its pre-1665 size. Charles bowed before the storm: the new regiments were disbanded, leaving only the standing army remaining. The Prince of Orange, with hatred in his heart, was left dreaming of revenge against France, even before the ink was dry on the Treaty of Nymwegen.[12]

19

The Popish Plot and Exclusion Crisis

Some truth there was, but dashed and brewed with lies,
To please the fools and puzzle all the wise.

So wrote the Poet Laureate, John Dryden[1]

One day in August 1678, Charles was taking his customary morning walk in St James's Park, when a man employed as a chemist in the royal laboratory accosted him with a story of a Catholic plot to assassinate him. Charles, accustomed to plots and stories of plots, at first dismissed the tale. 'After all,' he joked, 'who would be so dull-witted as to want to see me replaced by my brother?' But when a Catholic member of the Queen's household, Sir George Wakeman, her physician, and Edward Coleman, the Duchess of York's secretary, were named as conspirators, the King handed the investigation over to the Earl of Danby and the Privy Council.

The principal witnesses were Titus Oates, a renegade Jesuit novice, one-time chaplain on the frigate *Adventure* and son of a chaplain in the New Model Army; and Israel Tonge, chaplain to the Dunkirk garrison and then for two years chaplain to the Tangier garrison. Oates claimed he had been admitted to secret Catholic conclaves. In an age when professional perjurers could be obtained cheaply, Oates proved so convincing and the allegations so widespread that the Council sat amazed. 'If he be a liar,' wrote Secretary of State Henry Coventry, 'he is the greatest and most skilful I ever saw.'[2]

His accusations multiplied – all fuelling Protestant fears in an age when hatred, intolerance, fear and fanaticism were at their worst. The City of London would be fired; Catholics in Ireland would revolt; the French would invade, backed by the 'Popish' English brigade in Louis XIV's service. The King was to be assassinated, the Duke of York installed in his place, and 20,000 Papists would rise to murder all Protestants and impose Catholicism on the country by the sword. The whole operation had been ordered by the Pope and financed by the Jesuits.

Five elderly Catholic peers were named as senior officers or ministers of state, appointed by the Pope in the new Popish army and government: Arundel (aged 70), Powys (52), Petre (56), Stafford (64) and Belasyse (64, and bedridden with gout). When the last name was added to the list as the proposed commander-in-chief, Charles, who attended some of the interrogations personally, could not help smiling. He told Sir John Reresby, being with the King at the Duchess of Portsmouth lodgings, that 'he took Oates's story to be some artifice and that he did not believe one word of the plot'.[3]

Then in October Sir Edmund Godfrey, the Protestant magistrate who had taken down Oates's deposition, was found murdered: savagely beaten, strangled and with a sword thrust through his body. He was lying face down in a ditch at the foot of Primrose Hill, three miles from Charing Cross. The murder was never satisfactorily explained,[4] but the Jesuits, without a scrap of evidence to justify the charge, were blamed for killing a man who knew too much.

The murder proved a godsend, however, to the Protestant fanatics – especially Shaftesbury, who wanted to give reality to the plot, become the Protestant champion, ruin Danby and replace him as Lord Treasurer. A tremendous howl for vengeance swept the country. At every street corner, in the taverns and in the coffee-houses, the cry arose, 'The Papists have murdered Sir Edmund Berry Godfrey'.[5] Arrests followed wholesale. While Shaftesbury incited the Whigs in Parliament to challenge the legitimate succession to the throne, his wife carried a small pair of pistols in her muff and persuaded other ladies to follow her example. Many worthy citizens carried concealed daggers, and the Pope's effigy was burnt in the streets by the mob:

> God's pamper'd people, whom, debauch'd with ease,
> No King could govern, nor no God could please.[6]

Special measures were taken to protect the King. Monmouth, as captain of the guards and master of the horse, was responsible for the safety of the sovereign. He supervised restricted access to the King's person, placed sentries round the rambling palace and strengthened the guard at the Tower. He placed three trusted officers as a close bodyguard 'to be in attendance on the King's person on foot, wheresoever he walk, from his rising to his going to bed'.[7] He was also made responsible for the safety of Titus Oates, now the favourite of Parliament, who was given an armed bodyguard, lodgings in Whitehall and a pension of £1,200 per annum.

Oates did not create the national hatred against Catholics; he exploited it and raised it to a frenzy. Despite the absurdity of the claims, the obvious perjury of witnesses and the small size of the Catholic population in England,[8] Catholics were feared throughout Charles's reign as a source of plots against

King and country. Popery was associated with absolute monarchy and a standing army; it was anti-Parliament, pro-French, and supportive of Louis XIV's attempts to dominate Europe. It was also associated with Louis's persecution of the Huguenots, many thousands of whom settled in England and contributed to its prosperity with their skills.

Charles had shown himself to be ambivalent in his religious policy. Publicly he supported the Anglican church, but he had married a Catholic and kept Catholic mistresses. He was lukewarm, if not antagonistic, to anti-Catholic legislation. In 1663 laws had been passed to expel priests and Jesuits from England and forbid Catholics from practising any profession, including the military, holding office or transferring land. Catholic marriages were not valid in law. Clearly these laws were not being enforced.

Now Parliament, alarmed by Oates's accusations, petitioned that all Papists should be disarmed, banished 10 miles from London and confined to their homes. Charles reluctantly issued the necessary orders but in private he maintained the whole plot was a trick. Critics also pointed out that the King received large subsidies from Louis, which enabled him to dispense with Parliament, attack Protestant Holland and leave Catholic France triumphant at the Treaty of Nymwegen in 1678.

Parliament, led by Anthony Ashley Cooper, first Earl of Shaftesbury, who was 'resolved to ruin or to rule the State',[9] saw in the accusations an opportunity to harass the King and his Catholic court. Shaftesbury, an avowed enemy of the Catholics, was a master of the art of propaganda and in arousing the rabble against the court party in Parliament, later to become known as the Tories. He aimed his attack at the Duke of York, an acknowledged Roman Catholic, by supporting a bill in November 1678 to exclude Catholics from sitting in either House. The Earl of Danby managed to exempt James from its provisions. But Charles asked his brother to withdraw and assured Parliament he would help to secure the Protestant religion, provided that Parliament would not call into question the lawful succession of the throne.

While the country was being searched for priests and hidden arms, Charles did what he could to protect individuals from the worst excesses of these terrors. Father Huddleston, who had helped him at the battle of Worcester, was given exemption from the proclamation against priests. Charles refused to dismiss from his pay several humble Catholic officers, who had long served their country, when Parliament once again put pressure on him to disband his army, alleging it was largely composed of Papists.

A Disbandment Act was passed on 15 July 1678, voting £200,000 to pay off the troops. Charles, fearing mob violence as a result of Oates's anti-Catholic accusations, wanted to defer demobilisation. He ignored the Act, even though peace between France and Holland was secured two weeks later by the Treaty of Nymwegen.

In April 1679 Parliament returned to the attack, resolving that 'the continuing of any Standing Army in this nation, other than the Militia, is illegal and a great Grievance and Vexation to the People'.[10] In May it passed a second Disbandment Act and voted money to disband all the troops raised since September 1677. This time Charles gave his assent and the army was broken up during the spring of 1679. But when Parliament presented him with a bill to place the militia under its control (the very issue which had precipitated the Civil War in 1642) Charles vetoed it. He told Parliament he would not let command of the militia pass out of his hands even for half an hour.

Meanwhile, Oates continued to make fresh discoveries every day. In October 1678 he informed the House of Commons that Hortense Mancini, recently arrived from France, was the chief agent for Popish activities in England. Now he went further. In November, at the trial of Sir George Wakeman, the Queen's Catholic physician, Oates implied that the Queen knew of the plot to poison her husband and had consented to his murder, because 'she would not endure the violations of her bed any longer'.

Wakeman was acquitted, thanking God for his deliverance; a verdict which was greeted with violent abuse by the mob, as a perversion of justice at the prompting of royalty. Evelyn called it an extraordinary triumph for the Papists. The King was furious at Oates's accusation and had him imprisoned. The attack aroused all the King's chivalry towards his Queen – not for a moment did he believe her guilty. To Burnet, who had once before been Buckingham's emissary to try to persuade the King to divorce his barren Queen, he said: 'They think I have a mind to a new [Protestant] wife: but for all that I will not see an innocent woman abused.'[11]

The opposition, having been thwarted in different ways by the King's firmness, now resumed its attack on Danby. He was the leader of the court party in Parliament and Charles's chief minister. Louis XIV, too, had been biding his time to gain his revenge on Danby for his pro-Dutch policies and supporting the marriage of William of Orange to Mary. His opportunity soon arose and proved 'another example of the most important part played by love affairs in the epoch's diplomatic field'.[12]

Ralph Montagu, English ambassador in Paris during the Franco–Dutch war, was a vindictive enemy of Danby – who, as Lord Treasurer, had snubbed Montagu by refusing to allow him to buy the post of secretary of state. Montagu wanted his revenge. He had received two very confidential letters written by Danby at Charles's command during March 1678, asking for a subsidy of six million livres a year for three years from Louis XIV, as the price of England remaining neutral in the war. Montagu suggested to Barrillon that, in return for a large pension from Louis, he would reveal this confidential correspondence in Parliament and thus lead to Danby's certain impeachment.

Unfortunately for the plotters, Montagu was as energetic an adventurer in the boudoir, as he was in the diplomatic service, and incurred the anger of the Duchess of Cleveland. The two had conducted a passionate affair in Paris early in 1678, which ended abruptly when Barbara discovered that in her absence Montagu (who was adept at gaining the affection of young ladies, having, for example, fathered a child by Jane Middleton)[13] had carried off from her convent and seduced Anne, Countess of Sussex, the 16-year-old daughter of Charles and Barbara.

The outraged mother wrote a spiteful letter to Charles telling him of disgraceful remarks that Montagu had made about the King, his brother and the government, and gave details of the plot to ruin Danby. She freely admitted that Montagu's hold over her was governed by lust. She complained of her daughter's behaviour 'joining with the worst of men to ruin me', and assured the King she wished no harm to Lady Portsmouth (also involved in the French deal) nor the Lord Treasurer.[14] To defend himself against these accusations, the panic-stricken Montagu left his post in Paris without permission. He crossed to London, where Charles, a former lover, an outraged father and an angry employer, dismissed him from his embassy. He deprived him of all his offices and struck his name off the Privy Council.

To assure Montagu immunity from arrest, Parliament granted him a seat in the Commons. On 20 December 1678 Montagu handed the Speaker the damaging letters, in which Charles requested the subsidy from Louis as payment for not convening Parliament. Parliament was shocked by this revelation and Danby was impeached, charged with planning to overthrow the constitution with the aid of a standing army and French money, misappropriating the funds to pay off the army, and negotiating a peace on unfavourable terms.

To try to save Danby, Charles dissolved the Cavalier Parliament, which had sat for nearly 18 years. But he could not save the Catholic peers accused by Oates from impeachment, nor the indictment of three wretched servants of the Queen, charged with Godfrey's murder, nor the condemned Jesuit priests in Newgate, where the mob howled daily for their execution. Edward Coleman, the Duchess of York's secretary, was condemned on Oates's perjured evidence and executed, 'cut open alive, his bowels torn out and burned before his eyes'.

Alone, vilified on every side, Charles remained calm and patient. The middle-aged roué was now fighting, almost single-handed, to preserve the English monarchy against unscrupulous politicians and the blood-lust of the populace.[15] Despite all the foul defamations made against him, Charles was still popular with the people. Calmly and courageously, he faced the elections for a new Parliament and, to clear the ground, he tried to save the succession to the throne at the price of the successor. In affectionate terms he commanded the Duke of York and his wife to leave England with a small retinue for the Hague. At the same time he made it known publicly in council that he would have no tampering with the succession by declaring that in the presence of Almighty God, I was never married nor gave contract to any woman whatsoever, but to my wife Queen Catherine, to whom I am now married.[16]

Thus he forestalled claims to make the Duke of Monmouth legitimate. Finally, on the day before a new Parliament assembled (5 March 1679), he gave Danby a free pardon for all offences he had committed before 27 February 1679, a pension of £5,000 a year for life, and the rank of marquis. Then he requested Danby's resignation.

The new Parliament showed at once that it was going to pursue its investigations into the Popish Plot and the impeachment of Danby. Despite his plea that he was only obeying the King's orders, and despite the King's efforts to save him, Danby was committed to the Tower. From there in safety for the next five years he continued to advise the King, without success, to take control of the army, navy and garrisons, and secure the Tower to deal with possible insurrection. In May 1679 the Commons introduced the First Exclusion Bill to bar the Duke of York from the throne 'of the three Kingdoms', with perpetual banishment from the country. Led by Shaftesbury, the Whig faction passed the bill's second reading. Impoverished, his household officers unpaid, his naval and army garrisons without stores and needing repair, and with open rebellion imminent, Charles seemed to have no alternative but to surrender. After signing a number of bills, including the famous Habeas Corpus Act, Charles prorogued the House, stating:

I shall find means to pay the Fleet and manage economically and it will be difficult and uncomfortable for me but I will submit to anything rather than endure the gentlemen of the Commons any longer.[17]

The pamphleteers joined in on the attack on 'the Popish successor', even though he was in exile in Brussels, frightening the people with what they could expect, if he ever became King –

troops of Papists ravishing your wives and daughters, dashing little children's brains out against the walls, plundering your houses and cutting your own throats by the name of heretic dogs.... When James governs by an army, what will all your laws signify? You will not then have Parliaments to appeal to: he and his council will levy his arbitrary taxes and his army will gather them for you.[18]

The arguments over the right of succession ceased to be academic, when the King suddenly caught a fever, after a game of tennis on 21 August, and was thought likely to die. He was saved by the recently-discovered quinine, but not before the Duke of York had returned hurriedly from his exile in Brussels. He was secretly invited to return by Sunderland, Essex and Halifax, who feared that in the event of the King's death, Monmouth, who controlled the armed forces, might seize the throne.

Monmouth became angry at James's warm reception at court, where the royal mistresses and leading politicians took sides. Protestant Nell was never a political schemer like Castlemaine and Portsmouth, describing herself as a sleeping partner in the ship of state, but now supported the Whig faction, Shaftesbury and Monmouth. Catholic Louise supported Halifax, Essex, Sunderland, and those members of the court who believed Charles dare not support his brother much longer. They felt Charles should yield to the pressure from the Whigs and name his successor. The court party suggested a compromise whereby both dukes should be sent into temporary exile, allowing the King, who quickly recovered from his illness, time to make his decision.

When Monmouth received his orders from the King to go into exile he was astounded. From being personal bodyguard to the sovereign and captain-general in England and Scotland, he was now to be banished. Despite his pleas to remain, he was instructed to leave for Utrecht on 12 September 1679. He was followed the next day by the Duke of York, whom Charles ordered with his wife to Scotland, where the Test Act did not apply. In this way Charles ensured that James would succeed in the event of his sudden death. James kept in touch with negotiations for his eventual return through the Duchess of Portsmouth, the price of her support being a share in the Duke's post office revenues.[19]

Open warfare now developed between Charles and Shaftesbury, the one determined to manage without Parliament, the other to exclude the King's brother from succession to the throne and replace him with the Protestant Monmouth. Monmouth, defying his father, slipped back into London and into his lodgings at the Cockpit, where the populace gave him a tumultuous welcome. In the playhouses there was uproar as his supporters called 'all the women whores and the men rogues, the Duke of York a rascal and God bless His Highness, the Duke of Monmouth'.[20]

Encouraged by Shaftesbury in his ambition to be recognised as heir to the throne, the vain and easily led Monmouth spent a month in the west country. Under the pretext of hunting and taking the waters at Tunbridge Wells, he gathered support wherever he went 'as the Protestant Duke and because of his abnormally good looks, perfect manners and charming disposition'.[21] He was back in London in November, in time to celebrate the festivities centred on the burning of the Pope's effigy, while the rabble drank to the health of the King and the Duke of Monmouth simultaneously.

Charles was furious at his son's disobedience. He ordered him to leave

Whitehall, stopped his annual pension, and deprived him of his civil and military posts. He gave the posts of Master of the Horse to Charles Lennox and Colonelship of the Grenadiers to Henry Fitzroy and command of the King's Horse Guards to Christopher, second Duke of Albemarle. In the City, to which Monmouth retired, all the people acclaimed him. He paid court to Nell Gwynn, supping with her nightly, hoping her influence with the King might get him to change his mind. She begged hard for Charles to relent, but the King 'bid her be quiet for he would not see him'.[22] When the partisan Londoners, seeing her gilded coach, mistook her for her Catholic rival, she put her head out of the window and shouted: 'Be silent, good people, I am the Protestant whore!'

In January 1680, Charles ordered that Monmouth be formally banished from the kingdom by order in council; when he refused to go, Charles ordered the Duke of York to return as his legitimate heir. Monmouth still believed he could change his father's decision to banish him. In this he was encouraged by the Duchess of Portsmouth's example, who 'to show her power with the King (which was very great) would often make the King break his engagement' to those promised office or preferment.[23] If she could do it, could not the King's spoilt and favourite son do as well?

Shaftesbury, unable for the moment to impose Monmouth on the King, now counted on Charles's lack of money to make him change his mind, to force him to abandon his wife and brother, even to remarry if necessary, but at least to leave the matter of the succession to Parliament. Shaftesbury went to the palace with a petition and told the courtiers that,

> though now they had neither meat nor money, if their master would give way, they should have both and new wenches, too, if their old ones would let them.[24]

Such tactics only made Charles more resolute. Supported by the Duchess of Portsmouth, Laurence Rochester (Clarendon's second son, the Earl of Hyde) and Sunderland,[25] the King continued to rule without Parliament, refusing to budge on the exclusion issue or acknowledge the legality of Monmouth's claim. Nor would Monmouth agree to the absolute submission demanded by his father. His honour was at stake and his birthright called into question. Pride, vanity and ambition prevented any possible reconciliation between father and son.

Shaftesbury now tried another line of attack. On 26 June 1680 he persuaded a grand jury in Middlesex to indict James as a Catholic recusant (ie. an opponent of the Anglican communion), and the Duchess of Portsmouth as a common whore. The penalty for the royal mistress was humiliation in the stocks or the ducking stool. Parliament, in open debate, talked of 'popery being found in the King's bed'. The grand jury was packed with Protestant supporters, while Oates and a large body of anti-Papist Whigs crowded into the courtroom. The Lord Chief Justice, Sir William Scroggs, earlier a captain of a foot company in the Civil War and a member of Gray's Inn, was due to preside over the court. Charles had knighted him soon after his restoration, but Scroggs was known as a great debaucher and companion of the high court rakes, and one of the worst judges that ever disgraced the English bench.[26] Forewarned by the King, Scroggs had the jury discharged before it could pass a verdict.

This attempt to indict the King's brother and mistress caused a sensation, both in Europe and among the royal ministers. It so frightened Louise that she agreed with Shaftesbury, in return for a large sum of money and the dropping of all charges against her, to persuade Charles to accept the Exclusion Bill and any successor that Shaftesbury should name. Indeed, there was a possibility that her own son by the King, the Duke of Richmond, who had been brought up as a Protestant, might be a candidate, 'since she was so absolutely the mistress of the King's spirit', wrote Burnet.[27] Louis XIV considered her now not only as the undisputed *maîtresse en titre* but as virtually the Queen of England. Shaftesbury, however, was using her for his own ends, trusting she would make Charles see that the English would never tolerate a Catholic succession.

When the new Parliament assembled in October 1680, Charles hoped it would vote him desperately needed funds, especially for the defence of Tangier. Instead, it passed a Second Exclusion Bill, sponsored by Shaftesbury, which proposed that James's elder daughter Mary, a convinced Protestant and obedient to her husband, Prince William of Orange, should inherit the throne. To the King's relief, Lord Halifax, Charles's elder statesman, helped with his eloquence to defeat Shaftesbury's Bill in the House of Lords, which Charles attended in person and by his presence influenced the result of the debate. The Commons was furious, demanded Halifax's removal and attacked Scroggs for daring to doubt Oates. That night Charles ostentatiously supped and spent the night with the Queen instead of with Louise, as was his custom – a clear snub to Louise, Shaftesbury and his supporters. Despite all her tears and arguments, the best loved and most politically active of all the King's mistresses could not move him to agree to exclusion. Once again Parliament was dismissed.

By the end of the year, the Whigs had aroused anti-Popish hysteria almost to the point of revolution and were openly talking of civil war. Charles, knowing that Shaftesbury's supporters would be protected by the London trained bands and the City's Pope-burning populace, decided to summon his fourth Parliament to meet him outside London. He chose Oxford, retreat of kings in time of war and pestilence, no doubt hoping to convey the belief that, away from Westminster, tempers would be calmer and conciliation easier. But secretly the King was taking measures to secure the throne for himself and confound his enemies.

After the defeat of the Exclusion Bill, Louis XIV realised that, if Charles were forced to sacrifice the principle of legitimate succession to defeat his foes and agree not to Monmouth but to Mary and William of Orange as his successor, England might unite with Holland against France. Through Barrillon and Louise, he assured Charles that he would provide the necessary financial help to avoid the need for Parliament to be recalled, so Charles could continue his defence of the legitimate succession. Charles, apologising to Louis with shame for having to traffic in this way,[28] made one last attempt to make peace with Parliament and obtain the money he needed from them; he would offer in exchange reasonable political and religious concessions. Failing agreement, he would accept the French offer.

Before he left London for Oxford, Charles took precautions against any insurrection. He appointed the veteran Royalist, the Earl of Craven, commander-in-chief of all the troops left in London, with orders to secure the capital against public disorder. Then he lined the road from Windsor to Oxford with soldiers, sent his Guards to Oxford, and distributed his Household troops in the neighbouring villages. The undergraduates lit bonfires and cheered 'Charles the Great'. The King commandeered Christ Church to lodge himself and his Life Guards, and Corpus Christi and Merton colleges as accommodation for the royal party, which included the Queen, Nell Gwynn, the Duchess of Portsmouth, and the court. The Whig members of Parliament could not bring the London mobs with them, but they rode into the city with bands of retainers, heavily armed with swords and pistols, and flying blue streamers bearing the legend 'No Popery, No Slavery'.[29] Shaftesbury, with most of the exclusionist lords, was accommodated at Balliol for an exorbitant rent; the Commons met in Convocation House, the Lords in the Geometry School.

In his opening speech on 21 March 1681, Charles repeated his opposition to exclusion, but promised to remove all reasonable fears that might arise from the possibility of a popish successor to the crown by putting the administration of the government into Protestant hands. He was ready to listen to any expedient by which the Protestant religion might be preserved and the monarchy not destroyed. But Charles still needed money. His soldiers, sailors and civil officers were unpaid and mutinous, his cannon were unmounted, his magazines empty. He had to find £201,000 for the cost of his 'guards and garrisons', which numbered 6,872 men including the Tangier regiments. Even his own table was replenished with difficulty.[30] Parliament was not impressed. 'Hang Tangier,' growled one of the members. 'We resolve to raise no money to pay the whores at Whitehall and arbitrary government.'[31]

But the real issue was the future of the English monarchy. Shaftesbury told the King that, if he would declare the Duke of Monmouth to be his successor, the whole matter could be settled in a day. Charles replied that such a solution was contrary to both the existing laws and to divine justice. Much as he loved

Monmouth, he would rather see him hanged at Tyburn than own him as his legitimate son. Shaftesbury offered a bill to legitimise Monmouth. Charles replied: 'let there be no self-delusion. I will never yield and I will not be intimidated.'[32] Through Halifax Charles offered his expedients: the Duke of York to be banished for life; his sons educated as Protestants; and on Charles's death the government to be vested in the regency of Mary of Orange or, after her, of Princess Anne. The Commons, riddled with factions, refused every offer and resolved to return to the Bill 'to disenable James, Duke of York, to succeed to the imperial crown of this realm'.[33]

On Monday – the day fixed for the introduction of the Bill – Charles, 'with the crown carried between his feet in the sedan and the robes sent privately before',[34] assembled both Houses and, to their utter amazement, dissolved Parliament. That was the end of Parliamentary government, as far as he was concerned, and of Shaftesbury and the Whigs. He countered Shaftesbury's threat of an uprising by lining the streets with his First Foot Guards. The MPs, believing Charles, protected by his Life Guards, would turn his foot guards upon them, fled madly to their homes as from a city besieged. The price of horses doubled in a quarter of an hour. The Earl of Rochester, celebrated for his amorous lyrics and obscene rhymes, which so often amused the King, wrote:

> And so, red hot with wine and whore,
> He kicked the Commons out of door.[35]

Having dined, the King drove swiftly out of Oxford, spending the night at Windsor and reaching Whitehall next morning. Here Lord Craven, keeping watch with the guards, reported that all was quiet. Two days later the secret treaty with France was concluded. No definite conditions were named, except that Louis would pay a subsidy of £400,000 spread over the next three years 'without receipt'. French gold had made Parliament unnecessary -exactly as Charles had requested through the Duchess of Portsmouth some weeks earlier, when Barrillon had written to Louis XIV:

> I saw Madame de Portsmouth, to whom the King has confided all his affairs. She told me that, if your Majesty would pay four millions a year for three years, the King would agree to carry Your Majesty's wishes but that without this sum it would be impossible for him to refuse to call Parliament.

Louis thanked Louise for 'carefully fulfilling all she knew of his intentions and those of the King of England, my royal brother'.[36] The following year Louis would reward her in more tangible form, with a title and the duchy of Aubigny.

Charles had Shaftesbury arrested on 2 July 1681 and committed to the

Tower, charged with intending to use force, if the Exclusion Bill were not passed, to start a rebellion and establish a commonwealth. Since Shaftesbury could not be legally tried outside London, and no jury would convict him in the city, the Whigs obtained his release in November. Charles ordered a declaration to be read from the pulpit of every church, severely criticising the actions of his recent Parliaments and recalling the horrors of the Civil War, when 'religion, liberty and property were all lost and gone, when the monarchy was shaken off and could never be revived, till that was restored'. But neither the Whigs nor the Tories[37] wanted civil war. Deprived of a Parliament, the Whigs lost their power base. Monmouth urged Shaftesbury to force another exclusionist Parliament but with his Whig supporters deserting daily to the Tories, he bided his time.

The Popish Plot has been described as one of the most damaging practical jokes in the history of England,[38] and an indelible disgrace upon the English nation. The violence of the Whigs had alienated all moderate men; the tension in the country had been severe and prolonged. Shaftesbury's patronage of Monmouth had driven away many supporters: the country had been growing rich, and the well-to-do classes, especially, dreaded the thought of another commonwealth. With the court everywhere triumphant, and Charles persuaded at last to curb his expenditure and settle down to domesticity with Louise, peace seemed to reign in 1682. The crisis of his reign, which Charles had faced practically alone and unaided, appeared to be over.

But the calm was deceptive. Shaftesbury had one more card to play.

20

Charles's Final Curtain

In the autumn of 1682, Shaftesbury and some of his exclusionist friends persuaded Monmouth to make a ducal tour of north-west England. They remembered his success two years earlier at winning hearts in his tours of Sussex, Kent and the west country, and hoped the Whiggish Midlands would show their support, by insurrection if necessary, for 'a people's prince', England's first constitutional monarch. Monmouth travelled to Coventry, Cheshire and Stafford, to be met everywhere by cheering crowds, bonfires, ringing bells, and shouts of 'The King's son', 'the Protestant Duke', 'Let Monmouth Reign'. With the cries ringing in his ears, Monmouth pondered the situation. The rebels in London and the west were nearly ready; the Scots were well ahead with their preparations; in Kent and Sussex his following was assured.

At Whitehall, Charles kept a careful watch on his son's tour and reception, and decided it was nothing less than incitement to national rebellion. It must be stopped. Monmouth was arrested at Stafford by a sergeant-at-arms and conveyed back to London. He was soon released on bail, but Charles forbade him to enter the park (where his apartments lay) or any part of Whitehall. Shaftesbury accused Monmouth of indecision, suggesting he return to Cheshire to set up his standard and declare for a free Parliament.[1] But Monmouth was a soldier who understood what a rabble was and what regular troops were, and thought this would be a mad exposure of themselves and their friends.[2]

In November, after a last unsuccessful attempt to rouse the mob on Guy Fawkes' Day, Shaftesbury fled to the Continent, ill and distraught, and died there a couple of months later. Dryden wrote his epitaph in his masterpiece *Absalom and Achitophel*,

A name to all succeeding ages curst . . .
In friendship false, implacable in hate,
Resolved to ruin or to rule the State.

Monmouth now joined the aristocratic Whig lords, Essex, Grey, Russell and Algernon Sidney, in a plot to overcome the Life Guards, seize Whitehall, the City, the Tower and the King, call the country to arms and put Monmouth on the throne. During the spring of 1683, a former Cromwellian officer called Captain Richard Rumbold and some 40 other fanatics planned to assassinate Charles and his brother during one of their frequent visits to the Newmarket races. Rumbold's home was Rye House at Hoddesdon on the London-Newmarket road, and the plotters planned to obstruct the road at this point as the royal coach was passing. By an act of providence, a few days before the assassination attempt was due to take place, a royal groom carelessly set fire to the royal stables. Charles and James left Newmarket 10 days earlier than intended, and the plot had to be postponed. Otherwise,

> this tale would have ended with a cart of hay blocking the highway. While waiting horsemen galloped towards London to rouse the city and proclaim Monmouth, England's Majesty and his brother would have been killed with a dozen bullets through their bodies.[3]

The delay proved fatal. In June the plot was betrayed by one of the conspirators. As with the Popish Plot, much of the evidence was false and pre-fabricated. But the Rye House Plot gave Charles and the Tory court supporters the pretext and opportunity to turn the tables on the Whig exclusionists and their larger plan for a Protestant rising. With the help of judges who believed it was their duty to crush the King's enemies, it was easy to intimidate juries and obtain convictions for high treason. The result was a crop of Whig martyrs to match the Catholic and Irish martyrs in the years 1678 to 1681.

The principal conspirators were arrested, among them Lord William Russell, who was tried at the Old Bailey on Friday 13 July 1683. The prosecutor was George Jeffreys, who had been a student at the Inner Temple, but spent more time in the tavern than at his law studies.[4] He began his career by cultivating fashionable society; with introductions from the Duchess of Portsmouth and the assistance of Chiffinch, the handsome young lawyer obtained entry to the court. In 1677 he was appointed solicitor-general to the Duke of York and knighted.

Jeffreys took a prominent part in the Popish Plot trials; in September 1683 Charles agreed to his appointment as Lord Chief Justice of England, though he well knew 'Jeffreys had no learning, no sense, no manners and more impudence than ten carted street-walkers'. His legal learning may have been small, but he had a great talent for cross-examination and was a master of scurrilous invective. He obtained a conviction for high treason against Russell, who was executed on a black-draped scaffold at Lincoln's Inn Fields, despite pleas to the King by his desolate wife and father, the Duke of Bedford, who offered £100,000 to Charles through the Duchess of Portsmouth for a reprieve.

Colonel Algernon Sidney, son of Robert, the second Earl of Leicester and elder brother of Henry ('the handsomest man in the kingdom, a terror to husbands and dismissed the court for an affair with Anne Hyde')[5] was a leading Republican who had been wounded, when fighting for Parliament at the battle of Marston Moor. For 17 years after the Restoration he had tried unsuccessfully to persuade Louis XIV to finance another rebellion in England. As one of the leading Whig conspirators, he was the next to be tried and found guilty. Judge Jeffreys gave him the dreaded sentence of being hanged, drawn and quartered. For the sake of his family, however, this was commuted, as in the case of Russell, to beheading on Tower Hill.

The day after Sidney's execution, Jeffreys attended the wedding of a Mrs Castle, daughter of a rich broom manufacturer, to her fifth husband, a lieutenant-colonel in one of the City regiments. Evelyn, who was present, watched with disapproval Jeffreys dancing, drinking and talking with the bride in a manner that 'was exceeding merry – much beneath the gravity of a judge, who had but a day or two before condemned Mr Algernon Sidney'.[6]

The privilege of beheading was denied to another of the conspirators, Colonel Thomas Armstrong. He was a cousin of both Lord Rochester and Anne Hyde, the Duke of York's first wife, and a colonel in the Household Cavalry. Surrounded by a huge party of guardsmen, some of whom he had commanded, he was hanged, his body quartered and then disposed of 'at his King's pleasure'.

Another conspirator was Arthur Capel, Earl of Essex, whom the Duchess of Portsmouth had known well and whose father had died on the scaffold for Charles I. Essex had been one of Charles's most respected ministers. When lord lieutenant of Ireland, as part of his attempt to stamp out English corruption, he had refused to agree to the King's grant of Phoenix Park in Dublin to Barbara Castlemaine, thus saving one of the largest parks in the world for posterity. Later, as first lord of the Treasury, he advised the King in vain not to increase his army by raising new royal guards, which he said would antagonise Parliament. His involvement in the Rye House Plot, as a Whig exclusionist, greatly distressed the King, who remembered his father's execution for the Stuart cause. Essex, however, committed suicide, cutting his throat in the Tower.

Lord Howard of Escrick, who turned King's evidence, was pardoned; Lord

Grey, a strong supporter of Monmouth, fled to Holland with his mistress, Lady Henrietta Berkeley, his sister-in-law, to join Shaftesbury in exile. Jack Ketch, the public executioner, was kept busy 'despatching the humbler Whigs to another world'.[7] Titus Oates was sent to prison – not for perjury, but because he was unable to pay a prohibitive £10,000 fine and costs imposed by Jeffreys for slandering the Duke of York.

Charles was well aware that the Duke of Monmouth was also implicated in the plot but was reluctant to convict his son. A grand jury found him guilty but Halifax, Monmouth's wife, Anne, and finally the Queen begged Charles to spare him. Monmouth had, in fact, confirmed to the King details of the conspiracy before a committee of the Privy Council, headed by the Duke of York, gathered in the Duchess of Portsmouth's apartments. He also confirmed the names of the conspirators, but denied all knowledge of any design against the King's life. He admitted his part was confined to the planning of three simultaneous risings in London, Cheshire and the south-west, with a fourth in Scotland.

In return for his confession and a promise to avoid political intrigues in the future, the King pardoned him. He banished Monmouth from court, but allowed him to hide at the Toddington home of his 21-year-old mistress, Lady Henrietta Wentworth, whom he regarded as his 'real wife'. She had once been maid of honour to the Duchess of York, until removed from court by her mother because of Monmouth's attentions. Henrietta was desperately in love with Monmouth, and joined him in exile in Brussels accompanied by her mother, where, according to Bishop Burnet, they lived in a large house with a substantial retinue of servants. The Duke was hospitably received by William of Orange, who believed that Charles, despite the exile, was still fond of his son, and that the safest place to keep an eye on his chief rival to the throne of England was close beside him.

The Rye House Plot, according to Evelyn, left Charles very melancholy 'and not stirring without double guards'. On 9 September 1683 a public thanksgiving day was observed for the King's lucky escape, 'preserved from this horrid and damnable conspiracy by Divine Providence'. But Charles and his brother had not heard the last of Monmouth and, as long as he was at large, he was bound to attract intrigues and dissenters.

The final months of Charles's life passed peacefully, after all the storms of the preceding years. Abroad, England was no longer at war; with the return of the Tangier garrison in 1684, the army could return to its peacetime establishment. Ten years earlier, the standing army had consisted of three foot regiments of guards and three of the line (the Royal Scots, the Queen's Regiment and the Buffs, to give them their modern names) and a marine regiment. These foot soldiers were supported by the cavalry of the Horse (Life) Guards, Oxford's Blues and the Tangier Horse (First Dragoons). Between

1674 and his death in 1685, Charles only added the Scots Greys (1681) and the Second Tangier Regiment (later the Fourth King's Own) to his army, which now numbered some 16,000 compared with the 4,000 household troops he had embodied in 1661.

The Scots Greys were founded to help to stamp out religious dissent in Scotland. In 1678, Charles had raised three companies of dragoons, armed and equipped like infantrymen but mounted like cavalry. They could move faster across country than foot soldiers and were cheaper to pay and maintain than cavalry. They proved so successful under Monmouth's command that the King formed them into a regiment of six companies in 1681 and placed them under the colonelcy of General Thomas Dalyell. In this way he added the Royal Regiment of Scots Dragoons (Second) to the English establishment – the oldest regiment of dragoons in the British army.

Although pro-French, and with French subsidies running out, Charles managed in his last years to keep his small army free of European entanglements. But Louis XIV's increasing ambitions began to alarm Europe – first Holland, then Germany and Sweden. These fears increased after the Truce of Regensburg (1684) had secured France's eastern frontier by the annexation of the Flanders forts, Luxembourg, Franche Comté, Alsace and Strasburg.

To his people the final years of Charles's reign brought increasing prosperity. While Europe was plunged into war, they remained at peace and free to send their merchant ships to every part of the world in search of wealth and treasure. Trade boomed, protected by navigation laws which ensured an English monopoly of the carrying trade with the developing colonies. In the course of his reign Charles's merchant navy doubled in size, and the King's revenue from customs increased correspondingly.

Politically, with Shaftesbury dead and Parliament in abeyance, the power of the Whigs was broken: the angry debates in the two Houses had ceased and the plots and trials were over, though the country remained strongly Protestant and Parliamentarian. Charles was now free to rule personally, without a chief minister. Carefully balancing one minister with another, in 1682 he replaced Laurence Hyde, Earl of Rochester (Clarendon's son) with Robert Spencer, second Earl of Sunderland, as Secretary of State. He retained Halifax, president of the Privy Council, as a counterweight to the Duke of York.

Sunderland, after sowing his wild oats, had in 1665 married the great beauty and heiress Anne, daughter of the second Earl of Bristol; a marriage which gained him access to political influence more than actual wealth. In 1667 he had been commissioned into Prince Rupert's regiment of horse, where he met Halifax, who was serving in the same troop. His political activity at this time seems to have been limited for the most part to paying assiduous court to the royal mistresses – Lady Castlemaine (whom he invited to his seat at

Althorp) and later Louise de Keroualle, through his wife (who with Lady Arlington had arranged the burlesque wedding at Euston).[8] He became one of Louise's intimate political friends and looked after her interests in France, while serving there as ambassador.

Sunderland lost royal favour by joining the exclusionists, but was readmitted to the Privy Council by the King in September 1682 at Louise's request. There he supported Charles's Tory, pro-French policies, hoping to supplant Halifax, now his brother-in-law, who favoured William of Orange's claims to the succession and led the opposition Whigs in Parliament. But, as an additional political precaution, the crafty Sunderland began to cultivate relations with the Prince of Orange through his wife, a born intriguer and his equal in duplicity, whose 'gallant' at the Hague was the English envoy, his own uncle, Henry Sidney.

With the Whigs broken and the court Tory party dominant, Charles made no attempt during the years of his personal rule (1681-5) to increase the powers of the monarchy. He ruled without calling a Parliament; but in a country so beset with sectarian strife, it needed a king like Charles to bring calm and understanding to the handling of government. His wit and charm, his undoubted popularity with the common people, his complete immunity from all kinds of fanaticism and his considerable political and diplomatic skills 'came like a cooling draught administered to a fevered patient'.[9]

Charles was now in his fifties, but still kept himself alert in mind and body. He continued to play tennis every morning and, to escape the onerous duties of Whitehall, he moved to Windsor in August. There he could hunt in the forests and hawk on the downs around the new palace Wren was building for him at Winchester, the ancient capital of England. In September he sailed his yacht around the Isle of Wight, inspected the fortifications at Portsmouth and Southsea and supped with the Duchess of Portsmouth, who had come to see the castle.

In these final years, Louise functioned almost as an alternative Queen, entertaining ambassadors and helping the King with his ministers. As an example, Evelyn describes a great banquet of sweetmeats and music given to the Moroccan ambassador and his Moorish retinue in January 1682 in her apartments. It was attended by the King, the King's natural children (Lady Charlotte Lichfield and Lady Anne Sussex), the Duchess of Portsmouth, Nelly Gwynn, 'and concubines and cattle of that sort, as splendid as jewels and excess of bravery could make them'.

Charles settled down with her domestically, treating her more like a wife than a mistress. Evelyn believed her source of power lay partly in her capacity for business but chiefly in her personal beauty. Quiet and refined, sweet and loyal, she was many a man's ideal mate – a pretty, alluring, uncomplicated woman, who devoted all her energies to one overmastering ambition: to be the best kept mistress in Christendom.[10] She no longer feared a serious rival in his affections, although Charles never lost his taste for attractive new faces. For the last few years, she had resigned herself to his many infidelities, variety seemingly a necessary stimulant for his blunted appetites. But she knew these were passing fancies, unlikely to challenge the accepted favourite. Bishop Burnet complained:

> The King's fondness to Lady Portsmouth increased much and broke out in very indecent instances. The King caressed and kissed her in the view of all the people: which he had never done on any occasion or to any person formerly.[11]

The Puritan Evelyn also disapproved of Charles spending his last couple of years in inexpressible luxury and profaneness, gaming and dissoluteness.[12]

Parliament continued to dislike Charles's sexual extravagancies, not because they objected to his mistresses as such – how could they when most of its members kept mistresses themselves – but on account of their cost. Antonia Fraser compares his mistresses at the end of his life to

> the great ships he also loved, floating grandly on the tide of the royal favour, their hulls weighed down with jewels and other riches and flying their ducal titles like pennants.[13]

The nation at large, albeit Puritan, having passed through a period of cant, humbug and hypocrisy in sex matters, found his amorous dalliance healthily open and refreshingly shameless. Perhaps the sporting sense of the people responded to a king who would rather spend his time in the enjoyment of feminine society than in talking politics with his ministers.[14] Unlike other monarchs, he did not cast off his mistresses but remained on friendly terms with them, and they in turn provided the peace and companionship he needed away from affairs of state.

In 1684, Charles performed one more great service for his favourite mistress. He told Barrillon that the Duchess of Portsmouth and her son, the Duke of Richmond, were the persons above all others in the world whom he loved the most. He would be deeply obliged to the King of France if he were to agree to reconvert the estate of Aubigny into a duchy for her, with the reversion to her son and his future issue. Barrillon was privately not persuaded that Louise merited the right to sit on a ducal 'tabouret', whenever she went to pay her respects to the Queen at Versailles. Nevertheless, he wrote to his master that Louise had shown great, constant and intelligent zeal for Louis's interests and given numberless useful hints and pieces of information.[15] In due course, Louis recognised her services to France and himself by naturalising her son, so that he could inherit her estates in France. He created her a duchesse with rights over the duchy of Aubigny and gave her the coveted tabouret. As the Duke of York had also helped her over this affair, Louise used her influence with the King to have the Duke reinstated as lord high admiral in March 1684. She also helped to negotiate the marriage of James's daughter Anne to Prince George of Denmark.

On 24 November 1684 the Queen's birthday was celebrated with a splendid display of fireworks on the Thames in front of Whitehall. Afterwards the young ladies and gallants of the court danced in the great Banqueting Hall. Evelyn, describing the scene, wrote that the court had not been seen so brave and rich in apparel since Charles II's restoration. But the sands of time were fast running out for the King. At peace with himself, he was nevertheless worried about the future of his country and of his successor. Walking one day in Hyde Park with the English resident at Brussels, he confided:

> I know not what my brother will do, when I am dead and gone. I am much afraid that when he comes to wear the crown, he will be obliged to travel again. And yet I will take care to leave my kingdoms to him in peace, wishing he may long keep them so. But this hath all of my fears, little of my hopes and less of my reason. I am much afraid that when my brother comes to the crown, he will be obliged to leave his native soil.[16]

Time would prove the truth of this observation!

Drama, which had been a feature of Charles's life, now set the stage for the King, as he courageously faced death and his final curtain. On Sunday evening, 1 February 1685, John Evelyn visited Whitehall palace and strongly disapproved of what he saw:

> I was witness of the King, sitting and toying with his concubines, Portsmouth, Cleveland and Mazarin, a French boy singing love-songs in that glorious gallery, whilst about twenty of the great courtiers and other dissolute persons were at basset round a large table, a bank of at least two thousand in gold before them – a scene of utmost vanity. Six days after was all in the dust.

This scene, which so outraged the Puritan Evelyn, was no more than a domestic picture of a middle-aged man surrounded by loved companions, but it proved to be the last such evening at Whitehall.

Charles had not been well for some days but that evening he seemed in high spirits. After a good supper and his customary visit to the Duchess of Portsmouth's apartments, he retired to bed chatting excitedly to Lord Thomas Bruce, a young gentleman of the bedchamber. Bruce idolised the King and it is to him we owe many of the details of Charles's last illness. The King talked about his new palace at Winchester and promised Bruce an appointment in the Guards for a cousin of his. Bruce, sharing the King's room according to custom, noted that the King tossed and turned unusually in his sleep and, when he awoke, his normally olive complexion was 'pale as ashes'. His speech became impaired – 'an ill-omen'. He was bled by his doctors and purgatives forced down his throat: since he was, in fact, suffering from a kidney disease, this treatment proved fatal in the long run.[17]

The Duke of York was summoned and the rest of the Privy Council, as more remedies were applied. When news of the King's seizure reached the outside world beyond the barred gates of the palace, a vast and silent crowd assembled, anxious for their King. The Duke of York, to prevent any possible insurrection, ordered the sentries to be reinforced, the Horse and Foot Guards to be posted around the palace and the ports to be closed, lest any whisper of the crisis should reach Monmouth.

The following day the King appeared to be better but the relief was short-lived. Next morning, Tuesday 3 February, the King was seized with another 'fit' or convulsion. His doctors frantically cupped, blistered, purged and scarified his tortured body, applying every remedy known to their limited repertoire. Over the next two days, Charles had further convulsions and more bleedings, with spells of lucidity during which he was visited by the Queen, the Duchess of York and the Duchess of Portsmouth and talked from time to time to the company around his bed. But it was clear the King was dying, his sufferings borne with great fortitude.

While the Protestant bishops were imploring Charles to take the last rites of the Anglican communion, the grief-stricken Louise, whom decency bade should remain in her own apartments, sent for Barrillon, the French ambassador. In some agitation, she told him

a secret, although its public revelation would cost me my head. The King is in the bottom of his heart a Catholic and there he is surrounded by Protestant Bishops. I cannot decently enter his room. Besides, the Queen is now there constantly.

She implored Barrillon to give her message to the Duke of York, who was too busy with his own affairs to trouble himself about the King's conscience.[18] Barrillon told James, who in a whisper asked the King in the crowded bedroom if he wished to see a priest. Charles replied, 'Yes, with all my heart, but do nothing that might endanger yourself.'

To introduce a Catholic priest into the royal bedroom, even if one could be found at such short notice, was a problem. The chamber was cleared by the Duke of York, except for the Earls of Bath and Feversham, both army officers (the latter being the commander of Charles's Third, and later Second, Troop of Horse Guards) and Protestants, which helped to pacify the attendant bishops and Captain Trevannion of the guards. Barrillon, searching for a priest, came across Father John Huddleston, who happened to be in the palace. He had helped to rescue Charles at Worcester and had been rewarded by appointment to the households of Queen Henrietta and Queen Catherine. Now an old man, he was smuggled in disguise into the King's bedroom through the secret door by the resourceful Chiffinch (who had used the same door for other purposes on many occasions). According to Lord Bruce, Charles said to Father Huddleston: 'Father, you who once saved my body are now come to save my soul.' After hearing his confession, Father Huddleston administered the last rites of the Catholic church.

Later that evening Charles apologised to those crowding round his bed for being such an unconscionable time dying. He asked forgiveness of the Queen, 'begging her pardon with all my heart', and gave his blessing to his children. During the long night, Charles begged forgiveness of his brother James, weeping with his wife beside the bed, for the hardships he had inflicted on him from time to time, handed him the keys of his cabinet and begged God to give him a prosperous reign. Charles made no mention of Monmouth but asked repeatedly after Louise – 'I have always loved her and I die loving her', he murmured to James, commending her and Barbara to his care. A little later he said: 'Do not let poor Nelly starve.' As dawn broke, he asked to be propped up, so that he might once more see the day and hear the sounds of his beloved river. He died just before noon on Friday 6 February 1685. He was only 54.

The King's body lay in state for several days in the Painted Chamber at Whitehall. It was laid to rest on the night of 14 February, privately according to custom, in the chapel of Henry VII in Westminster Abbey: later many of his natural children would be buried near him.[19] The court and the army went into mourning and theatres were closed for three months.

In a valedictory epitaph to the King, to whom he had been a close adviser, Evelyn wrote:

> Thus died King Charles the Second in the 36th year of his reign. A Prince of many Virtues, and many great Imperfections, Debonaire, Easy of Access, proper of person, every motion became him . . .. An excellent prince doubtless had he been less addicted to Women.[20]

He added, 'he was ever kind to me and very gracious on all occasions.'

Evelyn noted that he had not heard Charles on his deathbed saying anything of the church or his people, now falling under the government of a prince suspected for his religion. God was incensed to make Charles's reign very troublesome, concluded Evelyn, and unprosperous by wars, plagues, fires, and loss of reputation caused by a universal neglect of the public for the love of a voluptuous and sensual life, which a vicious court had brought into credit. Such moral judgements would find little support in today's society, although one could fairly ask whether his private life damaged Charles's political ability or conduct.

Charles's earlier biographers stressed his personal immorality and suggested that it weakened his capacity to govern. The ruin of his reign and of all his affairs, wrote Burnet,[21] was occasioned chiefly by his delivering himself up after his restoration to a mad range of pleasure – in particular, his passion for the Duchess of Castlemaine, who did so disorder him that he was not master of himself, nor capable of minding business. Burnet blamed him especially for showing no sign of remorse at the last for his ill-led life and his recommending only his whores and his bastards to his brother's care.[22] Pepys joined the general condemnation of Charles as the political plaything of his mistresses. Parliament certainly considered them expensive and the Puritans could hardly be expected to be enamoured of his excesses.

But today's judgement[23] would be that Charles's cynicism, opportunism and unsurpassed skill in dissimulation gave him a superiority over all his ministers, and that he remained master over them and his mistresses. It is accepted that two of the latter, Louise and Barbara, had considerable influence over his affairs and appointments, especially when their views coincided with his own. As for his overall achievements, subsequent events proved unkind to Charles. He has been described as, on the whole, a successful politician without being a great statesman, whose reign could show a record of solid achievement. Yet nearly everything he struggled to achieve would be destroyed during the short reign of his successor.[24]

James honoured, as far as his financial means allowed, the dying wishes of his brother towards his mistresses and their children. Nell Gwynn died of a stroke two years after her royal master, robbed by his death at the last minute of the coveted title of Countess of Greenwich. James conveyed the freehold of Bestwood Park in Sherwood Forest to her (Charles had only given her the lease), gave her an allowance of £1,500 per annum, and saved her from a debtors' prison on at least two occasions.[25]

The death of Charles was a terrible blow to the Duchess of Portsmouth. Although the new King, James II, visited her within an hour of his brother's death to assure her of his protection and friendship, she knew he disliked her for her intrigues with Monmouth and her influence with Charles. Now, deserted also by the fickle courtiers and hated by the common people as a 'French whore', she realised she had lost all claim to political importance. In August 1685, with her debts cleared and James's promise to look after her interests in England and keep up her apartments in Whitehall,[26] she set sail for France and her estates near Brest in Brittany with an armada of ships, carrying her furniture, jewellery and other valuable possessions. She was accompanied by her son, the Duke of Richmond, who received an allowance from James, which helped him to buy Goodwood for use as a hunting lodge in 1697. He would receive the favour of Louis XIV, a handsome allowance in France, and serve with distinction in the French army. He later returned to England, became ADC to William III, married into the family of the Earl of Cardigan, and founded a long line of Richmonds who became distinguished and high-ranking military officers.

Louise settled down in France with an annual income of 130,000 francs, much of it provided by Louis XIV in recognition of her services to him. The Protestant William III saw no reason to help the Duchess of Portsmouth and stopped her pension from England on his accession. Louise's extravagant life style meant she would be constantly pursued by hordes of creditors and she gradually descended into poverty. She returned to England in 1686–7, and again in 1688 for the marriage of her niece Charlotte, the daughter of her sister Henrietta and Lord Pembroke, to the notorious judge Jeffreys. She would survive by almost 50 years the King she had loved. Voltaire, who met her in Paris when she was about 70, commented on her beauty even in her old age. She died in Paris in 1734, aged 85, and was buried there in the Church of the Barefooted Carmelites, where there was a chapel of her mother's ancestors.

The Duchess of Cleveland lived until 1709, dying at the age of 69 in her house in Chiswick Mall (known today as Walpole House, after Sir Robert Walpole who lived there). Unlike Nell Gwynn and the Duchess of Portsmouth, she did not remain faithful to Charles's memory. Her lovers multiplied and, when she became a widow after 40 years of official matrimony, she remarried – or so she thought! She accepted the proposal of General Robert Feilding, 'commonly called Beau Feilding, the universal flame of all the fair sex',[27] and went through the marriage ceremony with him, only to discover her new husband was already married. The general, having already married one virgin, one widow and two heiresses and 'survived all four blessings', was now looking for another wife and fortune. Two weeks earlier he had mistaken a recent inmate of Bridewell for the rich heiress she claimed to be, and married her. Before the bigamy was discovered, Feilding had taken all Barbara's money, sold her furniture, locked her up, beaten and starved her. Feilding was arrested and convicted. Queen Anne pardoned him – all to no purpose, for marrying yet again, he accumulated more debts and landed once more in Newgate. Barbara was buried in the graveyard at Chiswick, but no stone marks her resting place.

Hortense, Duchess Manzini, died 10 years earlier than Barbara at her home in Chelsea. Her husband paid her debts and, unable to get his hands on his wife during her lifetime, he brought her body back to France and buried her in Brittany, where, according to legend, miraculous cures took place at her tomb.[28]

Charles's long-suffering Queen, Catherine of Braganza, retired to her native Portugal. On her death she was buried in the monastery of Belem, near Lisbon.

21

King Monmouth and an Expanded Army

On the death of Charles II, there were fears that the accession of an openly Catholic king would provoke public disorder. Precautions had already been taken by the principal Secretary of State, the Earl of Sunderland, who instructed mayors at the ports to detain and search 'all suspected persons', and the lords lieutenant to alert the militia and garrison commanders to suppress any dangerous political demonstrations. Regular soldiers were deployed around London, always a source of potential disturbances. But the legitimate succession passed peacefully, the nation greeting the proclamation of the new King with shouts of approbation and joy, while the soldiers saluted him with their cannon.[1] James promised to preserve the established order in church and state and to defend the prerogatives of the crown. Elections were held for a new House of Commons, where the Tory court party, persons of approved loyalty and affection to the government, received an overwhelming majority.

On his accession on 6 February 1685, James immediately assumed the title of commander-in-chief of the English army and issued new commissions to all the officers, for which they had to pay a fee to the Secretary at War. He also informed assize judges that it was his will and pleasure that all persecution of his Catholic subjects should cease forthwith. He calmed Louis XIV's protests against his summoning Parliament by assuring him that it was only to obtain his revenues.

Economy would be the keynote of his reign. The funeral of the late king was conducted frugally, some might say with parsimony. James did his best to reform the court – 'its gaiety and diversions disappeared', according to Burnet. He no longer openly pursued women, but still smuggled them up the backstairs to his private apartments. A number of household servants and officials were dismissed and, to placate the new Queen, the most expensive of his mistresses, Catherine Sedley, was moved from her Whitehall apartment to the house in St James's Square occupied by his former mistress, Arabella

Churchill. James gave up seeing her, albeit briefly, and in compensation doubled her annual pension to £4,000.

On 23 April James was crowned in Westminster Abbey with pomp and ceremony, and with high hopes for the future. His military escort, the officers of the First Regiment of Foot Guards, were exceedingly richly dressed; some in coats of cloth of gold, others in crimson velvet, embroidered or laced with gold or silver. Most were in fine scarlet cloth buttoned down the breast, with silver plate on the facings of the sleeves. The Coldstream officers were similarly dressed but differing in their embroideries. All wore crimson or gold sashes round their waists, and hats adorned with white feathers. The privates wore red coats, the Grenadiers lined and faced with blue, blue breeches and worsted stockings. Coldstreamer's coats were lined with green, with red stockings and breeches. Both regiments favoured black, turned-up hats, garnished with blue or red ribands respectively.[2] It would be James's proud boast that

> he had formed a very complete body of men, tho' not numerous, with the reputation of being the best-paid, the best equipped and the most sightly troops of any in Europe.[3]

Londoners would certainly notice the difference between James's smart, well-dressed English soldiery and the slovenly appearance of the foreigners who came to occupy the capital with William of Orange.

But six weeks after his coronation, James was confronted with armed rebellion on 11 June. Parliament was aware by the middle of May of the threats posed by the exiled Earl of Argyll and Duke of Monmouth, and of their plans for simultaneous risings in Scotland and England. Not only did Parliament vote the revenues normally given to Charles to the new monarch for life and pay off Charles's debts, but they also promptly voted the necessary supply to reinforce James's army. (In February 1685 the army numbered some 7,500 men, with another 1,400 permanently attached to various garrisons.)[4]

As a result, James II started his reign with an income of nearly £2 million (almost double that granted to Charles II at his accession). It was enough to allow him to manage without parliaments for the rest of his reign. Parliament also passed a Bill of Attainder, which declared Monmouth a traitor and permitted his execution without trial. At the same time, the House of Commons debated the dangers of a standing army, officered by Roman Catholics, being used to overthrow the established church. Mindful of the Popish Plot seven years earlier, and in constant fear of Catholicism, both Houses insisted that the Test Acts and Penal Code should be retained completely. James's reply was to dissolve Parliament.

James had studied the art of war on the Continent, having taken part in four campaigns under Louis XIV's great commander, Turenne, and two more under the Spaniards. He had proved himself to be a capable general, trained in military administration by Louvois, and had both admired and encouraged England's armed forces – he regularly attended their parades, mock battles and sieges. James put little faith in the county militia, which he considered militarily inept and politically unreliable, but regarded his regular troops and those in Scotland and Ireland as a reserve force to be used in a crisis. And just such a crisis loomed on the horizon with the invasions of Argyll and Monmouth.

The rebellions of Monmouth and Argyll are tragic stories. The Duke of Argyll had been exiled, and in the spring of 1684 started to plan an invasion force to return to his native Highlands to fight the English. Argyll's rebellion was short-lived. With £10,000 given to him by the widow of a London merchant, who had followed him to the Netherlands, Argyll fitted out three small vessels and set sail in May 1685 with 300 men for Scotland. There he hoped to raise an army from his clansmen and Presbyterian supporters. But he failed to rouse the Lowlanders, his followers deserted him, and his ships were captured. Royalist troops intercepted his force and soon he was a fugitive. As Trevelyn phrased it, the rest of his story was to prove little more than the hunt, capture and execution of an incompetent leader who knew how to die.[5]

Monmouth's landing at Lyme Regis on 11 June 1685, with only 82 men and half the amount of money available to Argyll, proved a different proposition, illustrating the importance of effective leadership in military operations. Monmouth has been criticised for being politically incompetent and militarily indecisive; personally handsome, but weak and empty-headed. Nevertheless he possessed charisma, 'a glamorous and popular figure, who had all the qualifications to raise a great mass movement and to lead it to total disaster'.[6] For all his ineptitude during the rebellion, which lasted less than a month, he was able to raise and bind together an army of over 7,000 men in a matter of days. Moreover, he gave his motley collection of followers from the west country, ready to fight and die for their cause, a confidence which he himself did not feel. As an experienced army officer, he could have had little faith in such an ill-equipped and inexperienced collection of men pitted against the regular soldiers of the royal standing army, which he had once commanded.

The events of the early life of the Duke of Monmouth help to explain his character and his reasons for launching the rebellion. His mother, Lucy Walter, grew up in the fashionable neighbourhood of Covent Garden, where at 14 she became the mistress of one of Cromwell's officers. According to Lucy herself, the handsome Colonel Algernon Sidney, 'trafficked for her first for 40 broad pieces'. When he had to leave with his regiment for Ireland, he handed her over to his younger brother Robert, a colonel serving in Holland. There she joined the circle of young Royalist aristocrats at The Hague.

When Charles arrived at The Hague in July 1648 from Paris, he heard of her charms and quickly took the place of Robert, who apparently surrendered her willingly for 'she was already sped' with child. Evelyn, who saw Lucy in Paris, described her as a brown, beautiful, bold but insipid creature,[7] while Pepys added that it was well-known she was a common strumpet before the King was acquainted with her.[8] Historians consider it highly unlikely that Charles married Lucy Walter: the King himself publicly and strenuously denied any marriage, calling on Almighty God as witness, the faith of a Christian and his word as a King (2 January 1680). He accepted James as his child, albeit illegitimate, and always treated him as the eldest and most favoured of his sons.

Deserted by Charles when he left Holland to lead his army at Worcester, Mrs Barlow, as Lucy now called herself after a maternal uncle, supported herself and her child in the only way she knew – as a court whore. Scandal surrounded her and Charles took his son away from her in 1658, placing him in the care of William Crofts (later Baron Crofts of Little Saxham, Suffolk) and a tutor. Lucy died a few months later, aged 28, 'of a disease incident to her profession'.[9] Unremembered and unmourned, she was laid to rest in an unmarked grave in the Huguenot cemetery in the Faubourg St Germain.

On his father's restoration, Monmouth exchanged the poverty and neglect of his childhood for the luxury and licence of the court at Whitehall. He grew into a handsome youth, inheriting his mother's beauty and instability. He was outrageously indulged by his doting father and became a favourite with the Queen and ladies of the court. In 1663 Charles created him Duke of Monmouth, with precedence over all other dukes except the Duke of York, and heaped other honours, both civil and military, upon him. He was given apartments in the palace and a sizeable annual income, and in 1668 his father bought him a captaincy in the Life Guards, with seniority over all other regular army officers. He was made personally responsible for the safety of the King and his court.

He rose rapidly in his chosen military profession, becoming a general in the French army. His gallantry at Maestricht (17 June 1663), in company with Captain John Churchill and 12 gentlemen privates of the English Life Guards and the celebrated French musketeer d'Artagnan, earned him a military reputation, which was acknowledged by Louis XIV and by Monmouth's supporters in the exclusion crisis. At the age of 30, Charles gave him command of the royal army in Scotland at Bothwell Bridge (22 July 1679), where Monmouth defeated the Covenanters. Mercifully he checked the slaughter which ensued. 'I cannot kill men in cold blood; that is work only for butchers,' he told the King, who blamed him for taking prisoners. Charles made him captain general of his 'Kingdom of Scotland'.

His tour of the west country in 1680 had demonstrated his popularity with the common people, whose Protestant faith he shared. Encouraged by

Shaftesbury, he believed he had also the support of the Whig gentry: the Whig exiles and the conspirators played on his ambitions. They persuaded him the English people supported his claims to the English throne and promised him that with the right leader, and the support of Argyll in Scotland, they would rise in rebellion. He may also have believed that the army and the regiments he had once commanded, together with his brother officers, would support him against a Catholic succession. But his father's firm and consistent line on hereditary succession and Charles's support during the exclusion crisis for his brother in preference to his son, whom he refused to legitimise, dashed his hopes.

Monmouth's final banishment in 1683, stripped of all his honours and military and civil appointments, alienated him from his father. It reinforced his hatred for James, whom he blamed for all his misfortunes. True to his promise to his father, during his short but unsuccessful visit to London in 1684 to seek reconciliation with him, he had spent his year of exile avoiding politics and the intrigues around him. The news of his father's death caused him great grief, and James's succession offered him only the prospect of an indefinite exile. All that remained for him was to live by his sword, on his wife's generosity or in domestic bliss with his young mistress Henrietta Wentworth (a peeress in her own right, who had left her home and family and sacrificed her honour to share his exile). Unless he returned home as a conqueror, England and his rightful inheritance would be gone forever!

From the beginning, James realised the dangers of a foreign-led insurrection against himself and his throne. He shared the mutual hatred of his nephew, Monmouth, a bastard upstart with his graceful manners and easy popularity. As a teenager, Monmouth had successfully challenged his social position as the second man in the kingdom, mocked him at court, and even supplanted him in the bed of a mistress (the actress, Moll Kirke). Social rivalry became political challenge when Monmouth joined Shaftesbury and his Parliamentary supporters to exclude him from the throne. James hated these Parliamentarians: nonconformists and republicans who had murdered his father, Charles I, and forced him into exile and 11 years of poverty. Now they posed a threat to his Catholic policies and his divine right of legitimate succession to the thrones of England, as James II, and of Scotland, as James VII.

It was Argyll and his plan to invade Scotland with a supportive or diversionary invasion of England, which finally persuaded Monmouth to move. The two men had met in Rotterdam in April, when Monmouth, much against his will, had given his promise to lead the English invasion. As the King's son and heir, and a former commander-in-chief of the royal army with a distinguished military record, he could not leave the leadership to lesser men, however risky the venture in his professional judgement. Bishop Burnet wrote that the Duke was pushed into it against his own sense and reason; but he could not refuse to hazard his own person when others were so forward.[10] Dryden expressed it more poetically –

> The ambitious youth, too covetous of fame,
> Unwarily was led from virtue's ways,
> Made drunk with power and debauched with praise.[11]

To have any hope of success he had to move quickly, for Argyll's plans were well advanced and he had the larger resources. By pawning his goods and plate and his wife's jewellery, Monmouth raised £3,000. Clearly he would have to rely on English support for manpower, equipment and money. He had chosen a landing spot, beside the Cobb at Lyme Regis, which was easy enough to reach from Holland but reasonably far from the King's base in London. Moreover, it was in an area which had received him enthusiastically in his 1680 tour of the west country. But bad weather delayed his sailing for a month, which destroyed any hope of co-ordinating his invasion with that of Argyll. In fact, Argyll was captured on 18 June, only a week after Monmouth arrived in England.

So Monmouth landed at Lyme Regis with 82 men in three small ships, in resplendent uniform and declaring himself 'Captain-General of the Protestant forces of England', with a legitimate and legal right to the throne. He accused James of murdering his father, promised the country annual Parliaments, no standing army and toleration for all Protestants.[12] When he reached his rallying point at Taunton, he was received with rapturous enthusiasm, and presented with a bible by girls from a local ladies' seminary led by a teacher with sword in hand. He was declared King of England by the mayor on 18 June 1685.

His army had grown to around 7,000 men, but Monmouth noted with some foreboding that he was short of experienced soldiers and that not a single Guards officer had defected to his colours. Only one gentleman of distinction, John Speke of White Lackington, had joined him at the head of a company of ragged horse.[13] Few Whigs, in fact, among the west country gentry openly supported him, London proved apathetic, and the promised diversionary risings in the north did not materialise. Nevertheless, alarmed at the support given to Monmouth, Parliament passed an Act of Attainder outlawing him and voted an extra £400,000 to help defeat him.

Moving slowly because of the size of his army and the inclement weather, Monmouth made his way via Glastonbury, Wells and Shepton Mallet towards Bristol, the second city in the kingdom, strongly nonconformist and rich in provisions, money and arms. James had been alerted, and reconnaissance forces under John Churchill were already harassing the rebel army. Churchill knew Monmouth well, often having served under his command and had saved his life at Maestricht. He, too, was a Protestant; but a realist – not a man to support a doomed cause. Riding with him were four troops of the Earl of Oxford's regiment of Horse Guards (the Blues) and two troops of Churchill's own regiment, the First Royal Dragoons. This regiment was originally Monmouth's Horse, which the Duke himself had commanded in Scotland and in the service of France. There were fewer than 400 troopers in total, but they were all experienced cavalrymen, trained to reconnoitre, protect the flanks of an advancing army, and harass the enemy.

James had given titular command of the royal army to the Earl of Feversham, older and senior to Churchill, a French Roman Catholic and nephew of Marshal Turenne, whom James much admired. He had come to England with the Duke of York, was naturalised in 1665 and given an English peerage in 1673. But Churchill, the better soldier, was really in command, and was promoted brigadier as compensation for the lack of official control.

The King's army was ordered to assemble at Bath. Colonel Percy Kirke set off thither with five companies of infantry, some 500 men of the Queen's Regiment, veterans of Tangier, to join Churchill's cavalry. The Duke of Grafton, Barbara Castlemaine's second son and Monmouth's half-brother, followed with 2,000 grenadiers, representing two battalions of the First Foot Guards, and a train of light artillery. En route, too, was a battalion of the Coldstream Guards under Colonel Sackville and five companies of Dumbarton's regiment, the Royal Scots, escorting the main artillery train from London and easily recognisable in their red coats, white breeches and deep white cuffs. There were also three Scots regiments from the Low Counties, reviewed by the King himself in Hyde Park before leaving for the west country. Completing the field army were five companies of Trelawney's Regiment (later the 4th Foot), under John Churchill's younger brother Charles. They were the escort for the heavy artillery from the fortress at Portsmouth, transported by civilian drivers enlisted for the occasion. In support were elements of the militia from Devon, Gloucester, Somerset and Wiltshire.

Monmouth, pondering his forces before Bristol, considered them reasonably well-officered but lacking in training, short of artillery and with inferior cavalry. He had superiority in numbers and had got the better of early skirmishes with the militia. But he doubted the ability of his troops against the regulars of the royal army, many of whose regiments he had personally commanded in battle over a period of 17 years. He hesitated to attack Bristol and this hesitation proved fatal.

Although heavily outnumbered, Feversham and his 4,000 Royalists stood firm inside the city, whose inhabitants were threatened with bombardment from the castle should they demonstrate support for Monmouth. With his army drawn up on the hills overlooking the city, the Duke sent a herald to order the citizens to surrender; the city guards shot him dead. Looking in the direction of Bath, Monmouth knew the entire Royalist army was advancing steadily towards them. Daunted, he withdrew his forces towards Frome, where he learned of Argyll's defeat. Here, 2,000 of his followers deserted him, disappointed at his failure to fight a decisive battle, miserable with the atrocious weather, and tempted away by the warmth and proximity of their homes and families. One who remained was Daniel Defoe, author of *Robinson Crusoe* and *Moll Flanders*.

Monmouth decided to occupy and fortify Bridgwater, as his headquarters and base for future operations. The London Gazette for 16 July gives a lurid, if exaggerated, account of his dispirited troops as they passed through Wells. En route they robbed and defaced the cathedral, drinking their villainous healths at the altar, plundered the town, ravished the women, and committed all manner of outrages.[14] Monmouth later swore that the only wrong his troops had done was to strip the lead from the cathedral fabric to make bullets. But Lord Grey, his cavalry commander, was seen standing at the high altar with a drawn sword to protect the sanctuary from violation.

From the church tower at Bridgwater, the Duke surveyed with a military eye the Royalist dispositions five miles away around the small village of Weston Zoyland, near Sedgemoor. He decided to attack from the flank at night to avoid the enemy's artillery and most of its cavalry. The manoeuvre involved a three-mile approach march by foot and horse, in the dark over bog and moorland. The plan might achieve surprise, but it was a dangerous and difficult gamble, even for seasoned and well-trained troops.

The royal army expected a frontal attack down the main road and had deployed its troops and posted its sentries accordingly. On the right flank were Dumbarton's Royal Scots under Lieutenant Colonel Douglas: in the centre were two battalions of the Grenadier Guards – one commanded by the young Duke of Grafton. The Coldstreams under Colonel Sackville were stationed on the left with the five companies of Trelawney's Regiment under Lieutenant Colonel Charles Churchill, and five companies of the Queen's Regiment under Colonel Percy Kirke. The cavalry were concentrated in the village of Weston, with the artillery behind the left flank.[15]

When darkness fell, Monmouth, on foot, led the winding column of more than 3,000 men. He had nearly achieved the surprise he needed, when a single shot, either fired accidentally by one of his officers or, more generally agreed, deliberately by an alert sentry of Lord Oxford's blue-coated troops, aroused the sleeping royal army. Thanks to John Churchill's coolness (as general officer of the day, while his commander slept), and to the precautions taken by Dumbarton's regiment in marking out their battle positions with tapes during daylight hours, the royal army recovered quickly after some initial disorder. The result was a massacre, as their superior artillery destroyed Monmouth's cannon, and at dawn, Feversham's infantry and cavalry routed and pursued the rebel army. It is estimated that Monmouth lost 300 killed in battle and 1,000 in the pursuit, with 1,200 taken prisoner. The royal army lost 400 killed and wounded.

Monmouth had fought bravely but was captured, haggard and exhausted, trying to escape. He was escorted to Whitehall under a strong guard and imprisoned in the Tower. James refused to spare his life and, after saying farewell to his wife and children, he walked through the Traitor's Gate to his execution on 15 July 1685. His last words were once again to express his love for that 'virtuous and godly lady', his true wife and mistress, Henrietta Wentworth, claiming that he had been too young when he had married Anne, the Duchess of Buccleuch. Evelyn gave him an epitaph –

> Thus ended the quondam Duke, darling of his father and the ladies, being extremely handsome and adroit, an excellent soldier and dancer, a favourite of the people, debauched by lust, seduced by crafty knaves . . . He was a lovely person.[16]

Many ladies thought so, too. Many tears were shed, and many handkerchiefs were dipped in his blood as it trickled down the scaffold, for many regarded him as having died a martyr for the Protestant cause. He was buried in the Royal Chapel of St Peter ad Vincula in the Tower beside the bodies of two Queens (Anne Boleyn and Katherine Howard) and Lady Jane Grey – all, like Monmouth, beheaded. Henrietta died nine months after her lover, some said from a broken heart.

Clemency was not a Stuart virtue, and to fight against the sovereign was high treason. James took a savage revenge on the rebels, even if judged by seventeenth century standards. For six weeks after the battle, Feversham and Colonel Percy Kirke (who, as in Tangier, was to earn for himself and his soldiers, however unjustly, a reputation for savage cruelty) rounded up the fugitive rebels to face trial as traitors, on the King's orders.

> To Kirke was to be attributed every injustice and brutality, every rape, theft and plunder, every murder and degradation that was done, or said to have been done, by all the King's soldiers and loyal subjects in the West.[17]

He was accused, for example, of hanging 17 prisoners in the market place at Taunton, where he established his headquarters in the White Hart, and of using its signpost as a gallows.

The courts, too, were kept busy, as parish constables sought out those who had made war on the King. Over the next nine months, until James issued his 'most gracious and General Pardon' on 10 March 1686, some 2,600 men and women were herded into the prisons and bridewells to be tried as political pris-oners by the magistrates. Eight hundred rebels were sent to forced labour in the West Indies, and at least 150 were hanged in the 'Bloody Assizes' presided over in Winchester Castle, Salisbury, Dorchester, Exeter and Taunton by Judge Jeffreys, who was given the powers of an army general in the west country.[18]

Some suffered the awful punishment of being hanged, drawn and quar-tered. The town officials were required to provide the necessary equipment – the gallows and halters, faggots and tar for furnace and cauldron, spears and poles 'to fix their heads and quarters on' and an axe and cleaver 'for quartering the said rebels'.[19] Eleven rebels, for example, were hanged and quartered at the landing place at Lyme Regis and their remains hung in chains in various parts of the town, such as Cobb Gate. Another 12 were hanged elsewhere in the town. Others, spared disembowelment and mutilation, were simply hanged and left to die.

For women traitors, for whom 'the decency due to the sex forbids the expos-ing and publicly mangling their bodies', the punishment was burning alive. Elizabeth Gaunt was burned at the stake for having saved one of the conspir-ators of the Rye House Plot. Lady Alice Lisle's sentence of burning was altered to beheading: she was deaf and over 70 but the widow of a regicide, and found guilty 'on evidence so clear,' said Jeffreys to the jury, 'that had she been my own mother, I would have found her guilty.'

Other rebels suffered the lesser punishment of whipping, often at the cart's tail, 'until his or her body be bloody', as the law stated. Titus Oates was flogged with merciless severity from Aldgate to Newgate by the famous hangman, Jack Ketch and his assistants, followed two days later by another whipping from Newgate to Tyburn, tied to a sledge, because he was too ill to walk. Judge Jeffreys, in passing the sentence, did not expect Oates to survive the ordeal; but Oates did survive, witnessed by dense crowds, who thronged the streets to see him take his punishment of over 2,250 lashes from a whip of six thongs. He lived to enjoy, except for an annual appearance in the pillory, a comfortable retirement on a pension awarded by Parliament after the revolu-tion in 1688.

The sale of pardons to delinquents, especially rich landowners like Edward Prideaux, who paid £15,000 for his pardon, provided large sums of money for King and judges alike. Even the humbler prisoners were priced at £10 to £15 apiece by Jeffreys. It proved a profitable investment, too, to secure consign-ments of prisoners sentenced to transportation to the notoriously unhealthy West Indies for 10 years of bondage instead of the usual four. This was a traf-fic in which individual courtiers, the Queen and her maids of honour (to whom James 'gave' the girls of Taunton who had presented 'King Monmouth' with an embroidered banner and the pocket bible) made a considerable profit.[20] The

Taunton girls, for instance, fetched about £2,000: an average of £70 a piece for the maids of honour.

Transportation 'to parts abroad' was regarded as a less severe penalty than execution but it was also regarded as a chance for a criminal to redeem himself (or herself) and become a useful settler and for the state 'to quit itself of the undesirables' from prisons such as Newgate, Bridewell and the Marshalsea. It is interesting to note that transportation also provided the first foundation of our system of colonial defence. During their servitude these white servants or 'slaves' were obliged to serve in the ranks of the colonial militia, not as free men but as the subjects of their masters. Every planter was required by law to furnish his quota of men and to take his place at their head to act as officer. The colonial militia was more efficient than the militia in England because it had three big advantages. There was the presence of powerful (and often hostile) neighbours, native or European; little help was to be expected from the mother country; and, in the tropics, there was the eternal dread of a negro uprising. For instance, Barbados, an island no larger than the Isle of Wight, had in 1685 six regiments of foot and two of horse, some 6,000 men in total. Jamaica had seven regiments of 4,000 men.[21]

Passing through Windsor on his return from the 'Bloody Assizes' in the west country, Judge Jeffreys was given the Great Seal of England, the office of Lord Chancellor. At the age of 40 he had reached the pinnacle of his profession – the youngest man ever to have held that office. Four years later he was to die in the Bloody Tower!

Monmouth's rebellion gave James a pretext to bring the Regiment of Guards in Scotland (established on 1 May 1661) to London, and create a larger and more efficient regular army. With this he aimed to secure the country from invasion from abroad, defend his throne from internal rebellion, and control his sullen and recalcitrant citizens – especially those in London, whose loyalty he distrusted. Although the royal army at home had been strengthened by the return of the regiments from Tangier, he now demanded the return of two foot regiments (Monck's and Belasyse's) from the Anglo-Dutch brigade in Holland. In due course they became the 5th and 6th Regiments of Foot on the English establishment.[22]

The money voted by Parliament, once granted, was entirely at the King's disposal. Between June and August 1685, armed with this money, James set about raising 10 regiments of cavalry, nine of infantry and a train of artillery (comprising men, guns and horses and specialists, in addition to artillery and engineer officers).[23] At the same time he formed the independent garrison companies in Ireland into 19 new regiments, one of which survived into the next reign as the Royal Regiment of Ireland (18th Foot).

To raise and command the English units, James relied on leading nobles and old county families; men of substance, who had a stake in the land and a duty to their King. These 'Trusty and Well-Beloved Subjects' commanded the militia, and most had seen previous active service. Of the cavalry regiments, for example, only the Second Horse (The Queen's Regiment of Horse) was raised by a commoner, Sir John Lanier. Seven earls and a viscount were responsible for the rest. Charles Seymour, the sixth Duke of Somerset, and Lord John Berkeley, a younger son of Viscount Fitz-Hardinge, recruited the Third and Fourth Regiments of Dragoons respectively.[24] Charles, Earl of Shrewsbury, and Sir Thomas Grosvenor (MP for Chester and ancestor of the present Duke of Westminster) with his son Hugh and nephew John raised troops of horse in Lichfield and Chester. On 29 July, at the King's command, they took their troops to Hounslow to form the Seventh Regiment of Horse.

Title and wealth also combined in the raising of the foot regiments. Two were formed by dukes (the 11th Foot by Beaufort, the 12th by Norfolk), two by earls (the 10th by Bath, the 13th by Huntingdon), two by barons (the 7th by Dartmouth and 8th by Ferrers of Chartley), while two baronets, Sir Edward Hales and Sir William Clifton, raised the 14th and 15th respectively. The only untitled new colonel was Henry Cornewall, who raised the Ninth Foot and came from a leading Herefordshire family.[25]

In addition to title and position, wealth played its part in the formation of these regiments. The Duke of Somerset, for instance, married Lady Elizabeth Percy, the richest heiress in England, in 1682. She was the daughter of Joscelyne, the eleventh and last Earl of Northumberland, and bore her husband 13 children in a union which lasted 40 years. The Duke of Somerset owed all his wealth and at least half his importance to his marriage.[26]

Sixteen-year-old Lady Elizabeth, pursued by every fortune-hunter in the land, had already been married twice. In 1679 her grandmother, the widowed Duchess of Northumberland, who brought her up, refused her ward's hand to Charles II's son, Charles Lennox, Duke of Richmond. She bestowed it instead on the Earl of Ogle, a sickly boy of 15 who was heir to the second Duke of Newcastle. On his death a year later Elizabeth married 'that well-battered rake', Thomas Thynne of Longleat, colonel of the Wiltshire militia and companion of Monmouth, with whom he frequented London's brothels and gaming rooms. The marriage was not consummated, for the 14-year-old bride fled to The Hague and took refuge with Lady Temple, the ambassador's wife. Within months Thynne was killed in Pall Mall (where the United Services Club now stands) by three assassins hired by the Swedish nobleman, Count Königsmark, one of Elizabeth's unsuccessful suitors.

In accordance with the legal position of married women during the seventeenth century, by which –

> That which the man hath is his own.
> That which the wife hath is her husband's –

the Duke of Somerset owned his wife's vast estates and property, including her Northumberland House in the Strand. His position entitled him to be the second mourner at Charles II's funeral, where his handsome figure appeared to advantage. He also took the chief part in similar pageants in the funerals of Mary, William III, Anne and George I, and bore the orb at four coronations. It was due to his wife's wealth that Somerset was able to raise and command the 3rd Regiment of Dragoons.

The first of James's new regiments was raised on the day Monmouth invaded England, 11 June 1685. The King issued a warrant:

> To our trusty and well-loved counsellor, George, Lord Dartmouth, Colonel of our Royal Regiment of Fusiliers and Captain of a Company in the said Regiment . . . These are to authorise you, by beat of drum or otherwise, to raise volunteers to serve as soldiers in your own company in our Royal Regiment of Fusiliers, which we have appointed to be raised and whereof you are Colonel.[27]

Dartmouth had served at sea against the Dutch, commanding Prince Rupert's flagship *The Royal Katherine* in 1673. James equipped his regiment (later designated the 7th Foot) whose second colonel would be John Churchill, the future Duke of Marlborough) with new flintlock muskets, the equivalent of the French *fusil* (hence the name of the regiment), which the French army had found useful for guarding their artillery because it was safe with gunpowder. The Royal Fusiliers were thus designated an 'ordnance regiment', a trained and disciplined body of men to guard and escort the guns and prevent panic among the drivers. Drivers were hired or impressed civilians who were likely to flee, usually with their horses, on nearing a battlefield.

Dartmouth had been responsible for the miners at Tangier and knew their value, so he added a company of miners to his regiment. He was already master-general of the ordnance at the Tower of London, responsible for the royal artillery and all artillery and engineer commissions. He also commanded one of the two independent companies which had garrisoned the Tower for many years. These two companies were incorporated into the new regiment, to which the King gave the royal title and its emblem, the Tudor rose inside the garter, all under the crown.

Twelve companies of fusiliers and the one of miners were thus recruited and based in the City (which the regiment still regards as its home). Each company had three officers, three sergeants, two corporals, two drummers, and 100 private men. In August the regiment marched out of the Tower to the King's camp on Hounslow Heath, resplendent in their new uniforms of wide-skirted red coats, lined and cuffed with yellow, grey breeches and stockings, with yellow bows at the knees. On their heads they wore conical red caps with a yellow turn-up. The officers sported felt hats with a feather, the brims turned up at one side. Their hair was long and curled, falling to the shoulders – colourful and romantic figures but as yet untrained.

The camp on Hounslow Heath, near the present site of Heathrow airport, had been established on 19 June, and also housed Princess Anne of Denmark's (8th) and Henry Cornewall's (9th) Regiments of Foot. The latter were part pikemen and part musketeers, 1,000 strong, and dressed in scarlet coats lined with orange. They would spend the first four years of their life on garrison duty in various parts of the country, before seeing action at Londonderry (1689) and in the Battle of the Boyne (1690), at Aughrim (1691) and at the sieges of Limerick and Athlone.

Within the next three days the l0th to15th Regiments of Foot were formed: raised and equipped with remarkable speed, recruits flocking to join, the yeomen bringing their own horses and swords with them. The Royal Fusiliers, for example, took over their duties at the Tower the day before the battle of Sedgemoor. Whatever their own moral shortcomings, comments Atkinson,[28] the nobles and gentry of England were not prepared to have Charles's reputed bastard imposed upon them as King; and in June 1685 James had not yet turned his subjects against him. But it was not the new raised men that James relied on to suppress the rebellion: it was the trained and experienced troops of the standing army.

One of these new regiments, the 11th Foot, The Duke of Beaufort's 'men of distinguished loyalty who resided in North Devon', would have the distinction of supplying the first soldiers of the royal army to the East India Company. In June 1687 the ship *Caesar* sailed for India with 100 soldiers of the 11th Foot, to whom 'His Majesty had been pleased to give leave to go into the said East India Company's service'.[29]

The warfare in Tangier had shown the need for, and lack of, a balanced proportion of cavalry in the royal army. One of James's first acts, as an able military commander, was to remedy this deficiency in the additional forces he created in 1685. He raised eight new cavalry regiments, six of which later became established as the 1st to 6th Regiments of Dragoon Guards.[30] Of these, the 3rd Regiment would become known as Princess Anne of Denmark's Dragoons, because its founding colonel, John Berkeley, was an intimate friend of James II's younger daughter, Princess Anne. (Berkeley was married to Barbara Villiers, daughter of Colonel Sir Edward Villiers, a younger brother of Barbara Castlemaine's father.) The other two cavalry regiments raised were the 3rd and 4th Hussars.

Typical of these cavalry regiments was the 4th Horse (Plymouths), recruited as six separate troops from the English counties of Worcester, Oxford, Northampton, Bedford, Huntingdon and Middlesex. Like most of the new cavalry regiments, the 4th Horse was not used at the battle of Sedgemoor. But on

15 July 1685, the day that Monmouth was executed, the King signed a warrant appointing Thomas, first Earl of Plymouth, to be its regimental colonel. The soldiers of Plymouth's Regiment would be used by James as pawns in his political designs for an absolute monarchy. Recalcitrant towns and cities which refused to accept his pro-Catholic measures had troops forcibly billeted upon them. Not only had the inhabitants to feed and house the soldiers and cavalry horses but, as in the case of the 4th Horse in Huntingdon in 1688, the soldiers were created freemen of the borough and allowed to participate in elections – as supporters of the King.

Lord Richard Lumley was appointed the first colonel of the Carabiniers (the 9th Regiment of Horse), raised on 31 June 1685. He had seen active service in Tangier, and was master of the horse and treasurer to Queen Catherine of Braganza, who became Queen Dowager after Charles's death. She honoured Lumley's regiment by naming it the Queen Dowager's Regiment of Horse. Lumley had previously commanded an independent troop of horse, raised in Hampshire, which was engaged in the mopping-up operations after Sedgemoor and helped to capture the fugitive Monmouth in the New Forest, escorting him to London for imprisonment and execution. The colonelcy of the 9th Horse was Lumley's reward – but, despite his Catholic upbringing, he was uncomfortable at James II's court. He became a Protestant and was one of the officers who signed the invitation to William of Orange to come to England. William created him first Earl of Scarborough shortly after his accession. On 2 April 1689 William appointed him colonel of the First Troop of Horse Guards, and he fought for the Protestant cause at the Battle of the Boyne.

While the standing army was dispatched to put a speedy end to Monmouth's ambitions in the west country, the King reviewed his newly-formed and untrained troops at Hounslow Heath camp. The camp would become an annual event for training and exercising his army every summer during his reign. Reviews were held with great pomp and ceremony, watched not only by the court circle but also by crowds from London, who came to see the spectacle. After his first inspection at his Great Review of 22 August 1685, James wrote to William of Orange:

> On Saturday I saw some of my troups at Hounslow: they consisted of ten battalions of foot, of which three were Gards and the other seven new raised regiments. Of horse there were twenty squadrons and one of Grenadiers on horse-back and really the new troups of both sorts were in very good order, and the horse well mounted.[31]

James, his staff, and the general officers had their tents in a special enclosure. The River Thames wound round the rear of the camp, with a regiment of fusiliers to guard both bridges. In the rear were the family tents, baggage, and the sutlers' tents, where the troops could buy their beer and rations, except the officially issued bread. There, too, were the hospitals, each directed by a matron, who had a maid servant or cook 'to dress the sick soldiers' diet' and three nurses or tenders to help in taking care of the sick and washing their linen. Nearby was another tent serving as a chapel.[32]

This concentration of regiments into a field army for the first time during peace was not only useful for training and for the King to exercise command in person, but also as an army encamped close enough to the City to overawe it. James failed to achieve this objective: instead, the Londoners took complete possession of his army and welcomed this new form of entertainment with delight.

A visit to Hounslow became their favourite holiday amusement. The Camp presented the appearance of a vast fair. Mingling with the musketeers and dragoons was a multitude of fine gentlemen and ladies from Soho Square, sharpers and painted women from Whitefriars, invalids in sedans, monks in hoods and gowns, lacqueys in rich liveries, pedlars, orange girls, mischievous apprentices and gaping clowns, all constantly passing through the long lanes of tents.[33]

The tents extended for some three miles, with the foot in the centre and the horse on either flank. 'In truth, the place was merely a gay suburb of the capital.' The camp became a fashion, for then as now the women loved a redcoat, and where the women led, the men followed.[34]

Sir John Rearsby, who had been commissioned in 1678 to raise an independent company of foot in York, visited the camp with his wife and daughter. They admired the spectacle: the manoeuvres, the mock battles and sieges, the great feasting, the great concourse of people, and the almost daily visits of the King, dressed in a red uniform and carrying his general's baton. But the young girl had to be shielded from some of the sights in the long line of tents, which were full of lewd women, some the companions of soldiers, others there 'to debauch them'.

In 1686 nearly the whole regular army – nine regiments of horse, three of dragoons and 15 foot battalions, totalling 18,000 men – collected at Hounslow for the summer camp. Regiments learned to manoeuvre in brigades and to take their places in a line of battle. The army would not get such regular and systematic instruction again until Aldershot and the Curragh came into being after the Crimean War. But, while the politicians grew daily more alarmed at the sight of mass being said openly in the camp chapel-tents on Sundays, and the continual increase in the number of Irish recruits, to the rest of London it was all vast entertainment. James gained a fortuitous, if fleeting, popularity by bestowing on his grateful capital a foretaste of what Battersea Pleasure Gardens would be for a later generation!

The 15th Foot (The East Yorkshire Regiment) paraded at the 1686 camp under its colonel, Sir William Clifton, a Yorkshire baronet. When the camp dispersed the regiment marched north to Carlisle, covering 300 miles in 30 days. Major Barker, in charge of the troops, was court-martialled for allowing his soldiers during the march to beat local inhabitants, break open several houses and cellars, and refuse to pay for their quarters. He detained commandeered wagons longer than necessary, refused to pay the recognised hiring fee, and he and the troops used bad language.[35]

The Scots Guards, newly recognised as part of the body of Foot Guards, were also at the 1686 camp. The Scots Guards were now spending the winter quartered beside the two regiments later known as the Grenadiers and Coldstreamers. In March 1642 Charles I had asked the Marquess of Argyll to raise a royal regiment, but it was defeated and scattered at the battle of Worcester. Charles II resurrected the regiment in 1660 as the Scottish Foot Guard to garrison Edinburgh and Dumbarton Castle.

Since the Restoration the English army had been used actively to repress Presbyterianism (the Covenanters) in Scotland and quell, with brutality, the resultant civil disobedience. For this task the ideal soldier-policeman was the dragoon, half soldier, half cavalry, excellent for covering rocky and boggy ground or for storming parties during sieges. During the 1670s the Covenanters regularly attended their open-air prayer meetings with sentries posted to warn of approaching soldiers. In 1678 three companies of dragoons were recruited in Scotland and used the following year with royal infantry soldiers under the Duke of Monmouth to fight and beat armed Covenanters at Drumclog and Bothwell Brig.

So effective were the three companies of dragoons that in November 1681 they were formed into six troops in a new regiment, the Royal Regiment of Scots Dragoons (later the Royal Scots Greys).[36] Command was given to General Thomas Dalyell, whom Charles II had appointed commander-in-chief in Scotland on 1 November 1679 after he cancelled the Duke of Monmouth's commission as captain general.

Dalyell was a remarkable man by any standards. He had fought for Charles II at Worcester but was captured and imprisoned in the Tower, from where he escaped to join his future King in France. With few prospects in exile, he became a Russian general, fighting for the Tsar of Muscovy against the Poles and Turks. Later he was summoned home by the restored monarch to become, for the first time, commander-in-chief in Scotland in 1665. He was an uncompromising disciplinarian, who had threatened 'to spit men and roast' them and who had killed some in cold blood when serving in Russia.[37]

Dalyell drafted the Articles of War for the forces in Scotland and rigorously applied them. Of the 86 Articles, 42 specified the death penalty for offences ranging from murder to rape, pillage, cowardice before the enemy, being drunk on duty, insubordination and blasphemy; other offences were punishable by mutilation and whipping.[38] Dalyell's dragoons (raised as a national regiment and commanded by Dalyell to the day of his death from apoplexy in August 1685) were used in the suppression of the Duke of Argyll's rebellion in 1685. Having completed this task, the Royal Regiment of Scots Dragoons was called south by James, as part of the Scottish forces whose loyalty he hoped he could rely on in 1688, when invasion by William of Orange appeared imminent.

Sedgemoor was the last pitched battle to be fought on English soil. As an experienced military commander, James required all his commanders to submit detailed reports of the battle for his *History of the Rebellion*.[39] From their reports he drew three main conclusions.

Firstly, the county militia had proved useless, whether from inferior training, poor leadership, cowardice or lukewarm loyalty to the crown – and James had no time for military incompetence.[40]

Secondly, 'his three kingdoms had been saved by a handful of men' – the small force of regular soldiers, less than 4,000 of whom had fought at Sedgemoor. The survival of the monarchy therefore depended on having a larger army of professional soldiers.

Finally, loyalty was essential. Could he depend on the loyalty of a largely Protestant army, or should he increase the ratio of Catholic officers and men in the standing army? Parliament, he knew, preferred the militia to a standing army and would oppose Catholic policies in the military, as it opposed them in civil life.

These were the questions, which would bedevil his short reign, and find an answer in the Glorious Revolution.

22

A Popish Army to Enslave a Nation

After the battle of Sedgemoor, James possessed an army of 15,700 men in England, which would rise to almost 20,000 by the end of 1685, when mobilisation had been completed. Though his standing army was twice as large as Charles II's had been, it was smaller than Cromwell's, less than a third of the army William III would maintain from 1691, and puny compared with that of Louis XIV. Nevertheless, this army would now become the focus of a political storm. After suppressing the Monmouth rebellion, James sought to retain his troops in defiance of constitutional practice, and Parliament accused him of seeking to impose Popery on his kingdom by military force.[1]

On 9 November 1685 Parliament resumed its session. In his speech from the throne, the King referred to the incapacity of the Devon and Dorset militia even to deal with Monmouth's peasants at Axminster. Some militiamen from Somerset had actually fought for the Duke at Sedgemoor. He announced he needed

> a good force of well-disciplined troops in constant pay, that can defend us from such as, either at home or abroad, are disposed to disturb us and even to increase the number to the proportion I have done.

He admitted there were officers in his army who had not taken the oaths under the Test Act of 1673 but, in view of their past service and possible future needs, the King said he intended to keep them to guard against all disturbances from without and from within:

> The gentlemen are most of them well-known to me, having formerly served with me on several occasions, and have always proved the loyalty of their principles by their practice. I think them fit now to be employed under me. And I will deal plainly with you that, after having had the benefit of their service in such a time of need and danger, I will neither expose them to disgrace, nor

myself to the want of them, if there should be another rebellion to make them necessary to me.[2]

This royal demand for an army in which Roman Catholics would have concessions appeared to many of the listening MPs to be the direct prelude to arbitrary rule, and reinforced their fears of Popery. Sir Thomas Clarges, the late Duke of Albemarle's brother-in-law, suggested the expansion of the standing army was a first step to the introduction of absolute rule. He reminded the House that, in the Exclusion Bill debates, it had been prophesied that a Popish ruler would have a Popish army. He would be under constant pressure from his confessor and the Pope to extirpate heresy and impose Catholicism on England's Protestant subjects. He would try to overturn all anti-Catholic laws, fill offices, including the armed forces, with Papists, and rule by armed force.[3]

Members complained of the unruliness and insolence of soldiers and the burden of free quarters. The very idea of maintaining an army of idle persons to lord it over other citizens was anathema to some. Others complained that such armies

> debauched the manners of all the people, their wives, daughters and servants. Men do not go to church, where they are quartered, for fear mischief should be done in their absence.

Instead of the £1,400,000 demanded by the King, Parliament voted £700,000, but only to be spent on the discredited militia – saying it would make the militia more efficient, until such time as it was agreed necessary for the army 'to be kept up'.[4]

James, unlike his brother, had no political gifts. He was honest and single-minded, but bigoted and inflexible. He was an autocrat, who believed everybody who disputed his commands, was disloyal and he modelled himself on Louis XIV. He had a terror of civil war, and of following his father to the scaffold. He had publicly declared himself a Roman Catholic: now he openly attended mass. In the face of mounting criticism from the two Houses of Parliament, he decided to forgo the prospects of a grant to support the army and prorogued Parliament on 19 November 1685. From now on, he dropped his earlier caution and adopted pro-Catholic policies to free Roman Catholics from all penal disabilities, such as fines for non-attendance at Anglican services (Penal Laws), and disbarment from all offices and paid employment under the crown (Test Acts). His intention now was to restore the Church of Rome in Britain alongside the Anglican church.[5]

He dismissed the anti-French Earl of Halifax and appointed Sunderland, whom Louis XIV preferred, to lead a Catholic Cabal for the management of Catholic affairs. He began to canvass peers and members of Parliament to

repeal the Test Acts and penal laws which discriminated against non-con-
formists. (He offered Sir Thomas Grosvenor, for instance, a peerage and
command of a regiment for his support, but the MP for Chester refused.)
James sought legal support for his view that the laws of England were the
King's laws, and he was therefore entitled under royal prerogative to dispense
with any law he thought fit. This offended the Tory belief in the constitution
and revived fears of links between Catholicism and absolution.

Soon James was issuing batches of dispensations, enabling Catholics to
hold office without taking the Tests, giving them immunity from the penal
laws, and refunding their fines. He expelled the Fellows of Magdalene College,
Oxford, for their refusal to agree to a Catholic president. There were signs of
mutiny in the fleet because some ships' captains allowed mass to be openly celebrated on board; James went from ship to ship calling the seamen his
children and ordered the priests ashore. Then he promoted the Catholic officer who had ordered the celebration of the masses to the post of vice-admiral.

Making liberal use of the royal prerogative to dispense laws, James appointed Roman Catholics as admirals, colonels and privy counsellors. By granting
indulgences, through which he suspended the penal laws against those who
did not come to church or receive the sacrament or 'for any other nonconfor-
mity to the religion established', he offended the Anglican church, which had
enjoyed a monopoly of officers in church and state since the second year of
Charles II's reign.

He extended his personal rule to America, where he annulled the charters
of all New England colonies in 1686 and combined them into one unit – the
Dominion of New England – to which New York and New Jersey were soon
added. All local and provincial self-government was eliminated in the colonies:
James attempted to impose his own rule through a governor, who acted as his
personal representative.

In Scotland he prorogued Parliament, issued a proclamation granting the
right to public worship to all nonconformists, and suspended all the penal
laws against Catholics. In England he alarmed Anglican clergy by suspending
the Bishop of London, Henry Compton, a former cornet in the Earl of Oxford's
'Blues', who opposed the granting of army commissions to Catholics. He
authorised the opening of Catholic chapels, including a new chapel at
Whitehall, received the papal nuncio at Windsor and issued a Declaration of
Indulgence to be read in all churches on two specified successive Sundays.
The papists now swarmed at court, noted Evelyn in his diary.[6]

On 18 May 1688 seven bishops petitioned him against his Declaration.
James told them they had raised the standard of rebellion and consigned them
to the Tower; a month later, in June 1688, to his annoyance, they were acquitted. He claimed he wanted Anglicans and Tories to accept Catholics as equals
in both civil and religious rights, and to allow Catholics into political

appointments. These demands, though not extreme, were interpreted as undermining the Anglican church. Anglicans believed James intended to fill the majority of places in church and state, including the army, with Roman Catholics. By starting with the army – the most politically sensitive of all areas – the King's motives were suspected and proved unacceptable.[7]

Most serving army officers were Protestants and came from the Tory and land-owning class. They certainly felt threatened in their careers by James's Catholic policies, even though in 1687 Catholic officers only amounted to some 12 per cent of the total.[8] They saw how Louis XIV, after revoking the Edict of Nantes in 1685, had intensified persecution of the Huguenots (whose members had served France loyally in both army and navy) by quartering dragoons in their houses and by pillage, rape and murder.[9]

Fears grew in the army that James would follow his cousin's example. Despairing of establishing Popery by a Parliament, James might employ his 'Janissaries' to convert Protestants in England in the same way. One could easily imagine what a few hands might be able to do when authorised by a Popish sovereign and seconded by a well-disciplined army commanded by Roman Catholics, a contemporary complained.[10] (William of Orange would make similar claims[11] that James intended to use his Popish army to impose Catholicism and enslave the nation. The Convention Parliament declared in the 1689 Bill of Rights that James had tried to subvert and extirpate the Protestant religion and the laws and liberties of the kingdom. These were really overstatements: propaganda issued to support William's new monarchy and a new constitution.)

Early in his reign Charles II had employed a small number of Catholic officers in the Life Guards, Royal Horse Guards and Foot Guards, because of their ability and experience. He also wanted to reward them for their loyalty in the Civil War. Their number amounted to perhaps one or two per cent of the commissioned officers in these regiments between 1661 and 1685.[12] The Tangier garrison contained a few Catholics, mostly Irish; while there were others in the Anglo-Dutch brigade and in the colonies, where they were far removed from the Test Acts. Others enlisted during the Dutch wars, but caused Parliament no concern because Charles disbanded his new forces at the end of the emergencies. In any case Parliament controlled Charles's military budget, despite French subsidies.

But James did not disband the increased forces raised to repel the Monmouth invasion, thereby continuing the careers of many Catholic officers who had enlisted in open defiance of the Test Acts. Charles had bowed before the Test Act of 1678; James did not. Both needed experienced officers quickly. But James did not flood the army with Catholic officers. All the evidence[13] indicates that James's army contained only about one Catholic officer in eight and that, until the threat of William's invasion in 1688, the English military establishment hardly changed from July 1685. Even when the real expansion came in 1688, Sir John Reresby noted that William of Orange declared he brought over 4,000 Papists in his army – nearly as many Catholics as in James's English army.[14] James, too, claimed that in his army of 18,000 he had less than 1,000 Roman Catholics.[15]

What preyed on the minds of contemporary Englishmen[16] was not the number or percentage of Catholics in the English army, but the great purge which James and the army commander, Lieutenant General the Earl of Tyrconnel, had carried out in the Irish army. Whole battalions of Protestant soldiers were discharged, without even leaving them the clothes for which they had paid themselves. A simple oath of allegiance was prescribed for all officers and soldiers; no other oath was required of them.[17] The presence of this Catholic army, positioned just across the Irish Sea and thought ready to destroy the liberties and religion of the English people, posed a real threat. In 1685 it numbered some 9,000 men and was almost as large as the English army, though decidedly inferior in quality. From March 1685, Tyrconnel gradually replaced the majority of English and Protestants in the Irish army with Irish and Catholics; the last were removed at the end of 1688. The total displaced was estimated to number 300 officers and 4,000 other ranks.

But neither James nor Tyrconnel had any intention of using this army to intervene in English political affairs. The Irish army remained in Ireland, although late in 1688 a brigade was sent to England, specifically to oppose the Dutch invasion. When, in 1689, James was forced to rely on the Irish army, as almost his only means of regaining his throne, he found it virtually useless against the trained troops of William of Orange. There is no evidence to show that James intended using this army to impose Catholicism on England by force.

But religion was certainly a factor in dividing the loyalty of James's English army. Henry Howard, the seventh Duke of Norfolk, stemmed from a family of traditional Catholic support for the crown but was a staunch Protestant himself. He was one of the peers who had signed the proclamation hailing James as King. James authorised him on 22 June 1685 to raise the 12th Foot, the Norfolk, and later the Suffolk, Regiment, both counties having supplied the initial recruits. The Duke became disenchanted with James's policies and resigned, the colonelcy of the regiment passing to the Earl of Lichfield.

The 12th Foot contained a number of Catholics; James ordered the men to parade before him on Hounslow Heath, where he asked them to sign a declaration agreeing to help procure the repeal of the Test Acts (which required all officers in the public service to take the sacrament of the established church). Such a request was certain to divide the loyalty of the regiment. The Catholic major, George Trapps, ordered those who did not wish to comply with these instructions to lay down their arms. To the consternation of the King, the whole regiment grounded arms, save for two officers and a few Catholic private soldiers. The King strode off the parade, remarking, 'Another time I shall not do you the honour of consulting you'.[18]

To win over the King for the Church of England and save England from another internal struggle, the Secretary of State to the Treasury (the Protestant Earl of Rochester, Anne Hyde's younger brother and brother-in-law to the King) and Admiral Dartmouth, whose relationship with James was almost that of father and son,[19] devised a desperate plan. Bishop Burnet had tried without success to convert James from Catholicism: although James allowed his two daughters to be brought up as members of the Church of England and had assented reluctantly to the marriage of the elder to William of Orange, he himself remained firm in his faith. Now Rochester and Dartmouth proposed that Catherine Sedley, James's current mistress (whom he created Countess of Dorchester in January 1686, with an enhanced pension of £5,000 a year), should be given the same kind of official position (*maîtresse en titre*) as had been enjoyed by the Duchess of Portsmouth. A Protestant mistress would neutralise the influence of the Catholic Queen, Mary of Modena, and thus 'save the Lord's anointed from the Whore of Rome'.[20]

The Catholic faction opposing the scheme was headed by Sunderland, Tyrconnel, the commander-in-chief in Ireland, and Father Edward Petre, James's Jesuit confessor. They feared the danger of this royal contamination with heresy and the advantage a Protestant mistress gave to the enemy.

Queen Mary, a strong supporter of her husband's Catholic policies but outraged by his continuing attachment to his mistress, threatened to retire to a convent if he did not give Catherine up. Catherine Sedley became, for once in her life, a figure of political importance. She resisted attempts to remove her, but James eventually dispatched her to Dublin, where her friend Rochester was now viceroy. In August she was back at court, where James found her as irresistible as ever and visited her in great secrecy.[21] The King was also seeing other women 'in his closet at Whitehall', and his promiscuous amours distressed the Queen and her religious advisers. Louis XIV, who always thought highly of Mary's attractions, could never understand how such a beautiful woman could remain faithful to an erring husband 26 years her senior.

The Queen's jealousy upset her husband, who scourged himself in penitence for having lived so many years in almost a perpetual course of mortal sin and for 'letting myself go too much to the love of women, which for too long got the better of me: I have paid dearly for it.'[22] It would help to cost him his throne.

On 10 June 1688, at about two o'clock, the citizens of London were startled to hear the Tower ordnance fired and the bells of the city ringing. James's wife, Queen Mary of Modena, had given birth to a son in St James's Palace. As Mary had had four previous miscarriages, it was rumoured that the child had been smuggled into the bed in a warming pan! (Mary had little success at child-bearing – in addition to her miscarriages, four of her children died in infancy.) The boy took precedence in the succession over his half-sisters Mary and Anne, and was promptly baptised according to the rites of the Catholic church and christened James Edward. Queen Catherine and Barbara's husband, Roger Palmer, were signatories to the event. The Pope agreed to become one of the god-parents. It looked as if a Catholic succession was assured; but Fate had another card to play in the Stuart story!

23

A Simpleton, Who Lost Three Kingdoms For A Mass

With the birth of his son to assure the succession, James believed he had an army and a navy to protect it. As a last resort, if civil war threatened, he could rely on French support. But his Catholic policies and attempts to subvert English Protestantism from the top were uniting all classes against him. For most Protestants the birth of his son only helped to underline the dangers of Popery and absolute monarchy, and encouraged those plotting his downfall to open negotiations with William of Orange. In the autumn of 1688, the rebellion which James had long feared became a reality.

On the Continent his relationship with his son-in-law, William of Orange, was at first reasonably friendly. William, as captain-general of the United Netherlands, had agreed to return the English and Scottish regiments in Dutch service to help against the Monmouth rebellion – even offering to command them himself. But William's wife, Mary, was an enthusiastic Protestant, and William wanted to protect her right to succeed her father on the English throne. He also had a strong personal claim as a grandson of Charles I. He had agents and friends in England, who kept him fully informed of events there. He soon realised that James's use of his dispensing and suspending powers was alienating supporters of the Protestant religion. The birth of James's son meant that Princess Mary ceased to be heiress-presumptive by dynastic law, and it was reported that James planned to alter the succession in favour of his Catholic son. So the unscrupulous William supported the claim that James's son was an imposter. Despite the fact that 20 ladies and 46 gentlemen, including 18 Privy Councillors, had been present at Queen Mary's lying-in in her bedchamber at St James's Palace, each of whom made a signed statement at the public inquiry which followed, the substitution story was widely believed – prompted by the fear that a Catholic succession was now assured.[1]

Little did James know, in that summer of 1688, that William was contemplating an invasion of England. William had received assurances from six leading peers of the realm and the Anglican Bishop of London that most of England would welcome a rebellion, if a force strong enough to defend itself could be landed. William feared that James would conclude, or had already concluded, an alliance with France, as Charles had done before him. Worse, he feared that James's policies would provoke his subjects into civil war, which would render England impotent against Louis XIV's designs in Europe. In reality, James had no intention of making war on the Dutch or of allying himself with France. The suspicious Dutch Republic assembly, the States-General authorised William to take a force over to England to compel his father-in-law to alter his policies, regarding it as a private venture on William's part to protect his wife's claims to the English throne.[2]

It was Louis XIV, with his better intelligence network, who alerted James to the Dutch preparations and to his peril. He offered military assistance – some 12,000 to15,000 men, according to Burnet – to hold Portsmouth and keep open communications to France. But James feared that such a large army from France would unite the country against him. Right up to the last, Sunderland, his Secretary of State, whose 'command of connections and expedients' the King admired, convinced James that all his designs could be accomplished through a Parliament packed by Sunderland's supporters prepared to vote for the King's measures. Not until 28 September 1688 did James realise what everybody else seemed to know: an invasion was imminent.

On that day, James issued a proclamation warning the country that 'a great and sudden invasion from Holland with an armed force of foreigners and strangers' was posed to invade the kingdom, with the aim of 'utterly subduing and subjecting us and our people to a foreign power'. James recalled the writs for a new Parliament because of the serious military situation. To guard against the expected landing on the east coast, the Norfolk militia were put on a state of readiness; the Chatham and Medway towns, refortified after the 1667 débâcle, were alerted. Only then did James begin to equip and reinforce his army and navy, raising between September and November 5 regiments of horse and 7 of foot, 11 independent troops of cavalry and 30 independent companies of foot soldiers. He quartered 6 Scottish regiments (3 cavalry and 3 infantry), some 3,800 men, in and around London, while the Irish establishment provided 5 cavalry and 13 infantry regiments (some 5,000 men) to add to James's standing army of 22 cavalry and 24 infantry regiments. This made a total of some 40,000, according to James's own computation.

Two of these regiments, Douglas's (16th Foot) and Richard's (17th Foot) became regular regiments of the English establishment, together with the 18th Foot (the Royal Irish Regiment). This regiment was the only survivor of 19 regiments raised in Ireland from Cromwell's independent garrison and placed on the Irish establishment by Charles II in 1684. The oldest of the Irish regiments, they would fight against King James at the siege of

Carrickfergus, the Battle of the Boyne, the siege of Limerick and the engagement at Aughrim. Also transferred to the English establishment was the Royal Regiment of Scots Dragoons, the future Royal Scots Greys.[3]

The King sought, too, to pacify his Protestant subjects by putting his entire domestic policy in reverse. He set up a weather vane, which is still conspicuous on the roof of the Banqueting Hall at Whitehall, so that he might see from his own apartments when the wind was in a favourable quarter for his son-in-law to set sail: to determine whether the wind is Protestant or Popish, as a contemporary expressed it.

It was this wind which saw the birth of a regiment, according to the military historian of the Lancashire Fusiliers. A westerly wind confined William of Orange and his fleet to Dutch waters, while allowing James II to reinforce his army with troops from Ireland. But on 1 November 1688 the wind changed to 'Protestant'. William kissed his wife a tearful farewell (urging her to remarry if he failed to return – but not to a Papist), and sailed for Torbay; but the wind prevented James's ships from leaving the Thames to intercept him. On 20 November William issued commissions to raise three new regiments, one of them to Sir Robert Peyton, a soldier of fortune, who raised and became the first colonel of the Lancashire Fusiliers (20th Foot).[4] The regiment was sent to garrison Carrickfergus and would receive its baptism of fire at the Battle of the Boyne and the village of Aughrim.

James, in the meantime, might still have saved himself, had he shown resolution and a spirit of compromise. But he was wracked with indecision – unwilling to summon a Parliament, slow to make any concessions about religion, hesitant to commit himself to a French alliance, uncertain what help he could expect from France, unconvinced that William was engaged in designs against him.

The cause of much of this impotence was the Earl of Sunderland, who had personal and family connections with the great Whig and Protestant families of England and Scotland. In Charles's reign he had been dismissed from the post of Secretary of State, but was restored to office with the help of the Duchess of Portsmouth. He had learned how to survive disgrace, to make use of petticoat influence, to remove patiently those in office who stood in his way and, by royal example, to profit from religious conversion to the Church of Rome at the right moment. Interested in neither wine nor women, he devoted himself to his career 'with the ardour and asceticism of a monk'. He retained his place by pandering to the King and pretending to support his religious policy, while secretly ingratiating himself with the Prince of Orange – the best exponent of his times in the art of double-crossing.

Sunderland knew James's policies were suicidal, but he remained a sycophant in office because he desperately needed the money to pay off his gambling debts. While secretly pledging himself to support William in May

1687, he was guaranteeing an Anglo-French treaty of alliance in return for French money. Too late James II smelled treachery and dismissed him. Dressed in woman's apparel, he deserted his master and fled to Holland, where he reminded William of his services to the Protestant cause. But the Revolution in England ended his public career: thereafter 'he was considered beneath even the low-level requisite for politics. He was the craftiest, most rapacious of all the politicians of the second half of the seventeenth century.'[5]

What finally sealed James's fate and persuaded William to invade was a conspiracy in the army, many of whose principal officers had long had close professional contacts with the Dutch. In July 1688 James conducted a census through General Dumbarton to find out which officers and men in the army were Catholics. The army suspected this would lead the King to discharge the Protestants, or transfer them to service in Ireland, and replace them with Catholics. e.g. The Duke of Berwick enlisted 50 Irishmen into the 8th Foot.[6]

The conspiracy was effectively hatched during the 1688 summer camp on Hounslow Heath. It involved the élite regiments of horse and foot guards which were regularly stationed in or around London and in constant attendance on the court.[7] Regiments stationed further afield, in Scotland, Ireland and the outlying English garrisons, were unaware of the plans and would have been genuinely surprised at the early defections which occurred.

John Churchill, newly promoted lieutenant-general, was the central figure. He had a wide circle of contacts in the army and navy, and with the Anglican and Tory plotters at court and James's own daughter, the Protestant Princess Anne, through his wife Sarah. Every decision except those of hour and method had been taken. Churchill's mind had long been made up, his pledge given and his plans laid, wrote his descendant Winston Churchill. 'Churchill, Grafton and leaders of many of the King's trusted regiments were awaiting only a safe opportunity of going over to William.'[8]

The conspiracy was neither large nor widespread, and only when the military intervention of William was a certainty did the leading conspirators act. Besides Churchill, these conspirators were Prince George of Denmark (husband of James's daughter Anne), the Dukes of Ormonde and Grafton (James's nephew), Viscount Cornbury (eldest son of the Earl of Clarendon), the Earl of Oxford, and Colonels Kirke and Trelawney. They joined with the six peers Devonshire, Danby, Shrewsbury, Bishop Henry Compton, Admiral Edward Russell and Henry Sidney, who had assured William of their support. Together they began the practical task of arranging for the defection of the bulk of the armed forces, as soon as William landed at Torbay on 6 November – a task they did not succeed in achieving!

The King refused to recognise the existence of disloyalty in his armed forces. He could not believe that his senior officers, who had enjoyed his friendship and patronage during their military careers, could be so base as to rebel against him. The conspiracy itself was a poorly-kept secret, and James had been informed at the time of Dumbarton's census of the names of the leaders and the aims of the likely political and military defection. But he failed to appreciate the extent of the opposition lining up against him.

James assumed his army would remain loyal to the crown and to its paymaster, despite the political and religious rumblings to the contrary. In fact, his Protestant subjects in the army reacted to William's invasion with the same mixture of blind loyalty, apathy or organised betrayal as the civilian population. Substantial sections of the army and militia proved loyal: but the shock of the defections and obvious signs of rebellion destroyed James's faith in his army and with it his will to fight.

James had allowed the militia to fall into decay, so when he concentrated his troops into a field army first at Salisbury and then in battle positions along the River Thames to oppose William's advance on London, he left the provinces unprotected. William's supporters in England were thus able to seize the main provincial centres – Chester, York, Nottingham, Hull, Northampton and Norwich – during the last days of November. But James's army on Salisbury Plain totalled some 30,000, outnumbering William's by two to one. He also possessed as a potential reserve 8,000 to 9,000 garrison troops distributed around the country, mainly in the ports. The garrisons of Portsmouth, Tilbury and the Tower of London remained loyal to him.

William landed unopposed at Brixham Harbour in Devon with an expeditionary force of some 11,000 foot and 4,000 horse, the backbone of which were three English and three Scottish regiments from Holland. He entered Exeter four days later, and was received as enthusiastically as Monmouth had been at Taunton. The defections in the royal army began almost immediately and morale fell, for no army, however well disciplined, could fight under such a divided command. The appointment of Feversham as commander also ensured inaction and delay. Lord Cornbury, who had taken over command of the 'Royals' when John Churchill was promoted, led his dragoon regiment out to join the invaders. To their credit, most of the men refused to desert, so Cornbury and his officers crossed over to the enemy lines, leaving the men to fend for themselves.

At St James's, the Coldstream Guards were on guard and their colonel, the 80-year-old Lord Craven, prepared to fight in the streets, but Feversham forbade him to resist. James, who was having his portrait painted by Kneller for Samuel Pepys when news of William's landing reached him, had already sent orders to his commander to disband the regiments which remained loyal to him. Now James dismissed the Guards from their duty before the palace. A few hours later, William's blue-coated Dutch troops replaced them. The Bishop of London, Henry Compton, abducted Princess Anne from her Whitehall lodgings, rode off with her to join the Prince of Orange, and then reoccupied his see at the head of a troop of horse – the last of the soldier bishops!

Fortunately, Feversham was able to obey James's command and disbanded the main body of the royal army in a leisurely fashion. But many regiments of both horse and foot went over to William complete, though in most cases without some of their officers. Colonel Percy Kirke, asked about quitting the Church of England, replied that unfortunately 'he was pre-engaged for. When at Tangier, he had promised the Sultan of Morocco that, if ever he changed his religion, he would turn Mohammedan.'[9] Kirke was now able to forget his promise to the Sultan as he led his own regiment (the Queen's) and another Tangier unit, Trelawney's Foot, into William's camp. Prince George, Ormonde and Trelawney himself joined them, while Churchill and Grafton with 400 officers and troopers rode out of James's camp at Salisbury to join William at Axminster.

In December 1688 Aubrey de Vere, Earl of Oxford and Colonel of the Blues, forfeited his regiment when he joined William; a few weeks later (13 February 1689) he was promoted a lieutenant-general of horse and foot with a day's precedence over the future Duke of Marlborough. Prior to that, James had given his place as head of the Blues to the Duke of Berwick, his eldest illegitimate son by Arabella Churchill and a nephew of John Churchill. The Earls of Shrewsbury and Dorset also gave up their regiments of horse and followed Oxford to William's side. James's trusted Earl of Lichfield was transferred to the command of the First Foot Guards. The Duke of Norfolk, attended by 300 armed and mounted gentlemen, assembled in the market-place at Norwich and declared for William, bringing most of East Anglia to William's cause.

The Royal Fusiliers Regiment had already made a political statement to indicate their support for the Protestant cause. Among the seven Protestant bishops sent by James to the Tower of London in spring 1688 for protesting at the Declaration of Indulgence was the Bishop of Bristol, brother of Colonel Trelawney of the Queen's Regiment. It was the duty of the Royal Fusiliers, garrisoned in the Tower, to guard the bishops. Instead of handling them as prisoners, the regiment had treated them as honoured guests, drinking their healths and seeing to their every comforts. When the bishops were released, the regiment joined the rest of the army and the people in rejoicing. (The Queen's Regiment still plays *And shall Trelawney die?* as its regimental slow march.) Colonel Billingsley, commanding the 15th Foot at Berwick, consulted the officers of the regiment in church and told them he was resolved to declare for William and the Protestant religion. All the officers agreed and invited the mayor and officials of the town to do the same.[10]

Colonel Sir Edward Hales, who raised the 14th Foot (West Yorkshire Regiment) originally in Kent remained loyal to the King, and would help him to escape to France. Hales was captured and spent 18 months in the Tower. He later joined James in exile and died in Paris. His son was killed, fighting for James, at the Battle of the Boyne.[11]

Another who refused to change sides was Sir Theophilus Oglethorpe, who led a charge of the Life Guards at the battle of Sedgemoor. He was made colonel of the Buffs in October 1685 but remained loyal to James. As a result his regiment was later given to the Duke of Marlborough's brother, Charles Churchill. Regiments and individuals were uncertain of their loyalties – to the King, who had founded their regiments or given them their commissions, or to Parliament and the nation, which shared their Protestant convictions.

James, though an experienced military leader himself, panicked and refused to take command of his army or navy, relying instead on Protestant commanders like Feversham, who failed him. With Churchill, his best general, gone over to the enemy, served by an army which showed little enthusiasm for his cause, disheartened and ill in mind and body, he resigned himself to his fate. He ordered his baby son to be brought back from Portsmouth, where he had been sent with his nurse for safety. The baby Prince of Wales was taken to Queen Mary of Modena in London, who escaped from England disguised as a laundress and reached Calais with her infant son on 11 December. Meanwhile, Lord Dartmouth, had gone over to William's side to avoid bloodshed and Feversham having surrendered the army, offered his personal surrender.

By now all organised resistance had ceased and, cheered on by an enthusiastic people, William's march towards London became a triumphant progress rather than a military campaign. James left Whitehall in the early hours of the morning by a secret staircase and fled; William quietly slipped into St James's palace to take possession of his Kingdom. On 14 December James was captured at Faversham, waiting for a favourable tide to take him to France. He was bought back to Whitehall with an escort of 240 loyal Life Guards and Horse Grenadiers. But William did not want to be saddled with his father-in-law as a prisoner. He allowed him to escape to France, where Louis XIV provided a refuge for James and his family at St Germain-en-Laye, where his mother had lived and died 40 years earlier. James spent most of the rest of his life here in piety and domesticity. 'With this his reign ended,' wrote Bishop Burnet. 'In the crisis of his destinies, his judgement deserted him and by his fatuous flight he placed his throne in William's power.'[12]

Had James been of a different mould, like that of his notoriously libertine grandfather, Henri IV of France, who decided that Paris and a kingdom were well worth a mass, he might have kept both his Protestant mistress, Catherine Sedley, and his kingdom by accepting that London was worth the 39 Articles (the doctrine of the Church of England, established by Elizabeth I in 1571).[13] In 1696 Catherine, at the age of 39 ('too old for lust and proof against all shame')[14] married Sir David Colyear, a veteran Scots soldier who had served with distinction under William III in Ireland and in Flanders. He was created Earl Portmore, promoted major-general and given command of the 2nd Regiment of Foot.

The spiritless attitude of the King and the undermining of the loyalty of his army, for which Churchill was largely responsible, jointly saved England from civil war. Critics accuse Churchill of treachery and deceit, but in no other way could the country have avoided another blood-bath. To be loyal to a Catholic King and a Protestant country was impossible and Churchill, with Grafton and the others, put country before King. Ironically, William gave Churchill and Grafton, who had largely been instrumental in causing the confusion in the army, the task of making good their work. All English regiments were ordered into winter quarters by William, and their officers told to repair to their respective commands and 'not to absent themselves upon any occasion or pretext whatsoever without leave first obtained from us'.[15] All their guard, garrison and ceremonial functions in England were taken over by 'ill-looking and ill-dressed Dutch and other foreigners of the Prince's army'.[15]

Anarchy had followed James's cancellation of the writs to convene Parliament and the disbandment of the army. Action now had to be taken to preserve public order, as anti-Catholic riots broke out in London and threatened to turn into general mob attacks on property. In the provinces, too, the disbandment of so many troops led to rumours that ravaging and murdering bands of soldiers were approaching the capital; there were 'Irish alarms' as groups of Irish Catholic soldiers tried to reach the ports to return to their own country, and the gentry mustered the semi-defunct militia to preserve the peace. On 31 December Cavendish's (10th) Regiment of Horse (later the 7th Dragoon Guards) was raised by William, Duke of Devonshire, who had left Chatsworth with a small number of his retainers and collected gentry and yeomen in Derby and Nottingham to defend the Protestant religion.

Only William could restore proper order and establish normal government. But was he King or conqueror? Nobody wanted civil war or more bloodshed: an early settlement was needed.[16]

William convened a 'caretaker' assembly over Christmas to advise him, composed of peers and surviving members of Charles II's House of Commons and London's aldermen and city councillors. Then a national convention was established to settle the nation's future, until a new Parliament could be convened. On 22 January 1689 the convention decided that James by his flight had vacated the throne. On 13 February the Lords and Commons met, waited upon the Prince and Princess of Orange in the Banqueting Hall and formally offered them the throne – to William and Mary jointly, since William refused to become his wife's 'gentleman usher'. The offer being accepted, William and Mary were proclaimed King and Queen of England 'by the will of the people and not as Divine Right'. Parliament and monarchy were restored by a joint

Declaration of Rights, afterwards embodied in the Bill of Rights on 16 December 1689.

The threat of a Popish succession was over. William (aged 39) and Mary (aged 27) were declared joint sovereigns of England, Scotland and Ireland, and crowned in Westminster Abbey on 12 April 1689. (It was a Blue – Henry Compton, Bishop of London, a former member of the Royal Regiment of Horse Guards – who crowned them!) It was decreed that any Papist, or anyone married to one, was henceforth barred from succession to the throne. The sovereign was required to swear to maintain 'the Protestant reformed religion, established by law, and to govern according to the statutes in Parliament agreed on and the laws and customs of the same'.

The House of Commons also resolved that Parliament's thanks should be given to the officers, soldiers and marines in the army and the fleet and read out to each regiment for having 'testified their steady adherence to the protestant religion and been instrumental in delivering this kingdom from popery and slavery'.[17]

Mary would die without producing an heir. William lived on with war and battle to become one of the least popular kings in English history. He married off his mistress, Elizabeth Villiers, cousin of Barbara, Duchess of Cleveland, to one of his regimental commanders and thereafter lived and died with a lock of his wife's hair and her wedding ring constantly in his possession.[18]

24

Battlefield in Ireland

James never recovered from his bloodless defeat, but he made one last attempt to regain his throne. He misguidedly accepted the advice of Louis XIV, his wife Mary, and the Earl of Tyrconnel, his commander-in-chief in Ireland, to strike back at England and win back his kingdom through Ireland and the Irish. Louis wanted to create a diversion in Ireland to prevent William from prosecuting a Protestant war on the Continent, as Louis pursued his designs on the Spanish Netherlands. In February 1689 the Dutch declared war on France: in May the three British kingdoms would join the struggle under their new Dutch King. In the meantime, Tyrconnel persuaded James there was no lack of support in Ireland, though he needed money and arms. Louis promised James both.

James landed at Kinsale, near Cork, on 12 March 1689 and made for Dublin, where his lord deputy called on the Irish people to rise in the Stuart cause. Cromwell in a brief and cruel campaign had written his name in blood in the annals of Ireland, wrote Fisher. Native Irish were driven from their homes to make way for Cromwell's soldiers and land speculators from England; thousands of humble Celtic families had to find refuge among the desolate bogs of Connaught. The Cromwellian settlement, far from promoting the Protestant religion, had deepened the hatred of the native Catholics, leading to religious intolerance and bigotry still very evident today. Thus Tyrconnel's call to arms would inherit this legacy of division, and the contest would become more of a religious struggle than a civil war: Irish against Saxon, a subjugated people against the dominant race.[1]

Tyrconnel had filled the army in Ireland, the bench and the boroughs with Catholics and, by the time of James's landing, 100,000 Irish Catholics had responded to the call to arms. James's journey to Dublin became a triumphant procession through a countryside of loyal peasants, who regarded him both as their King and their liberator from centuries of religious persecution by the English. He arrived in Dublin on 24 March, with a few French officers, engineers and artillery specialists and a small French force of about 1,800 men, created Tyrconnel a duke and established his court in Dublin Castle. Within a month he controlled all Ireland, except some Protestant towns like Londonderry and Enniskillen in the north. But James proved unworthy of such a cause. To him Ireland was just a stepping stone to Scotland and thence to England. An Irish Catholic army was a reliable instrument for achieving that end. For Irish aspirations he had nothing but contempt.

Tyrconnel's hasty and ill-considered actions not only alarmed Protestants in Ireland but also in England. William, who assumed the appointment of commander-in-chief on 13 February 1689, realised that Ireland could only be reconquered by force. He countermanded James's order for the disbandment of the army and Parliament voted financial support. With this he raised six regiments of horse, two of dragoons and 25 of foot (including O'Farrell's 21st Foot, Colonel the Earl of Mars' Regiment, previously raised in Scotland in September 1678). Three regiments (the 18th to 20th of Foot, under their respective colonels, Forbes, Luttrell and Peyton) would survive subsequent disbandment orders.[2]

On 8 March William asked nine of his influential supporters to raise regiments of infantry, each regiment to consist of eight or 10 companies of 60 private soldiers. One such was Henry, seventh Earl of Norfolk, who some years earlier had raised the 12th Foot.[3] He now 'beat up round Chester and the Wirral' for some 700 men, to be armed with pikes, muskets and grenades, to form the 22nd Cheshire Regiment.[4] As was the custom of the times the regiment was originally called after the colonel – Norfolk – who owned and equipped it. A few months after his enlistment, the London Gazette of 1689, published a notice concerning one of these recruits – the barber-surgeon, who performed both functions in a regiment:

> Run away, out of Captain Soames' Company, in his Grace the Duke of Norfolk's Regiment of Infantry (22nd Regiment), ROGER CURTIS, a barber-surgeon:-
> > A little man with short, black hair,
> > Round faced, fresh coloured,
> > Light-coloured cloth coat, with gold and silver buttons,
> > Red plush breeches and white hat.
> Information to Francis Baker, Regimental Agent, Hatton Gardens
> 2 GUINEAS REWARD FOR CAPTURE.[5]

After only a few months the Duke of Norfolk resigned the colonelcy and was succeeded by Sir Henry Belasyse, who had commanded the 6th Foot, when it had been in the Dutch service.

Another of William's nine influential supporters was Henry, fourth Baron Herbert of Cherbury, who raised the 23rd Regiment of Foot (the Royal Welsh

Fusiliers), which assembled at Ludlow.[6] Baron Herbert, who paid the customary £6,000 for the privilege, became the regiment's first colonel. His family had great possessions in the Welsh Marshes. Both the 22nd and 23rd Foot Regiments would fight in the battles of the Boyne and Aughrim, and both would survive to become part of Britain's permanent army establishment.

The third of William's supporters to raise a regiment which has survived to the present day (the other six of the original nine were disbanded before the end of the century) was Sir Edward Dering, who raised the 24th Foot. Dering was one of 17 children born to an ancient Kentish family, and succeeded to the title of third baronet of Surrenden, Kent in 1684. He had seen no previous military service before being commissioned as colonel of the regiment; although, like many landed gentlemen of the period, he had dallied with part-time service in the local militia. In those days a man's social standing and the capacity of his purse mattered as much as military prowess or qualifications. Dering recruited 900 all ranks, kitted, armed and paraded them in less than three weeks. His second-in-command was his brother Daniel, an experienced military and naval officer, who fled to England as a result of Tyrconnel's Irish purges and brought with him several of his experienced brother officers.

At first, William had no regular troops in Ireland on the Protestant side, except six companies of General Mountjoy's regiment under Major Gustavus Hamilton who had voted to join his cause, leaving the other seven companies supporting James. These six companies took part in the defence of Londonderry, the main stronghold of the Protestants, and six years later achieved 'the distinguished title of the Royal Regiment of Ireland, won at the sword's point'.[7]

The defence of Londonderry (or Derry as the Catholics call it) therefore rested mainly with its 30,000 inhabitants: to this day the 'Prentices of Derry of 1689' are remembered with pride among the Protestants of Ulster for their part in the 'no surrender' struggle, closing the gates against the Catholic Earl of Antrim and his men.

James attacked the city, behind whose ramparts were crowded almost all the militant representatives of the Protestants in Ireland. He called repeatedly for the citizens to surrender, promising them a free pardon. But they refused, though the governor was ready to make terms. The governor, Colonel Lundy, fled, leaving the besieged to face 105 days of starvation and disease, during which 'cats, mice and rats and even carrion horse flesh were selling at high prices. Half of the garrison died and over 100 officers and 8,000 men were lost to the enemy'.[8] The siege reached a stalemate, until some English ships appeared in Lough Foyle carrying supplies and men of the Queen's regiment and of the 9th and 11th Foot under General Percy Kirke and forced the boom across the river. Colonels Thomas Cunningham (9th Foot) and Solomon

Richards (17th Foot) were later 'broke for cowardice' in the first attempt to relieve the garrison. A few weeks later, James's French commander, Rosen, raised the siege.

The French troops were notoriously addicted to pillage and their commander allowed them the utmost licence, despite protests from James, who realised the damage being done to his cause. Their example was followed by the Irish troops, with the result that the inhabitants fled from the surrounding countryside to Inniskilling (Enniskillen).

> Soon that town was filled with men whose hearts were aflame with rage and longing for revenge. This one had seen his homestead burnt to the ground and his cattle driven off or slaughtered: another had seen his wife, sister or daughter brutally mocked and outraged or even carried away by the licentious French troops. All hated the French, all thirsted for the blood of the (to them) despicable Irish.[9]

The townspeople met together, elected officers and a governor, and formed themselves into strong bodies of horse and foot. Thus was formed Wynne's Inniskilling 6th Dragoon Guards (later the 5th). (The Governor, Gustavus Hamilton, commissioned Captain James Wynne, a gentleman of Ireland and a captain in Colonel Stuart's regiment, to form a regiment as Colonel on pay of 15 shillings a week.) On the same date, 20 June 1689, Sir Albert Cunningham's (or Conyngham's) 7th (later 6th) Dragoon Guards were created from various regiments formed in 1688,[10] and Colonel Zacharias Tiffin's (27th) Regiment of Foot, the Royal Inniskilling Fusiliers – all taken on the English establishment by William in 1690.

Cunningham's Dragoon Guards suffered heavily at the Battle of the Boyne, in which James Wynne's Dragoons were also engaged in desperate fighting. The official history records[11] the fighting during the sieges of Limerick and Athlone (1691):

> For three hours did a sharp fight continue, in which the Irish women boldly joined, and when they failed to obtain more deadly missiles, threw stones and broken bottles. At length when the ammunition was spent, while the Irish fire increased, the troops were recalled from the covered way.

Sir Albert Cunningham was killed in the last few months of the war and was succeeded in command of his regiment by his son, Henry.

The Royal Inniskilling Fusiliers also fought with great bravery, at times armed with little more than scythes and reaping hooks, from the Boyne to the fall of Limerick. They would earn the right to carry the badge of the castle of Inniskilling flying St George's banner.

Just after the relief of Londonderry, General Kirke sent Colonel William Wolseley to take command of all the Inniskilling forces. He was a man of exceptional military talent, who quickly organised the Protestant volunteers into an efficient, regimented force. Although outnumbered three to one, they defeated a strong detachment of James's army at Newton Butler on 30 July in one of the bloodiest battles of the Irish war. This success, together with the collapse of the siege of Londonderry, saved Northern Ireland for the Protestant cause.[12]

Meanwhile, in August 1689, William sent another large army to Ireland under a Huguenot general, the Duke of Schomberg. On 13 August Schomberg's force, which had sailed the previous day from Hoylake on the Wirral with 10,000 men, disembarked at Bangor on Belfast Lough. This was the first expeditionary force undertaken by the standing army so recently recognised by law, and was welcomed by the local Protestants,

> swarming down to the beach, weeping for joy, falling on their knees to thank God for their safety and regarding every red-coat as an angel of deliverance.[13]

The troops camped on the beach, while the 12th Foot pushed forward to occupy Belfast and 300 men marched to Antrim. They found the Irish army almost disabled by its unsuccessful siege of Derry–fever, dysentery and battle casualties had decimated the troops. The commander of Antrim had retreated south to Newry to cover the Duke of Berwick's forces advancing north from Dublin. Only Carrickfergus near the mouth of the Lough was defended, and even that garrison capitulated after a week. By the terms of the surrender the garrison was permitted to march to Newry; but the local Protestant inhabitants, enraged at their own treatment by 'these rebels, thieves and murderers', set upon them, when they were four miles out of town. They would not only have disarmed and beaten the Irish but possibly even massacred them had not Schomberg and the English officers intervened, annoyed at so gross a breach of the surrender terms.[14]

James decided to withdraw his forces to Dublin, after setting fire to Newry. This left Schomberg free to follow him – but his army was unfit for such an expedition. Instead, Schomberg decided to fortify Dundalk and remain on the defensive for the rest of the season. His 10,000 men had been landed in hostile country without an organised food supply or medical facilities: starvation was imminent and foraging showed corn lying rotting in the fields. Everything else had been burnt, devoured or carried away. The camp had been badly sited on boggy ground, the rain fell in torrents, and the men had no tents. The soldiers died at first by dozens, later by hundreds, many from exposure. By October, Herbert's regiment (23rd Foot) had lost 421 dead, over half its total, without firing a shot; Colonel Dering of the 24th Foot died of a fever and was succeeded by his brother. Sir Henry Belasyse (or Bellasis), having taken over the colonelcy of the 22nd Foot from Norfolk, moved his large number of sick from the camp to the ships in hired waggons, the corpses being left to rot on the roadside. Funeral ceremonies were forbidden for fear of further depressing the troops.

In two months Schomberg lost 6,000 men and scores of survivors were sick and ineffective. Schomberg dared not venture south after James, he told William, because his men were raw recruits, who for the most part were badly armed and clothed, and unable to fire a musket, even if they possessed one. He complained that English officers would neither train their soldiers in the art of war nor look after their bodily needs. This he attributed to cavalier officers believing their peacetime duties did not include any preparation for war, and that an officer when not actually fighting was free to enjoy himself.[15]

Schomberg spent the winter in restoring the health and discipline of his shattered forces and filling his supply depots for the spring campaign of 1690. The Irish, for their part, busied themselves with training their men, strengthening their fortresses and raising new regiments. Early in 1690, William decided to go to Ireland in person, with an army capable of obtaining a decision. He landed at Carrickfergus in June 1690 with an army numbering about 35,000 men – a motley collection of English and Dutch regiments, supplemented by detachments of Huguenots, Germans, Danes and Finns from the Protestant League of Augsburg fighting against Louis XIV. They were reinforced by the loyalists in Ireland.

William, backed by all the power and wealth of England and Holland, poured men, horses, arms, clothing and provisions into Ireland as fast as transport could be found for them. Regiment after regiment arrived from England or from the Continent. Learning from the past year's disasters, responsible contractors were engaged to provide the commissariat with transport and provisions.

This was in marked contrast to James, who had neither the financial resources nor home-raised produce to supply his forces. France alone could help, but Louis was more interested in the mainland of Europe than in providing large sums of money and men to Ireland, which had little part in his schemes of French aggrandisement. Nevertheless, he did send James a contingent of 7,300 well-armed and equipped soldiers, but demanded an equal number of Irishmen in exchange. James's forces totalled some 37,000 men.

The issue was decided on 1 July 1690 at the Battle of the Boyne, when William with 40,000 men totally defeated James's army encamped by the River Boyne, some three miles from Drogheda. It was a minor engagement in itself; but coupled with the battle at Aughrim a year later, where William decisively defeated Franco-Irish forces attempting to defend the line of the River Shannon, it sealed the fate of Ireland and of the Stuarts. It led to the political dominion of Protestant England over the Catholic Irish for the next 200 years. Today, the Battle of the Boyne has become part of Irish historical folklore.

James, a spectator of the battle, saw his troops defeated and fled to Dublin without striking a blow or receiving a wound.[16] With his flight the way to Dublin was open; the morale of the Irish was broken and the conquest of the rest of Ireland was a mere formality. As for William, the Battle of the Boyne was won without great credit to his skill and paid for rather dearly by the death of gallant old Schomberg. The 81-year-old general was buried with honours in St Patrick's Cathedral, Dublin.[17]

William was careful not to take James prisoner, since his capture would have proved an embarrassment. So James returned gladly to the comforts of St Germain and Versailles, believing the Irish debacle was God's punishment for his sins. There he lived always surrounded by his friars, noted a contemporary, and talked of his misfortunes with indifference.[18] His Regiment of Foot Guards in Ireland remained loyal to him and shared his exile, continuing to wear their old red coats with blue facings in the French service. The regiment would cease to exist during the Napoleonic wars. As for Tyrconnel, who despite his illness had fought bravely at the Boyne, he sent his wife to France with all the money he could scrape together. He died at Limerick after the disastrous battle of Aughrim, 12 July 1691.

James had hoped for help from Scotland, or at least a strong Jacobite diversion, but his hopes were dashed when the commander of his troops in the Highlands, the Earl of Dundee, was killed and his army overwhelmed in the pass of Killiecrankie on 27 July 1689. A month later, in the small cathedral city of Dunkeld, William Cleland, with little more than 1,000 of his Presbyterian psalm-singing Cameronians, defeated a much larger force of Highland clans in a savage battle which decided the Stuart cause in Scotland for ever. Two foot regiments, the Earl of Leven's 25th Foot (first known as the Edinburgh Regiment of Foot and later the King's Own Scottish Borderers) and the Earl of Angus's 26th Foot (better known as the Cameronians) were mustered at this time.[19] So too, were the Fifth Dragoons, raised by Lord Cardross, who because of his sufferings as a Covenanter had emigrated to North America and founded a plantation at Charlestown. Driven out by the Spaniards, he joined William in Holland and fought with his dragoons at Killiecrankie.

When James was expelled from England, Louis XIV had promptly declared war on Protestant Holland in February 1689 and reminded England of its treaty obligations to assist France. A force of 10 regiments under General Lord Marlborough (John Churchill) was shipped to the Continent. The Scottish soldiers of Colonel Dumbarton's regiment (the Royal Scots), one of the reformed units of James's army but with many Jacobite sympathisers in its ranks, were stationed at Ipswich ready to embark for France. They objected to a foreigner as their colonel-in-chief, and mutinied in March 1689. The mutiny was soon quelled and the ringleaders punished, but it illustrated the need for a special code of military law to regulate the conduct of soldiers, especially in cases of mutiny, sedition and desertion, for which the civil law made no provision.

The House of Commons was thus stirred to pass the first Mutiny Act, which became law on 3 April 1689. At first in force for only six months, it provided, with subsequent additions, a statutory basis for army discipline, authorised by Parliament and enacted annually, until a permanent Army Discipline and Regulation Act was passed in 1879. It is important also because its preamble, confirmed in the Bill (later the Declaration) of Rights, defined the legal basis for a standing army in peacetime: the crown could not lawfully raise or maintain military forces in peacetime without the consent of Parliament. All this was despite the fact that the standing army had already been in existence for nearly 30 years! The actual wording of the Act is:

> Whereas the raising or keeping a Standing Army within this Kingdom in time of Peace, unless it be with the Consent of Parliament, is against law.[20]

The prerogative of the sovereign to command the army is not specifically mentioned in the earlier Mutiny Acts, but it is tacitly recognised,[21] and all martial power is by those Acts legally to emanate from the sovereign alone. The sovereign is the sole head and commander of the army, the dispenser of military honours and titular rewards, and the source of all military authority – although in practice the sovereign has usually, but not always, delegated military command to an army officer.

The army today has every reason to remember James II kindly. Not only did he add eight cavalry and 11 infantry regiments to the line,[22] which have now given over 300 years distinguished service to crown and country, but he also did much to train and develop his army, which increased to 20,000 men in peacetime (34,000 if one adds the regular forces of Scotland and Ireland). The birth of the British standing army might have taken place on 14 February 1661, but its true creation came with the army's rapid expansion between 1685 and 1688 – and James II was its creator. As a younger man James had fought well in battle and the Duke of Wellington regarded him as the best master-general of the ordnance there had ever been.[23]

James loved his army, but he asked too much of his soldiers, most of whom shared the Protestant faith of the nation. He made the mistake of expecting his troops to fight for his Catholic-orientated policies and his army to support an authoritarian monarchy. His fatal error was trying, in the name of religion, to rid the English army of all but the most devoted to his service. This caused sufficient ill-will and suspicion among a small number of officers to ruin his whole design. After his overthrow the standing army was returned to the society from which it had grown: to it we are indebted for the political and religious freedom we enjoy today.[24]

Our story has chronicled the birth of the modern British army and told of its first 25 years as a small force of some 6,000 regular soldiers devoted to guarding the King and securing his throne. Its men were never popular, and the army itself was feared by Parliament and the majority of the population as a potential threat to civil and religious liberties. In times of emergency extra troops were recruited, to be disbanded as quickly as possible once the emergency was over.

In the next five years the baby grew lustier in strength and employment. It became a standing army of some 20,000 men, with another 14,000 in Scotland and Ireland. It was no longer supported by the monarch's pocket, but from funds supplied by Parliament intended for the militia. The fears of Parliament and the populace grew stronger, though threatened military rule never materialised. Its battles would be fought at home, where the numbers involved, though substantial, would never match Continental standards.

In the next two decades (1690–1713) the three separate armies united, and under a magnificent general (Marlborough) this British army with its allies would show its valour and capabilities on the European scene in a series of splendidly-won battles. It would not reach maturity until many years had passed and many campaigns been fought and won in all parts of the globe. At least the British army had made a healthy beginning.

Appendices

Appendix A

(See Adams – *History of the British Regular Army* Vol I)

Regiments formed from the Restoration to the Battle of the Boyne (1 July 1690) and taken on the permanent English establishment.

Charles II

1661   Life Guards (four troops)
        Royal Horse Guards (Blues)
        1st Royal Dragoons (Tangier Horse)

1 Foot Guards (Grenadiers)
2 Foot Guards (Coldstream)
Three Scottish regiments of Foot Guards (on Scottish establishment, moved to English establishment 1685)
1st Tangier Regiment of Foot (2nd Foot, Kirke's or Queen's)

1664   1st Maritime Regiment of Foot (the Lord Admiral's Regiment; disbanded 1689)
1665   The Holland Regiment of Foot (3rd Foot or Buffs)
1678   1st Foot (Dumbarton's Regiment; returned to England and placed on English establishment)
1680   4th Foot (2nd Tangier Regiment or Plymouth's)
1681   The Royal Regiment of Scots Dragoons (2nd Dragoons or Dalyell's)

At the end of the reign the regiments of 'Our Guards and Garrisons' were:

Household Cavalry	Horse	Dragoons	Foot Guards	Foot	Marine
4 Troops Life Guards	1	2	3	4	1
3 Troops Horse Guards					

James II

1685   5 Foot. Clare's (Monck's)   (James recalled both these
         6 Foot. Vane's (Belasyse's)   regiments from Holland. Previously
                                     known as 1st and 2nd. English
                                     Regiments of the Anglo-Dutch
                                     Brigade.)

1685   7 Foot. Dartmouths or the Royal Fusiliers
         8 Foot. Princess Anne of Denmark's
         9 Foot. Cornewall's Regiment of Foot
         10 Foot. Granville's Regiment of Foot
         11 Foot. Beaufort's Regiment of Foot
         12 Foot. Norfolk's Regiment of Foot
         13 Foot. Huntingdon's Regiment of Foot
         14 Foot. Hale's Regiment of Foot
         15 Foot. Clifton's Regiment of Foot
         3rd Dragoons. Somerset's
         4th Dragoons. Princess Anne of Denmarks (or Berkeley's)
         2nd Horse. The Queen's or Lanier's
         3rd Horse. Peterborough's
         4th Horse. Plymouth's
         5th Horse. Thanet's
         6th Horse. Arran's
         7th Horse. Shrewsbury's
         8th Horse. The Princess Anne of Denmark's or Scarsdale's
         9th Horse. The Queen Dowager's or Lumley's

1688   16th Foot. Douglas's Regiment of Foot
         17th Foot. Richard's Regiment of Foot
         18th Foot. Forbes's Regiment of Foot (transferred from Irish establishment)
         19th Foot. Lutterell's Regiment of Foot
         20th Foot. Peyton's Regiment of Foot

At the end of the reign the regiments of 'Our Guards and Garrisons' were:

Household Cavalry	Horse	Dragoons	Foot Guards	Foot	Marine
4 Troops Life Guards	10	4	2*	20	1
4 Troops Horse Guards					

* 3rd Foot Guards on Scottish establishment until 1686

Appendix A

William III
(to the Battle of the Boyne)

31 December 1688   10th Horse. Cavendish's (raised during the interregnum)
1689   21st Foot. O'Farrell's Regiment of Foot
      22nd Foot. Norfolk's Regiment of Foot
      23rd Foot. Herbert's Regiment of Foot
      24th Foot. Dering's Regiment of Foot
      25th Foot. Leven's (Edinburgh) Regiment of Foot
      26th Foot. Angus's (Cameronians) Regiment of Foot
      27th Foot. Tiffin's Regiment of Foot
      5th Dragoons. Cardross's
      6th* Dragoons. Wynne's (Enniskillen)
      7th* Dragoons. Cunningham's
January 1690   Two new Marine Regiments: 1st Torrington's and 2nd
      Montgomery's. Both disbanded 1699.
*Later 5th and 6th Dragoons respectively

Regiments of the standing army to the Battle of the Boyne

Household Cavalry	Horse	Dragoons	Foot Guards	Foot	Marine
4 Troops	10	7	2	27	2
Life Guards					
1 Troop					
Horse Guards					

225

Appendix B

Regiments of cavalry, dragoons and infantry raised by Charles II, 1660–1685 (Taken from John Childs *The Army of Charles II*. Routledge and Kegan Paul 1976, Appendix A)

For service on the English establishment
Second and Third Dutch Wars: Flanders 1678–1679: Home Service   57
   Most were later amalgated or disbanded.
For Tangier   5
For Colonies (Barbados(1667): Bombay (1661): Virginia (1676)   3
For Scotland (1679)   3
For Foreign Service (France and Portugal)   <u>14</u>

    82

Appendix C

Principal French Ambassadors during reign of Charles II

1661   Gaston, Comte de Cominges
1664   Honoré de Courtin
1665   Henri de Bourbon
1667   Henri de Ruvigny (1)
1668   Colbert de Croissy (brother of Jean Baptiste Colbert, Louis's Foreign
         Minister)
1673   Henri de Ruvigny (2) son of 1667 Ambassador
1676   Antoine Courtin
1677–85 Paul Barrillon (In 1678 Henri de Ruvigny (2) was also appointed)

Notes

N.B. All Pepys references are to the Braybrooke edition, unless stated.

Preface
1 Pepys, 15 May 1663; *Diary and Correspondence of Samuel Pepys* ed Lord Braybrooke. George Allen (1914) 4 Vols (Verbatim reprint of 1848–9 edition). Ed, Andrew Browning, *Memoirs of Sir John Reresby,* Jackson (1936), p 35.
2 Gilbert Burnet, *History of My Own Time* ed Airy, 2 Vols (1897) Vol II p 28.
3 Maurice Ashley, *The House of Stuart.* Dent (1980) p 167.
4 Oliver Millar, *Sir Peter Lely.* National Portrait Gallery p 15.
5 G M Trevelyan, *England Under the Stuarts.* (1904) p 335.
6 The only part of the old palace of 1660 still surviving above ground. Its marvellous ceiling by Rubens (1635) shows the early seventeenth century idea of monarchy, with Justice, Peace and Plenty abounding.
7 Arthur Bryant, *King Charles II.* Collins (Preface to 1955 edition).
8 Dr John Childs, *The British Army of William III.* Manchester University Press (1987) p 5.
9 A C A Brett, *Charles II and His Court.* Methuen (1910) p 285.

Chapter 1 *Our Trusty and Well-beloved George Monck*
1 Clarendon, *Selections from The History of the Rebellion* ed Huehns. OUP (1978) pp 361, 359; Burnet, Vol I p 178.
2 Correlli Barnett, *Britain and Her Army.* Allen Lane (1970) p 79.
3 H A L Fisher, *A History of Europe.* Arnold (1957) p 654.
4 Monck's chaplain, Thomas Gumble, *Life of Monck.* (1671) p 4.
5 Clarendon *op cit.*
6 Her brother, Thomas Clarges, was knighted by Charles II for his loyal services and became a member of Parliament. Pepys (Vol III p 291) states, 'General Monck married Anne, daughter of the regimental farrier, in 1652 at the Church of St George, Southwark. Her first husband was Thomas Ratford, from whom she separated in 1649. This would explain her low origin and vulgar habits.'

7 *Dictionary of National Biography* (DNB).
8 Sir John Fortescue, *History of the British Army,* Vol I. (1910) p 240.
9 Oliver Warner, *Hero of the Restoration. Life of General George Monck.* Jarrolds (1936) p 126.
10 Fisher, p 661.
11 Pepys.
12 Arthur Bryant, *The Letters, Speeches and Declarations of Charles II.* Cassell (1935) p 65.
13 Warner, p 132; J Griffith Davies, *Honest George Monck*, app C. Lane (1936)
14 'His officers and men declared unanimously they would live and die with him.' Colonel D Mackinnon, *Origins and Services of the Coldstream Guards,* Vol I p 72 (1833).
15 Griffith Davies *op cit.*
16 J R Jones, *Country and Court.* Arnold (1978) p 127; Griffith Davies, p 199.
17 Mackinnon, Vol I p 87.
18 *New Cambridge Modern History,* Vol V. CUP (1961) p 301; Pepys, 18 January 1660.
19 Mackinnon, p 90.
20 Pepys, 3 February 1660; Griffith Davies, p 206.
21 Pepys, 11 February 1660; John Evelyn, *Diary.* Dobson edition, 3 Vols. Macmillan (1906) Vol II p 143.
22 Pepys, 13 March 1660; Clarendon. *State Papers.* 3 Vols (1767–86) Vol III p 711.
23 Griffith Davies, pp 174, 227.
24 *Journals of the House of Lords,* Vol XI pp 7–10.
25 Pepys, 24 April 1660; Mackinnon, p 93.
26 Pepys, 2 May and 3 May 1660; Griffith Davies, pp 232–3.
27 Clarendon, p 366; Sir Sibbald David Scott, *The British Army.* London (1880).
28 Clarendon, p 370.
29 Godfrey Davies, *The Restoration of Charles II (1658–1660).* OUP (1955) pp 7–8. Griffith Davies, p 241.
30 Clarendon, p 367.
31 Burnet, Vol I p l78, n 1.
32 Evelyn, 29 May 1660. 'All this without one drop of blood.'

Chapter 2 *Enter King and Royal Mistress*
1 Evelyn, *Diary* 29 May 1660. Vol II p 145.
2 Clarendon, p 367; John H Jesse, *Memoirs of the Court of England. (*1857) Vol II pp 468-9; DNB; Andrew Marvell, *An Historical Poem.*
3 The blood of the Villiers was in the Duke of Marlborough and Sir Winston Churchill, in the Cecil, Russell and Bedford families, and even in Queen

Elizabeth II. Barbara herself is an ancestress of Lord Castlereagh, Lord Melbourne and Sir Anthony Eden: no fewer than 13 prime ministers can trace their line directly to her.

4   The baptismal register of St Margaret's, Westminster gives 27 November 1640.

5   Buried in Christ Church, Oxford, where Barbara (when Duchess of Cleveland) erected a white marble monument to him.

6   Abel Boyer, *Annals of the Reign of Queen Anne* (1722) p 48.

7   Burnet, Vol I p 168, n 3.

8   At first the child was named Anne Palmer and Roger Palmer, Barbara's husband, had no doubt the child was his. The King eventually acknowledged paternity 13 years later to make Anne's marriage to Lord Dacre easier, but the general opinion was that Lord Chesterfield was the father. Brian Masters, *The Mistresses of Charles II*. Blond and Briggs (1979) p 55.

9   See Alan Hardy, *The King's Mistresses*. Evans (1980) p 9.

10 Jesse p 494; Antonia Fraser, *King Charles II*. Weidenfeld and Nicolson (1979) p 284 quoting the Memoirs of Sir John Reresby 1735 p 7.   Pepys, 15 May 1663 and 8 December 1666 cf. Rochester's scurrilous *Satire* on Charles II for which he was banished from the court in 1676 [*The New Oxford Book of Seventeenth Century Verse*. OUP (1991) p 760].

11 George Savile (Lord Halifax), *Works* (1912).

12 Burnet *op cit.*

13 *Diary* 29 July 1667.

14 J P Kenyon, *The Stuarts*. Collins (1958) p 114.

15 DNB.

16 Masters, p 52.

17 Pepys, 13 July 1660. General Edward Whalley (Cromwell's cousin) had fled to New England on hearing that he was one of the regicides not covered by Charles II's general pardon.

18 Burnet, Vol I p 168.

19 DNB.

20 In the Irish peerage to avoid the royal confirmation by Clarendon (who hated her) and the Chancellor's Great Seal.

21 *The Complete Peerage.*

22 Elizabeth Hamilton, *The Illustrious Lady*. Hamish Hamilton (1980) p 100.

Chapter 3 *The Birth of the Army and a Royal Marriage*

1   Pepys, 9 November 1663.

2   Fortescue Vol I; Godfrey Davies, *The Army and the Restoration*. J.S.A.H.R. (1954) pp 26–29; Burnet Vol I, p 274.

3   Mercurius Publicus. February 1660 quoted MacKinnon Vol I p 101.

4 Thomas Gumble, Monck's chaplain and biographer wrote: 'This town of Coldstream hath given title to a small company of men, whom God made the instrument of great things.' 1671.

5 C Walton, *History of the British Standing Army (1660–1700)*. (1894) pp 1–8.

6 Instead, Charles had to make do with a succession of mistresses, said to have numbered 17 in all.

7 Bryant, p 104; Tony Palmer, *Charles II, Portrait of an Age*. Cassell (1979) p 60.

8 Brett, p177; Pepys 17 August 1661.

9 Charles Fitzroy. Created Duke of Southampton 1675. He was born in Barbara's house in King Street and baptised in St Margaret's, Westminster on 18 June 1662. Barbara's five children Charles acknowledged were: Anne (1661), Charles (1662), Henry (1663), Charlotte (1664) and George (1665).

10 Pepys, 21 May 1662.

11 To Minette, Duchesse d'Orleans, 23 May 1662. C H Hartmann, *The King, My Brother*. Heinemann (1954) p 39; Bryant, *Letters*, p 127, 23 May 1662; Clarendon, p 397; Burnett Vol I, p 307.

12 Bryant, *Letters*, p 128. 25 May 1662.

13 Pepys, 31 May 1662; C H Hartmann, *La Belle Stuart*. Routledge (1924) p 15.

14 Edmund Waller, *Tea Commended by her Majesty* c. 1680.

Chapter 4 *The Growth of the New Army*

1 F W Hamilton, *History of the Royal Grenadier Guards*. (1874) Vol 1 p 43.

2 Walton, p 843; John Childs, *The Army of Charles II*. Routledge and Kegan Paul (1976) p 17. The additonal companies cost £67,500 in June 1661, making £190,000 in total therefore for this army out of his annual revenue of £1,200,000.

3 French 'buffetiers' - cup-bearers or sideboard waiters. Founded by Henry VII in 1485.

4 See also Leonard Cooper, *British Regular Cavalry 1644-1914*. Chapman and Hall (1965) p 23.

5 It should be noted that Scotland and Ireland maintained their own military establishments, paid for by their own national revenues.

6 See Correlli Barnett p 115. The use of numbers to designate regiments at this period is an anacronism: until the middle of the 18th century regiments were known by the names of their colonels.

7 Walton, p 5.

8 Walton, pp 1-8.

9 Fisher, pp 645 and 651.

10 Car 11 Stat 1 Cap 6. *Statues of the Realm* 5, 308-9.
11 L G Schwoerer, *No Standing Armies*. Baltimore (1974) p 86.
12 A I Dasent, *The Private Life of Charles the Second*. Cassell (1927) p 95.
13 Hardy, p 15; Clarendon, p 396.
14 Bryant, *Letters*. July 1962, p 129.
15 Clarendon, p 406.
16 See Margaret Gilmour, *The Great Lady*. Long (1944).
17 The Complete Peerage lists 14 illegitimate children produced by seven of his concubines. John Dryden in *Absalom and Achitophel* (1681) expressed it more poetically:
      'When nature prompted, and no law denied,
      Promiscuous use of concubine and bride;
      Then Israel's monarch, after heaven's own heart,
      His vigorous warmth did variously impart
      To wives and slaves, and, wide as his command,
      Scattered his maker's image through the land.'
18 See Chapter 3, note 9.
19 Brett, p 185 and note. The French ambassador, de Comminges, called them 'les eaux de scandale, for they nearly ruined the good name of the maids and of the ladies (those, I mean, who were there without their husbands)'.
20 Brett, p 186.

Chapter 5 *The Palace of Whitehall*

 1 Sorbière, *A Voyage to England*. (1665).
 2 Edgar Sheppard, *The Old Royal Palace of Whitehall*. (1902) p 22.
 3 Evelyn, 6 July 1660.
 4 Pepys, 29 October 1666. In 1665 the Hall was adapted for use as a regular court theatre, replacing the cockpit. George Dugdale, *Whitehall Through the Centuries*. Phoenix House (1950) p 76.
 5 Evelyn, 2 September 1680.
 6 At the spot where Downing Street now runs into Whitehall.
 7 The original Eleanor Cross erected in the then village of Charing stood where the equestrian statue of Charles I now stands.
 8 His rapid rise to political power was due to Cromwell's favour and to a shrewd marriage to the sister of Colonel Charles Howard, one of Cromwell's major-generals. He served in Cromwell's army as a regimental preacher. Pepys, *The Diary of Samuel Pepys* eds. Latham and Matthews. Bell and Hyman, now Unwin Hyman, an imprint of Harper Collins (1983) Vol X.
 9 Sheppard, p 33.
10 Jeanine Delpech, *The Duchess of Portsmouth*. Elek (1953) p 48.

11 Pepys, 24 June 1664.
12 Evelyn, 4 October 1683.
13 Evelyn, 10 April 1691.
14 John Adair, *The Royal Palaces of London*. Thames and Hudson (1981) p 81.
15 DNB.
16 The present building was erected in 1750–1753.
17 Sheppard, p 72.
18 Pepys, 2 September 1667.

Chapter 6 *The Court*

 1 Jones, p 16.
 2 Ronald Hutton, *Charles II*. Clarendon (1989) p 134.
        As England's monarch in his closet lay
        And Chiffinch stepp'd to fetch the female prey.
     (Lampoon 1678) (DNB)
 3 Lord Guildford, *Life of Francis North*. (1742) p 210. DNB. (Chiffinch)
 4 *Works of George Savile, Marquis of Halifax*. (1912) p 256.
 5 David Allen, *The Political Function of Charles II's Chiffinch*. Huntington Library Quarterly (1976) Vol 39 Pt 3 pp 277 and 290.
 6 Hartmann, (Belle Stuart) p 2.
 7 DNB.
 8 Pepys, eds Latham and Matthews, Vol X; Patrick Morrah, *Restoration England*. Constable (1979) p 155; DNB, John Sheffield.
 9 Pepys, 6 June 1666, and note Vol II p 155 (Latham) 31 May 1669. Anthony Hamilton/Gramont, *Memoirs of the Court of Charles II*. Bell (1908). 'Winifred Well's father had faithfully served Charles I and believed, therefore, she too should serve her royal master no less devotedly'. DNB. Jane Middleton, 'after the succession of her old lover, James II, she enjoyed an annual pension of £500 paid from the secret service fund.'
10 Hamilton/Gramont, p 262.
11 Pepys, 30 October 1668, eds. Latham and Matthews. Lord Braybrooke has 'amours'.
12 Evelyn, 1 March 1671
13 Mrs A Jameson, *Beauties of the Court of Charles II*. (1861 edition).
14 Morrah, p 43; Gilmour, p 24.
15 John Childs, pp 58–60 and pp 64–5. The red coat was also used by Cromwell's soldiers. W Y Carman, *British Military Uniforms*. Webb and Bower (1982) pp 27–36.
16 Jameson, introduction.; Morrah, p 44.
17 2 November 1676. PRO 31/3/81.
18 General Viscount Wolseley, *Life of Marlborough*. (1894) Vol I p 183.

Jameson, p 31; H Forneron, *Louise de Keroualle, Duchess of Portsmouth (1649–1734)*. 1887 p 161; Bryant, *King Charles II* p 168; Morrah, p 44.
19 Pepys, 3 November 1662 and 27 July 1667; Clarendon, p 379.
20 J R Jones, *Charles II, Royal Politician*. Allen and Unwin (1987) pp 54–55 quoting Clarendon *State Papers*, Venetian 1659–61 p 297. Morrah, p 44.
21 E N Williams, *Life in Georgian England*. Batsford (1962) p 29; Daniel Defoe, *Moll Flanders*. (1722) Panther edition p 26.
22 After the marriage, Frances deserted her husband for a more congenial lover.
23 Bryant, *Letters* p 262;
24 Morrah, p 77; Peter Earle, *The Making of the English Middle Class*. Methuen (1989).

Chapter 7 *Tangier - An Expensive Wedding Present*
 1 Pepys, 20 February 1662.
 2 Childs, *Army of Charles II* p 17. The cost was £122,400 per annum.
 3 Near where the Imperial War Museum stands today.
 4 Colonel N T St John Williams, *Judy O'Grady and the Colonel's Lady*. Brasseys (1988) p 1; Enid M G Routh, *Tangier, an Outpost of Empire 1661–1684*. (1912) p 12.
 5 Routh, p 31 and Pepys, *Diary*, 31 December 1662.
 6 Routh, p 14.
 7 Christian Fielding, *The Occupation of Tangier*. History Today (1955) p 465. Pepys (15 Dec 62) noted 'I am sorry to see a Catholic Government appointed there, where all or the rest of the officers are such already'.
 8 Routh, Chapter IV
 9 For details of the warfare in Tangier, see Colonel Clifford Walton, *History of the British Standing Army (1660–1700)* 1894 ch 3; Lieutenant Colonel John Davis, *The History of the Second Queen's Royal Regiment* 1887 Vol I; Sir F W Hamilton, *The Origin and History of the First Grenadier Guards* 1874 Vol I.
10 Routh, p 125 n 1; DNB; Charles Dalton, *The Scots Army 1661–1688*. Greenhill Books (1989) p 10.
11 Routh, p 155; Pepys, eds Latham and Matthews Vol X p 410.
12 British Museum, Sloane MSS 1957–60, quoted in Walton pp 555–73.
13 London Gazette, 11–15 July 1678; 10 September 1686; 17 September 1687.
14 Walton, p 554.
15 Davis, p 114 *et seq*.
16 Childs, *Army of Charles II* p 47.
17 Calendar of State Papers (Domestic Series), 17 April 1675.
18 See Wenceslaus Hollar's watercolour sketches at Tangier; Carman, p 34.
19 Routh, p 282.

20 Davis, p 130.
21 Colonel L I Cowper, *The King's Own. The Story of a Royal Regiment.* OUP (1939 Vol I) p 17; Fielding, p 469; MacKinnon, Vol I; Hamilton, p 239 states: the combined battalion, 600 strong, to be divided into five companies of 120 men each, composed of drafts from the two regiments of Foot Guards (240 men from the First Regiment in two companies; 120 from the Coldstreams) and from some of the garrisons in England - 100 from the Portsmouth garrison, 80 from Plymouth, 30 from the three garrison companies in the Tower; 30 from the companies in the Isle of Wight. These last 240 men to be formed into two companies.'
22 Cowper, p 13.
23 *Army Quarterly*, July 1964 Vol 88 pp 216–17
24 Quoted Routh, p 203.
25 Cowper, p 15.
26 DNB; Kirke; Pepys, eds Latham and Matthews Vol X, p 411; Routh, p 250.
27 Cowper, Vol I p 16.
28 Pepys, *Tangier Papers* ed E Chappell. N Royal Society (1935) pp 89–90; Cowper, p 17; Childs, *Army of Charles II* p 120.
29 'A humble address of the Ladies of Pleasure' to King Charles quoted Morrah, p 62.
30 Routh, ch 15.
31 Cowper, p 17.
32 Cowper, p 22 and Proceedings of Court of QS 28 October 1679, quoted Routh p 278.
33 Walton, p 573.
34 See Williams for the details and subsequent story of army women and the army's attitude to marriage (from Charles II to present day).
35 Burnet, Vol I p 306 note.
36 DNB (George Legge).
37 Pepys, *Tangier Papers* p 4.
38 Pepys, *Tangier Papers* p 90.
39 Cowper, p 30; MacKinnon, Vol I.
40 DNB.

Chapter 8 *Royal Pleasures and Military Affairs*
 1 Pepys, 31 December 1662.
 2 Pepys, 7 September 1662.
 3 Burnet.
 4 Pepys, 31 December 1662.
 5 John Dryden, *Absalom and Achitophel*. 1681
 6 Dalton, ch 8.
 7 Pepys, 1 January 1663, 31 December 1662, 10 August 1663.

8 15 December 1662, 15 May 1663. Pietro Aretino's sixteenth century volume of illustrated erotic sonnets was a banned publication, although well-known in England in the 1660s. Pepys had a copy; see Dasent note p 100.

9 Jones, *Charles II* p 63; DNB.

10 Bennet's daughter, Isabella, married one of Barbara's sons (Henry FitzRoy) and founded the line of the Dukes of Grafton.

11 Clarendon, p 410.

12 Burnet, Vol I p 166

13 Pepys, 23 December 1662 and 31 December 1662.

14 Hesketh Pearson, *Charles II and His Likeness*. Heinemann (1960) p 180.

15 Allen Andrews, *The Royal Whore*. Hutchinson (1971) pp 76–7.

16 Burnet.

17 Rochester's verse.

18 Pepys, 15 May 1663; Reresby (1936) p 35.

19 Pepys noted 'Monmouth doth hang much upon my Lady Castlemayne and is always with her'. See also Count Gramont, and Gilmour p 72.

20 David Ogg, *England in the Reign of Charles II*. OUP (1956) p 149; Reresby, *Memoirs*. (1936) 10 September 1660 p 36.

21 Brett, p 260.

22 Pepys, *Diary of Samuel Pepys*. Dent edition (1953); 24 June 1667.

23 Pepys, 10 June 1666.

24 Pepys, 12 December 1666.

25 Pepys, 3 November 1662.

26 Hardy, p 48; Ann, Countess of Winchelsea, *Complete Peerage*; Antonia Fraser, *The Weaker Vessel*. Weidenfeld (1984) p 333.

27 Barry Coward, *The Stuart Age*. Longman (1985) p 243.

28 Pearson, p 138;

29 Childs, *Charles II* p 47 and p 66; Public Record Office, Warrant Books.

30 David Ascoli, *A Companion to the British Army*. Harrap (1983); Childs, *Charles II op cit*.

31 Frederick Myatt, *The British Infantry 1660–1945*. Blandford Press (1983) p 27.

Chapter 9 *The Girl Most Fitted to Adorn a Court*

1 Hartmann, 4 January 1662, p 38.

2 Pepys (Everyman edition), 15 November 1666.

3 13 July 1663, 26 August 1664 and 25 February 1667.

4 Pepys, *Diary* 25 November 1666.

5 Jusserand, *A French Ambassador at the Court of Charles II*. Comminges to Lionne, 31 December 1663; Pepys, 22 December 1663 and 20 January 1664; Philip Sargeant, *My Lady Castlemaine*. (1912) p 108.

6 Pepys, 8 February 1663 and 18 May 1663; Gramont, pp 110–11.
7 Clarendon, p 409.
8 DNB; Jusserand, p 88; Pepys, 9 November 1663; Burnet, Vol I p 451.
9 Agnes and Elizabeth Strickland, *Lives of the Queens of England*. 1851 5 Vols. Vol V p 561.
10 Bryant, *Letters* 19 May 1664 p 158.
11 Pepys, 6 November 1663; Burnet, Vol I p 451 note.
12 C H Hartmann, *La Belle Stuart*. Routledge (1924) p 61; Sir George Etherege, *Dominant, in the Man of Mode*. 1676.
13 Dennis Wheatley, *Old Rowley*. Hutchinson (1967) p 76.
14 Pepys, 15 July 1664, 8 February 1664, 9 January 1666, 15 April 1666 (Latham edition) and 12 December 1666.
15 Pepys, 26 April 1667.
16 DNB; Burnet, Vol I p 452; Gramont, p 369; Hartmann, p 108 et seq.
17 DNB.
18 Pepys, 29 January 1666, 27 July 1667, 29 July 1667, 7 August 1667 and 31 July 1666 (Everyman edition); Masters, p 80.
19 Pepys, 25 March 1668 and 6 April 1668. The Petition and Gracious Answer were printed in full in Dasent p 112 et seq.
20 Strickland, p 590; Burnet, Vol I p 452 note. Lord Dartmouth asserted 'after her marriage she had more complaisance than before'; Hartmann, p 189.
21 see Lawrence Stone, *The Crisis of the Aristocracy*. OUP (1965) p 388.
22 Jones, *Charles II* p 80; Andrews, p 125.

Chapter 10 *War and a Growing Empire*
1 Brett, p l97.
2 Pepys, 29 June and 18 July 1663. (Latham Edition: Bell and Unwin, now Unwin Hyman, an imprint of Harper Collins Publishing Ltd) Jones, p 77–8.
3 Arthur Bryant, *Restoration England*. Collins (1934, rep 1968) pp 30–31.
4 Jones, p 79; David Ogg, *England in the Reign of Charles II*. OUP (1956); Walter Besant, *London in the Time of the Stuarts*.
5 Childs, ch 8; Douglas Leach, *Arms for the Empire*, Collier (1973) p 9.
6 *Encyclopedia Britannica* (USA): *New Cambridge Modern History* Vol V 1961: *English Historical Documents* IV; see also Samuel Morison, *History of the American Republic*. OUP (1973).
7 Pepys, 22 February 1664 and 9 February 1664.
8 Bryant, *Letters*, Whitehall 2 June 1664 p 159, 19 September 1664 p 164.
9 Childs, p 157.
10 Sir George Clark, *The Later Stuarts*. OUP (1934) p 63.
11 C H Hartmann, p 152; J J Jusserand, pp 233 and 243; Hartmann, *Belle Stuart*, p 32.
12 Hartmann, p 176.

13 Clark *op cit*, p 63.

14 J W Fortescue, *History of the British Army* Bk IV. (1910) p 296.

15 Cecil Lawson, *A History of the Uniforms of the British Army* Vol 1. Webb and Bower (1940) p 54. The regiment was disbanded in 1689, many of the men being drafted into the Coldstream Guards. After many vicissitudes it was placed under Admiralty control in 1755, as the forerunner of the Royal Marines.

16 Pepys, 8 June 1665.

17 Hartmann, p 167.

18 Fisher, p 669; Patrick Morrah, *Restoration England*. Constable (1979) pp 159–60; Griffith Davies, p 262.

19 Ronald Hutton, *Charles II*. Clarendon (1989) p 234.

20 Pepys, 7 February 1667.

21 Pepys, 21 June 1667.

22 Pepys, 27 July 1667.

23 Pepys, 23 June 1667.

24 Pepys, 6 June 1667.

25 Pepys, 14 June 1667.

26 Jones, p 17.

27 See page 40.

28 Evelyn, *Diary*. 27 August 1667.

29 Burnet I, p 444 note.

30 Pepys, 27 August 1667.

31 Clarendon, p 478.

32 Richard Ollard, *The Image of the King*. Hodder and Stoughton (1979) p 138.

Chapter 11 *The Hand of God*

1 *Clarendon, p 410.*

2 Pepys, 7 June 1665; 15 June and 29 June. City Regulations required crosses to be one foot high and the house to be shut up for 40 days, often with the victims inside.

3 Gumble.

4 Pepys, 27 July 1665.

5 Pepys, 7 and 8 September 1666.

6 Pepys, 24 April 1665.

7 Pepys, 15 June 1666; 12 July 1666; 15 August 1665.

8 5 October 1665. (Latham Edition: Bell and Hyman, now Unwin Hyman (Harper Collins Publishing Ltd)) Antonia Fraser, p 238; DNB.

9 11 and 23 August 1665; 15 August 1664; 20 February 1665; 12 September 1666 (all refs Latham Edition). See also Richard Ollard, *Pepys* 1974 Ch.7; John H Wilson, *All The Kings Ladies*, Harvard (1958).

10 Pepys, 25 and 31 December 1665.
11 Burnet, Vol I p 391.
12 The official register recorded: 1665 December 28. George Palmer, sonne of Roger, Earl of Castlemaine was born at Merton College. His mother was Barbara, dutchesse of Cleveland. Filius naturalis regis Caroli ii.
13 Pepys, 2 September 1666 *et seq.*
14 Evelyn, *Diary* 3 September 1666.
15 Clarendon, p 416.
16 Clarendon, p 415.
17 Evelyn, Vol II p 261 (10 October 1666) and p 269 (6 March 1667).

Chapter 12 *Indecent Actresses and Decayed Soldiers*
 1 Burned down in 1672 and replaced by one designed by Sir Christopher Wren. The present building is the fourth on the site
 2 Allardyce Nicoll, *A History of English Drama 1660–1900*. Cambridge University Press (1952) Vol 1 pp 314 and 315.
 3 *Oxford History of English Literature*. Clarendon Press (1969) pp 3 and 35.
 4 Robert Gould, *The Playhouse* Vol II. London (1709) p 251. Quoted by the *Revels History of Drama in English* Vol 5. Methuen (1976).
 5 Allardyce Nicoll, *World Drama*. Oxford History (1949) p 276; Bryan Bevan, *Charles II's French Mistress*. Robert Hale (1972) p 66; Pepys Vol X and Vol XI Latham.
 6 John E Cunningham, *Restoration Drama*. Evans (1966) p 36.
 7 John Etherege, *The Man of Mode or Sir Fopling Flutter* (1676); Pepys 28 May 1665. Rochester was clapped in the Tower for abducting the heiress Elizabeth Malet. He was released on the King's orders and two years later married his heiress in 1667.
 8 Jeanine Delpech, *The Duchess of Portsmouth*. Elek (1953) p 52.
 9 *An Apology for the Life of Mr. Colley Cibber, Comedian*. Everyman (1914) Apology 4.
10 Pepys, 3 January 1661. 'The first time I ever saw women come upon the stage'. See Latham Vol X.
11 Pepys, 18 August 1660.
12 Bryan Forbes, *That Despicable Race*. Elm Tree (1980) p 27.
13 Allardyce Nicoll, *English Drama* pp 71 and 72; Pepys, 11 October 1664.
14 Evelyn, 18 October 1666.
15 Pepys, 17 October 1662 and 20 May 1662; Evelyn Vol II p 263, note 4. Ruperta married General Emanuel Scroope Howe
16 Thomas Brown, *Physick Lies A-Bleeding* (1697). Brown was buried in Westminster cloisters near his friend Mrs Aphra Benn.
17 John Wright, *Thyestes* 1674; Dryden, Epilogue to *Secret Love*, spoken by an actress in man's clothes.

18 See Allardyce Nicoll, *History of the Restoration Theatre* Vol 1 p 8.

19 It is also claimed Nell was born in Pipewell Lane (now Gwynne Street) in Hereford.

20 John H Wilson, *Nell Gwynn, Royal Mistress*. Muller (1672) p 9.

21 Pepys, 26 October 1667.

22 Gramont, p 252; Pepys, 28 December 1967.

23 DNB. *On a pretty little person.*

24 5 October 1667.

25 Adamson and Dewar, *The House of Nell Gwynn*. Kimber (1974) p 5; James Howard's 'All Mistaken' April 1667.

26 DNB; Pepys 13 and 14 July 1667, 26 August 1667. See Braybrooke Vol III p 239 for story that Buckhurst would not surrender her to the King, until the expenses, which he had lavished upon her, were repaid and until he was promised the Earldom of Middlesex for his compliance. His poem 'To all you ladies' is a recognised masterpiece.

27 G Burnet, p 475.

28 Pepys, 7 March 1667. See Braybrooke's note 'a tall, handsome woman, she captivated the King by her singing and dancing', especially when she danced, like Nell, in boy's clothes. Vol 3 p 46.

29 Bryant, *Charles II* p 159.

30 Pepys, 14 January and 31 May 1668.

31 The house was demolished in 1848 to make way for the Army and Navy Club

32 Burnet I, pp 474–5.

33 Pepys, 5 October 1667, 2 March 1667, 7 May 1668 and 27 July 1665 and note 4; Forneron, p 205.

34 *The Complete Poems of John Wilmot, Earl of Rochester, A Satyr on Charles II.*

35 Bevan, pp 75–6; Pepys, 26 April 1667; Braybrooke III p 184 and note.

36 Fraser, p 285.

37 Ogg, *England in the Reign of Charles II.*

38 Cibber, *Apology* 4.

39 Madame de Sévigny, Letter IV 11 September 1675.

40 T W E Roche, *A Pineapple for the King*. Phillimore (1971) p 84.

41 Dasent, p 236.

42 Walton, p 595.

43 Walton, p 596 *et seq.*

44 Pepys, 18 November 1667 and note (Braybrooke); Royal Warrant dated 7 December 1671. Their names are still commemorated in the locality.

45 David Ascoli, *A Village in Chelsea*. Luscombe (1974) p 106. The tombstone of the first army pensioner to die in the Hospital, Simon Box, bears the date 6 April 1692.

46 Captain C G T Dean, *The Royal Hospital, Chelsea.* Hutchinson (1950).

Chapter 13 *The Standing Army: From Ensign to Colonel*
 1 Godfrey Davies, *The Restoration of Charles II* (1955) Introduction.
 2 Architel Grey, *Debates of the House of Commons (1667–1694)* (1763) vi 280.
 3 *ibid* viii 357.
 4 *Journal of Modern History* Vol XVIII No 4, December 1946 quoting Trenchard and Moyle 1697 pp 28–29.
 5 John Childs, p 123.
 6 *Commons Journal* 1 April 1679 Vol 9, p 581.
 7 J R Western, *The English Militia in the 18th Century.* Routledge and Kegan Paul (1965) p 28.
 8 Walton, p 479.
 9 Correlli Barnett, *Britain and Her Army.* Allen Lane, The Penguin Press (1970) p 117.
10 George Farquhar, *The Recruiting Officer* (1706). Act 2 Scene 3, Act 1 Scene 1, Act 5 Scene 7.
11 See Walton, pp 664 and 668.
12 Two shillings and six pence a day for a trooper, one shilling and sixpence for a dragoon.
13 Barnett, p 139.
14 1664. Walton, p 671.
15 Walton, p 679 note.
16 Colburn's United Services Magazine August 1867 Pt 2, pp 506–9 and *Articles of His Majesty's Guards* (1663). See also Colonel N T St John Williams, *Judy O'Grady and The Colonel's Lady – The Story of the Army Wife and Camp Follower 1660–1980.* Brasseys (1980).
17 By an Order of 1678 but the shape of the garments had not been regulated and was dictated by civilian dress of the time. Red had gradually become the accepted colour of the soldier's coat, each regiment being distinguished by the colour of its coat linings, generally the colour of its colonel's livery. Cowper, Vol 1 p 11.
18 Act 31 Chas II C I S 32.
19 Davis, Vol I p 153; Walton, p 714.
20 Childs, p 29.
21 Walton, p 448 and notes.
22 Correlli Barnett, *Marlborough.* Methuen (1974) p 39.
23 Anthony Hamilton, *Memoirs of the Comte de Gramont Bell* (1908) Ed 1926 p 262.
24 Sir Winston Churchill, *Marlborough, His Life and Times.* Harrap (1938).
25 Hamilton, Vol I p 166.

26 Walton, p 21.
27 French Correspondence PRO Courtin to Louvois 16 November 1676; Jeanine Delpech p 107.
28 Gramont, p 262.
29 Henry Edwards, *A Short Life of Marlborough*. Bell (1926); Churchill I p 125.

Chapters 14 *Petticoat Diplomacy*
 1 Pepys, 23 October 1667.
 2 Pepys, 8 March 1661, 4 November 1666, 9 December 1665; Maurice Ashley, *General Monck*. Cape (1977) p 54; DNB.
 3 J D G Davies, *Honest George Monck* (1936); Ashley, p 246.
 4 Today remembered in Albemarle Street. Bond, Dover and Stafford Streets commemorate the speculators, who developed the area at the end of Charles's reign.
 5 *The Autobiography of James II*, see Walton, p 617.
 6 Bryant, *Letters* p 135; Hartman, p 524.
 7 DNB.
 8 *J S A H R* 1962 Vol 40.
 9 Bryant, *Letters* p 214.
10 Bryant, *Letters* p 224.
11 Dasent, p 173. See also Farneron and Gramont.
12 See appendix C for list of French ambassadors and dates.
13 Letter 20 January 1669. French Foreign Affairs Archives quoted H Forneron p 24.
14 Letters February 1669 quoted Forneron p 22.
15 Letters 3 and 23 April 1669 p 16.
16 A Lampoon of the Day (Rochester?) ridiculed her:
    Full forty men a day have swiv'd the whore,
    Yet, like a bitch, she wags her tail for more.
17 Forneron, p 24.
18 Colbert de Croissy to de Lionne, Letters 7 and 14 February 1669 quoted Forneron p 25.
19 De Croissy to de Lionne 9 February 1669; Pepys 16 January 1669. 'He was not ruled by his ministers' – Hartmann, *The King, My Brother* p 265.

Chapter 15 *The Grand Design*
 1 See letter dated St Cloud 12 September 1669; Hartmann pp 284–7; Fisher, p 671.
 2 Forneron, p 53.
 3 Letter dated 14 March 1670 from the Marquis de St. Maurice to the Duke of Savoy quoted Hartmann p 308. See also Prince Michael of Greece, *Louis XIV*. Orbis Publications (1983) p 145.

4 Hartmann, p 308.
5 Delpech, p 37; Dasent, p 187.
6 Keith Feiling, English Historical Review, *The Treaty of Dover* (1932) Vol 47 p 642.
7 Letter, St Cloud 29 June 1670 quoted Hartmann p 324.
8 Dryden, *Absalom and Achitophel*.
9 Delpech, p 66; Hester Chapman, *Four Fine Gentlemen*. Constable (1977) p 226. Anna Maria (neé Brudenall), the second wife of Francis Talbot, the 11th Earl of Shrewsbury.
10 *Diary*, 10 September 1677.
11 Burnet *op cit*.

Chapter 16 *The French Whore Will Do Her Duty*
1 Quoted Delpech, p 40.
2 De Croissy to Louvois 8 October 1671 (*Correspondence Angleterre*, Cl fol 167)
3 Forneron, *Louise de Keroualle. Duchess of Portsmouth (1649–1734)* (1887) pp 66–67.
4 Forneron, p 64.
5 Quoted Bryan Bevan, p 37.
6 Saint Evremond, *Oeuvres III. Problème à l'invitation des Espagnols*; Forneron pp 66–8.
7 *Correspondence Angleterre* Cl fol 167–8 October 1671; Bryan Bevan, p 39.
8 Delpech, p 61. Arlington purchased the estate, in near ruin, in 1666 and built Euston Hall 'in the French style'. It has been the family home of the Dukes of Grafton for over 300 years.
9 Forneron, p 72.
10 Evelyn, *Diary* 9 October 1671.
11 Ronald Hutton, *Charles II*. Clarendon (1989) p 280.
12 Forneron, p 93.
13 Burnet, Vol I p 599.
14 Delpech, p 64.
15 Burnet I p 599n.
16 Evelyn, 10 September 1675; Forneron p 278. The apartments were over the Stone Gallery, to the South of the Privy Garden.
17 Sir John Reresby, *Memoirs* (1735) p 24.
18 Forneron, p 92.
19 George Savile, Marquis of Halifax, *A Character of Charles II* etc (1750).
20 Reresby, (1936) p 93. A contemporary lampoon ran: 'Foe to England, spy to France' q.Bryan Bevan p 79.
21 Letters of the Marchioness de Sevigny IV quoted Bryan Bevan p 79.
22 Poem *Britannia and Ralegh*.

23 Patrick Morrah, *Restoration England*. Constable (1979) quoted p 57–8.
24 Burnet 11, 16. See also Alan Fea, *James II and His Wives* (1909).
25 Colbert 29 September 1671, *Correspondence Angleterre* C vii   fol 111
26 Burnet 11, p 20n.
27 Burnet 11, p 22n.
28 Alan Hardy, p 47.
29 Burnet 11 p 50 n ^{2}; DNB.
30 James had 8 children by his first wife, 7 by his second and acknowledged
    4 by his mistress, Arabella Churchill, and 1 by Catherine Sedley. DNB.

Chapter 17 *Men and Women at War*
 1 Bryant, *Letters* p 279.
 2 Bryant, *Charles II* p 176.
 3 Reginald Hargreaves, *The Bloody Backs*. Hart-Davis (1968) p 41.
 4 Fisher, p 671.
 5 Gilbert Burnet II, p 48 n 4.
 6 DNB.
 7 Burnet II, p 110 and n^1.
 8 Forneron, *Louise de Keroualle, Duchess of Portsmouth* (1887) p 83.
 9 Samuel E Morison, *A Concise History of the American Republic*. OUP
    (1983) p 19 and 37; The New Cambridge Modern History Vol 5 1648-88, p
    348; Fisher, p 609.
10 E J Burford and Sandra Shulman, *Of Bridles and Burnings*. Robert Hale
    (1992) p 189.
11 DNB.
12 John Childs, *The Army of Charles II* p 161.
13 C H Hartmann, *The Vagabond Duchess*. Routledge (1926) p 150.
14 Forneron, p 120 *et seq*.
15 Forneron, p 131.
16 Delpech, p 109.
17 PR0 (31/3/31) 20 January 1676.
18 Hartmann, p 160.
19 Courtin to Louis XIV 8 June 1676.
20 *ibid* 2 July 1676.
21 Louvois to Courtin 19 August 1676.
22 Forneron, p 187.

Chapter 18 *The Champion of Protestant Europe*
 1 Courtin PR0/31/3/132–6. 15 February 1677 and 25 March 1677.
 2 Fraser, pp 336 and 369; Delpech, p 113.
 3 Delpech, p 115; Forneron, p 189.
 4 Barrillon was the fourth French ambassador to the Court of St James's in

Louise's time, after Croissy, Ruvigny and Antoine Courtin. See Appendix C.

5   Forneron.

6   DNB; Delpech p 117; Alan Fea, *James II and His Wives*. Methuen (1908).

7   Forneron, pp 189 and 206–7; Delpech, p 118.

8   Burnet II, p 127.

9   Burnet II, p 131.

10 Childs, p 184. See Childs chap X for the detailed account of 'Flanders 1678'.

11 Dalton, *English Army Lists* i 201–220; Miller English Review Vol 88 p 43 gives 26,500 quoting Commons Journals IX, 487.

12 Delpech, p 122.

Chapter 19 *The Popish Plot and Exclusion Crisis*

1   John Dryden, *Absalom and Achitophel*, lines 114–5, 21 November 1681.

2   Burnet II, p 61; Bryant, *Charles II*, p 217.

3   *Memoirs* of Sir John Reresby, (1936) p 153. Reresby was a member of Gray's Inn, a Member of Parliament and High Sheriff of Yorkshire. His Memoirs, published in 1734, give interesting and valuable accounts of society and political events during his lifetime; DNB.

4   It is now generally believed Godfrey was murdered by the dissolute young Earl of Pembroke, a follower of Shaftesbury, who hated Godfrey. See J D Carr, *The Murder of Sir Edmund Godfrey*. Hamilton (1936).

5   Bevan, p 105.

6   Dryden, lines 47–8.

7   The origin of today's Gold Stick-in-Waiting, who takes precedence on State occasions over all other officers in the Armed Forces. Order dated 1678. Chamberlayne's Angliae Notita.

8   Estimated at 66,000 or just over 1% of the population. John Miller, *Catholic Officers in the Later Stuart Army*. English Historical Review (1973) Vol 88.

9   Dryden, 'and lent the crowd his arm to shake the tree'.

10 Anchitel Grey, *Debates of the House of Commons (1667–1694)*, (1763) 7.67–73.

11 Burnet II, p 180.

12 Jeanine Delpech, *The Duchess of Portsmouth* (1953) p 131.

13 Elizabeth Hamilton, *The Illustrious Lady*. Hamilton (1980) p 172.

14 Harleian MSS. 7006, fol 171. British Museum and Burnet II p.152 and note.

15 Bryant, p 225.

16 Whitehall 6 January 1678.

17 Bryant, p 231; Maurice Ashley, *The Stuarts in Love*. Hodder and Stoughton (1963) p 190.

18 C Blount, *An Appeal from the County to the City*. State Tracts 2 Vols 1689–92, Vol 1 p 401–2, quoted John Miller, *James II*. Methuen (1978), p 92.

19 D Ogg, *England in the Reign of Charles II*. OUP (1956) p 633.

20 Quoted Violet Wyndham, *The Protestant Duke*. Weidenfeld (1976) p 85.

21 Wyndham, p 87.

22 Quoted Bryan Bevan, *Nell Gwynn*. Robert Hale (1969) p 120.

23 Reresby, *Memoirs* (1936) p 248.

24 Bryant, p 239.

25 Burnet II, p 249.

26 DNB.

27 Burnet II, p 267.

28 Brian Masters, *The Mistresses of Charles II*. Blond and Briggs (1979) p 165.

29 G M Trevelyan, *English Social History*. Longmans (1978) p 398; Brett, *Charles II and his Court* (1910) p 236 *et seq*.

30 PRO AO/52/33 quoted David Ascoli p 29; Trevelyan, p 399.

31 Fraser, p 401.

32 Barrillon to Louis XIV 28 March 1681.

33 Burnet II, p 286; Reresby (1936) p 221.

34 *ibid*; (Burnett).

35 Brett, p 237; Rochester, *The Royal Buss*.

36 See Masters, p 165.

37 The terms, Whig and Tory, came into use at this time – see Burnet II, p 287 and note. At first they were abusive nicknames. A Tory = an Irish Catholic outlaw. A Whig = a Scottish Covenanting fanatic.

38 Wyndham, p 66; John Kenyon, *The Popish Plot*. Heinemann (1972).

Chapter 20 *Charles's Final Curtain*

 1 Quoted J N P Watson, *Captain-General and the Rebel Chief*. Allen & Unwin (1979) p 146.

 2 Burnet II, p 350.

 3 Bryant, *Charles II* (1931) p 268.

 4 DNB; *Memoirs* (1936) p 55.

 5 Reresby, Pepys and DNB

 6 Evelyn, *Diary*, 5 December 1683.

 7 Cambridge History of the 17th Century.

 8 DNB.

 9 Fisher, p 674; J R Jones, *Charles II. The Royal Politician*. Allen and Unwin (1987) p 162; Brett, p 240; DNB.

10 Masters, p 172.

11 Burnet II, p 455.

12 Evelyn, 4 February 1685.

13 Fraser, p 411.

14 Hesketh Pearson, *Charles II and His Likeness*. Heinemann (1960) p 250.

15 Barrillon to Louis XIV, 14 January 1684; Forneron.

16 Burnet II, p 409 note 3.

17 See Ashley, p 312. For Bruce's account of Charles's last illness see Brett, p 242 *et seq.*

18 Report of French Ambassador to Louis XIV in English Historical Documents VIII (1660 – 1714) p 166.

19 Earl of Plymouth (Catherine Pegge), Countess of Yarmouth (Betty Killigrew), Duke of Northumberland (Barbara Palmer), St Albans (Nell Gwynn) and Richmond (Louise de Keroulle). The latter's remains were transferred to Chichester Cathedral in 1750.

20 4 February 1685. See Vol III p 138 *et seq* for notes on Bruce's account.

21 Burnet II, p 168.

22 Burnet II, p 461.

23 See J R Jones, p 190; Fraser, p 469.

24 Ogg, Chapter XIX.

25 Donald Adamson, *The House of Nell Gwynn*. Kimber (1974) p 12.

26 They were destroyed in 1691 by the disastrous fire which swept Whitehall. Evelyn recording the fire on 10 April 1691 noted the fire began at the apartment of the late Duchess of Portsmouth (which had been pulled down and rebuilt no less than three times to please her) 'and consumed other lodgings of such lewd creatures, who debauched both King Charles 2 and others and were his destruction'.

27 DNB.

28 Delpech, p 202.

Chapter 21 *King Monmouth and an Expanded Army*

1 Calendar of State Papers, Domestic Series. 2, 7 and 17 February 1685; Reresby (1936) p 353.

2 Francis Sandford, *History of the Coronation of James II* (appendix). W Y Carmen, p 41.

3 Cecil Lawson, *A History of the Uniforms of the British Army*. Webb and Bower Vol 1 (1940) p 38.

4 The Irish Army possessed 7,500 soldiers in 1685 and Scotland 2,200 on separate establishments.

5 G M Trevelyan, *English Social History*. Longman (1978) p 413.

6 J R Jones, *Court and Country 1658–1714*. Arnold (1981) p 228.

7 DNB; Violet Wyndham, *The Protestant Duke*. Weidenfeld (1976); John Evelyn, *Diary*, 18 August 1649 and 15 Jul 1685 'a beautiful strumpet, who was familiar with Colonel Robert Sidney'.

8 22 February 1664.

9 DNB. She was also the mistress of Arlington 'She could deny nobody' (John Aubrey, *Brief Lives* 1898 Vol II p 283).

10 Burnet III, p 25. See also Robin Clifton, *The Last Popular Rebellion*. Temple Smith 119.

11 Dryden, lines 309-12.

12 Wyndham, pp 132–3.

13 Quoted Peter Earle, *Life and Times of James II*. Weidenfield (1972) p 26.

14 Wyndham, p 149.

15 Colonel Sir F W Hamilton, *The Grenadier Guards* (1874) 2 Vols, Vol I.

16 Diary, 15 July 1685; Alan Fea, *King Monmouth* (1902) pp 324 and 342.

17 Earle, p 138; DNB.

18 The War Office ordered, 24 August 1685, all officers in the West to furnish such soldiers 'as might be required by the Lord Chief Justice for securing prisoners and to perform that service in such manner as he should direct'. He was also given an escort of Dragoons.

19 B C Chenevix Trench, *The Western Rising*. Longmans (1969) p 246.

20 DNB; David Ogg, *England in the Reigns of James II and William III*. OUP (1984) pp 151–4.

21 Fortescue, Bk VII p 39; Charles Andrews, *The Colonial Period of American History*. Yale Univ. (1933) Vol 1 p 64.

22 These two regiments, raised 8.8.1674 as Clare's and 12.12.1673 as Vane's regiments, were known as the 1st and 2nd English regiments of the Anglo-Dutch Brigade. They were taken on the English establishment as 5th and 6th Foot (later becoming the Royal Northumberland Fusiliers and the Royal Warwickshire Regiment respectively).

23 These regiments became :- 7th to 15th Foot: 3rd and 4th Dragoons: 2nd – 9th Horse (Lord Oxford's Horse was numbered 1st Horse). The 5th and 8th Horse were later disbanded and the others were renumbered 1st – 6th Dragoon Guards. The Train of Artillery was raised by Royal Warrant dated 16 June. See Henry and Patricia Adams, *History of the British Regular Army*. Major Book Publications (1990) Vol I p 28.

24 C T Atkinson, *J S A H R* Vol 14 *James II and His Army* (1935) p 4.

25 *ibid.*

26 DNB.

27 Michael Foss, *The Royal Fusiliers*. (Famous Regiment Series) Hamish Hamilton (1967) p 13. Letter of Service was dated 20 June.

28 Atkinson, p 6.

29 Walton, p 46.

30 See ref 23.

31 Foss, p 16.

32 Cowper, p 46.

33 Macaulay, *History of England*.

34 Fortescue.
35 A J Barker, *The East Yorkshire Regiment*. (Famous Regiment Series) Leo Cooper (1971) p 4.
36 Stephen Wood, *The Royal Scots Dragoon Guards (The Carabiniers and Greys)*. Main Stream (1988).
37 Burnet, p 161.
38 Articles of War for the Forces in Scotland, 4 Jan 1666. See Charles Dalton pt II, p.84.
39 British Library, Harleian Manuscripts 6845, ff 289–296.
40 John Dryden satirised the 'rude militia' as -
      'Mouths without hands: maintained at vast expense.
      In peace a charge, in war a weak defence'.
    (Cymon and Iphegenia 399).

Chapter 22 *A Popish Army to Enslave a Nation*

1 John Childs, *The Army, James II and the Glorious Revolution*. OUP (1980) p 2; Barnett, p 118; Walton, (1894) p 497; Ogg, p 119.
2 Speech of James II in support of Standing Army and Catholic Officers 9 November 1685; Journals of the House of Commons, IX, pp 756 and 758. English National Documents VIII (1660–1714); Ogg, p 158.
3 John Miller, *Catholic Officers in the Later Stuart Army. English History Review* Vol 88 January 1973 p 36. See also L G Schwoerer, *No Standing Armies*. Baltimore (1974).
4 Journals of the House of Commons, IX, p 758; Anchitel Grey, *Debates of House of Commons 1667 – 1694* (1763), VIII 353 and 365.
5 DNB; Barnet, p 119; F C Turner, *James II*. Eyre and Spottiswoode (1948) p 236.
6 Evelyn, p 418; Reresby (1936) p 503.
7 Jones, p 231.
8 *Ibid*, p 247.
9 Fisher, p 677.
10 Quoted from a contemporary chronicler by Miller, p 37.
11 *Declaration of His Highness William Henry* – State Tracts (1692) 11 422 quoted Miller p 37; Reresby (1936) p 522.
12 Childs, p 18; Miller, p 38.
13 Miller, pp 39–40; Childs, p 21.
14 Sir John Reresby (1936) p 553.
15 Childs, p 21.
16 Miller, p 39.
17 DNB.
18 DNB; Guthrie Moir, *The Suffolk Regiment*. (Famous Regiments Series) Leo Cooper (1969); Walton, p 47; Reresby (1936) p 501.

19 DNB (Dartmouth).
20 Ogg, p l63; Alan Hardy, p 50.
21 Burnet III, p 13.
22 DNB (Catherine Sedley) and *Papers of Devotion of James II* II4.

Chapter 23 *A Simpleton Who Lost Three Kingdoms For a Mass*
 1 See J P Kenyon, *The Birth of the Old Pretender. History Today* (June 1963).
 2 Maurice Ashley, *The House of Stuart*. Dent (1980) pp l70–2.
 3 DNB and English Army Lists and Commissions Register (1661–89); Allan
    Fea, *James II and his Wives*. (1908) p 283 *et seq*.
 4 Cyril Ray, *The Lancashire Fusiliers*. Leo Cooper (1971) p 1; Henry and
    Patricia Adams p 29.
 5 David Ogg, pp 193–194; DNB.
 6 Reresby (1936) p 509.
 7 John Childs, p l44.
 8 Sir Winston Churchill, *Marlborough. His Life and Times*. Harrap (1933–8)
    4 Vols.
 9 DNB; Walton, pp 47–8, note 118.
10 Michael Foss, *The Royal Fusiliers*. Hamilton (1967) p 14.
11 A J Barker, *The Prince of Wales's Own West-Yorkshire Regiment*. (1974) p 1.
12 Burnet III, p 345 and DNB.
13 Hardy, p 51.
14 Antonia Fraser, *The Weaker Vessel*. Weidenfeld (1984) p 407.
15 Cowper, Vol I p 53; Reresby (1936) p 545.
16 Jones, p 250. See John Childs, *The British Army of William III*. Manchester
    University Press (1987) Chapter 1.
17 House of Commons Journals X 16, 18; Anchitel Grey Debates of the House
    of Commons 1667-1694 (1763) IX 164-6,110,112. See also Childs, p 26.
18 J P Kenyon, *The Stuarts*. Fontana Collins (1979) p 179. Elizabeth Villiers
    was the daughter of Colonel Sir Edward Villiers of Richmond, younger
    brother of Viscount Grandison, father of Barbara, Duchess of Cleveland.
    She went as maid of honour to Mary on her marriage to William of
    Orange. (DNB).

Chapter 24 *Battlefield in Ireland*
 1 Walton, p 50–1; Fisher, p 657.
 2 See Henry and Patricia Adams, p 31. 5,6,7 Dragoons and 27 Foot were
    raised in Ireland.
 3 See Chapter 21 p 189 and Chapter 22 p 200.
 4 Bernard Rigby, *Ever Glorious (The Story of the 22nd (Cheshire) Regiment*
    Vol I.
 5 John Laffin, *Surgeons in the Field*. Dent (1970) p 40.

6 Michael Glover, *History of the Royal Welsh Fusiliers*. Leo Cooper (1989) p 5–6.
7 Walton, pp 78–9. Hamilton's or The Royal Regiment of Ireland (18th Foot) Raised 8 1.4.1684.
8 Walton, p 54.
9 Walton, p 55 and note.
10 These two regiments of dragoons, raised on 20.6.1689 were later given precedence as the 5th & 6th Regiments of Dragoons.
11 W T Willcox, *The Historical Records of the Fifth (Royal Irish) Lancers*. London (1908).
12 Ogg, p 251.
13 Walton, p 63.
14 Walton, p 65.
15 F C Turner, *James II*. Eyre (1948).
16 *ibid*
17 Fortescue, Vol I Book V, Chap 1. An eyewitness account of the Battle appeared in the Belfast Telegraph 21 August 1937.
18 Ashley, p 176; Fea, p 283.
19 Raised 19 March and 19 April 1689 respectively.
20 1 Jul and Mar Sess. 2 Cap.2.
21 Walton, p 616.
22 1st to 6 Dragoon Guards, 3rd and 4th Hussars: 7th – 17th Foot.
23 C T Atkinson, *J S A H R* Vol 14 (1935). *James II and His Army*.
24 Walton, p 48.

Index

Index

Virginia 38, 77, 78, 82, 144
Visconti, Prince 13
Voltaire, François 176

Wakeham, Sir George 153, 156
Walcheken 128
Waldegrave, Earl Henry and Lady
    Henrietta 119
Wales 2, 102, 214
Wales, Princess of Wales (Diana
    Frances) 131
Wall Street 82
Waller, Edmund 21, 39
Wallingford House 33
Walpole House 176
Walpole, Sir Robert 176
Walter, Lucy (Mrs Barlow) 57, 83, 180,
    181
Wapping 74
War, Crimean (1854–6) 193
Wars, Civil (1642–6; 1650–1) 2, 3, 22, 24,
    32, 36, 37, 47, 97, 106, 116, 121, 122,
    143, 156, 161, 164, 199
Wars, Dutch 3, 36, 111, 121, 127, 128,
    141, 152, 156, 190, 199, 212
  First 1652–4 83
  Second 1665–7 37, 80 81–87, 90, 91, 94,
    102, 109, 110, 111, 123, 204
  Third 1672–1680 84, 109, 110, 111, 115,
    117, 122, 128, 141–143, 152
Weaver, Mrs Elizabeth 100
Wellington, Duke of 219
Wells 183, 185
Wells, Winifred 39
Wentworth, Colonel Lord Thomas 24
Wentworth, Lady Henrietta 168, 182, 186
West, Captain Joseph 38
Westminster 4, 31, 74, 76, 138, 161
  St Margaret's 12, 32
Westminster Abbey 18, 31, 51, 71, 120,
    121, 174, 179, 211
Westminster, Duke of 189
Westminster Hall 18, 70, 72, 75
Westminster, Treaty of 1674 142, 152
Weston Zoyland 185
Wexford 2
Whalley, General Edward 14
White, Lackington 183

Whitechapel 90, 95
Whitefriars 193
Whitehall 6, 18, 72, 93, 94, 95, 116, 145,
    166, 174, 186, 209
Whitehall Palace 6, 8, 11, 12, 15, 22,
    Chap 5, 43, 55, 57, 63, 65, 89, 90, 94,
    98, 123, 124, 130, 138, 160, 163, 165,
    172, 209
  Apartments 29, 30, 31, 32, 33, 58, 67,
    69, 84, 136, 154, 178, 181, 207
  Banqueting Hall 9, 29, 30, 31, 33, 39,
    172, 205, 210
  Bowling Green 30, 31, 33, 71
  Chapel Royal 31, 69, 198
  Cockpit 31, 103, 159
  Council Chamber 30
  Great Hall 30
  Holbein Gate 27, 30, 31, 173
  Horse Guards Parade 6, 30, 33
  King Street 14, 31, 33, 70
  King's Closet 30
  King's Gate 31, 173
  Laboratory 31, 61
  Palace Gate 30, 173
  Privy Garden 30
  Privy Stairs 14, 32, 35, 69, 105, 150, 174
  Royal Bedchamber 29, 30, 31, 61, 147,
    173, 174
  Scotland Yard 29, 32, 63
  Stone Gallery 30, 32, 104, 132, 172
  Sun Dial 30
  Tennis Court 31, 33, 61
Wight, Isle of 170, 188
William (of Orange) 29, 40, 113, 121, 134,
    142, 151, 152, 156, 161, 162, 168–170,
    179, 203, 204, 205, 207, 210
William III 176, 190, 192, 199, 200, 201
  Ireland 210–214, 217, 218
Wiltshire 88, 184, 189, 196
Winchester 170, 173
Windsor Castle 42, 108, 143, 162, 163,
    170, 187, 188, 198
Winthrop, John Jr. 39, 78, 80
Wirral, The 213, 216
Wissing, Willem 42
Wolseley, Colonel William 216
Wolsey, Cardinal Thomas 20, 30
Woolwich 80, 87, 91, 94